Richard Donald Lewis was born at Slack Farm, Billinge, in 1930. The author of several books on educational subjects, he holds a degree in Modern Languages and is at present head of the Linguarama organization.

THE BILLINGERS

by

Richard D. Lewis

Riversdown Publications
Pall Mall, London

To my parents.

ACKNOWLEDGMENT

It would not have been possible to write this book if I had not listened to many stories and picked many brains. I am indebted to such fine old Billingers as Minnie and Hugh Parr, Jem Bellis, Val and Elizabeth Cunliffe, Hugh and Beatrice Lowe, Polly Hill, Austin Durkin, Frances Lowe, Dick Fairhurst, Bessie Gaskell, Tom Lowe, Susie Ellen Mather, Bill and Minnie Roby and countless others who have contributed their time and patience. Rev. D. W. Harris of Billinge St. Aidan's and Rev. Ashton of Birchley St. Mary's were kind enough to aid me with the chapters dealing with their respective churches and I received further help from talks with Mr. R. Hart, Mr. E. Sharples and Mr. Jeff Hurst. The Rector of Wigan, the Rev. K. M. Forrest, gave me some interesting background on Wigan Parish Church, Mrs. Elisabeth Sumner let me read the notes she had made on Billinge life and Mr. J. J. Bagley kindly discussed some of the historical aspects of one or two of the chapters.
Mr. Arthur Jones and Mr. Clifford Webb helped me with the chapter on the dialect and Mr. Reginald Latham advised me on geography.

Author's note

The main personalities in this book are real people who lived in or near Billinge between 1840 and 1970. Some of the characters are composite and occasionally names and nicknames have been changed, but all the village stories have been related to me, over the last thirty-five years, by Billingers themselves. There are no bad people in this book and if any one of the characters mentioned had not figured in this portrait of the village, then Billinge would not have been the place it was.

The miners Jake and Tom, who lived on the fringes of the village and give us the outsider's view of Billingers, were real men, though their name was not Lancaster.

R.D.L.

RIVERSDOWN PUBLICATION LTD.

© Richard D. Lewis 1976.

First published 1976
2nd Edition 1985

ISBN 0 906256 08 9

Printed in England by
Wood Mitchell & Co. Limited, Stoke-on-Trent
for the publishers
Riversdown Publications Ltd., Pall Mall, London.

Contents

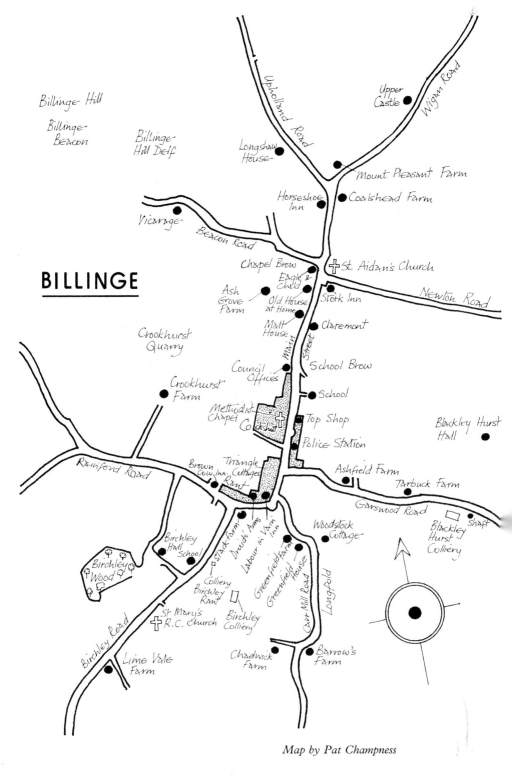

BILLINGE

Billinge Hill

Billinge Beacon

Billinge Hill Delf

Vicarage

Beacon Road

Crookhurst Quarry

Crookhurst Farm

Rainford Road

Birchley Hall School

Birchley Wood

Birchley Road

St Mary's R.C. Church

Lime Vale Farm

Colliery Birchley Row

Birchley Colliery

Stack Farm

Druids Arms

Labour in Vain Inn

Greenfield Farm

Greenfield House

Chadwick Farm

Carr Mill Road

Longfold

Barrow's Farm

Brown Cow Inn

Triangle Cottages Row

Methodist Chapel

Cockshut

Council Offices

Malt House

Ash Grove Farm

Old House at Home

Eagle & Child

Chapel Brow

Main Street

Top Shop

Police Station

School Brow

School

Claremont

Stork Inn

St Aidan's Church

Newton Road

Ashfield Farm

Tarbuck Farm

Garswood Road

Woodstock Cottage

Blackley Hurst Hall

Blackley Hurst Colliery

shaft

Longshaw House

Horseshoe Inn

Coalshead Farm

Mount Pleasant Farm

Upper Castle

Wigan Road

Upholland Road

Map by Pat Champness

The Billingers

There are few of us who do not believe that there is something special about the place in which we were born. We know its people and its streets, its houses and trees, the twist of its streams and the smell of the air. We cannot judge our birthplace objectively, for we are part of it. We can live in far-off places and learn to appreciate and love them, but we can never belong to them in the same way that we belong to our birthplace, for the chemistry is different. For both psychological and biological reasons, there is no place like home.

It is not uncommon for a man, at some time in his life, to sit down and pen a few lines about his native place. It is natural that an older person, having experienced his share of hopes and joys and sorrows, should wish to record these in some manner and perhaps give expression to his gratitude for having lived a full life in the spot where his forefathers lived before him. If he has a tendency to eulogize, it is more than understandable and indeed eulogy may be the principal and most worthy object of the exercise.

Such lines have already been written about my village and I have read them with pleasure. They echo sentiments which I myself possess and which I should be by no means averse to reiterating in words of my own.

But I have another reason for writing what I write. It has been my good fortune, in the last twenty years or so, to travel to many parts of the globe and to live in many different countries and places. I have resided in a large number of towns and villages and I have met people of various nationalities, races, religions and dispositions. In short, I have seen something of the world and of the persons in it. I do not claim to have learnt a great deal from my experiences and I envy those travellers who, with more insight than I, are able to sum up in their writings or lectures the psychologies and philosophies of the peoples they have encountered. While I venture from time to time to draw modest comparisons between this country and that and even on occasion feel qualified to pass judgement on someone or other, I find that the years bring more queries than persuasion, more doubt than certainty, to my reading of the human mind.

In the midst of my dubiety, however, I feel that I have learnt one or two things about people and places. One of the conclusions I have reached – and it first came as a surprise, though by now it has become an unshakable belief – is that some places are special. Special places are relatively few in number (I have only come across two or three in all my travels) and it may well be that many of us live and die without ever seeing one. Of course it all depends on what one means by "special", and I shall attempt to go into that definition in a moment,

1

but I can tell you that if you have ever been to one of these special places and encountered the type of atmosphere and characters to which I am referring, you will know immediately what I am talking about and you will automatically be an insider or semi-insider to this story. As I said, I have been to two or three of these places and the fact that my own village is one of them is something which I finally have come to regard as a coincidence.

                    *   *   *   *   *   *   *   *

Most of us are stereotypes, or soon will be. Mass communication has standardized our habits and it will not be long before we are all watching television over our cornflakes, whether we be in London, Paris, Tokyo or New York. There are still some remote communities, in undeveloped or inaccessible parts of the world, which lie in the backwaters of human civilization and which have retained the customs and speech of an earlier age. There are the people of Tristan de Cunha in the south Atlantic, the inhabitants of Gomera in the Canaries, and the anachronistic Icelanders with their fish, sheep and Old Norse. The geographical reasons for these conditions are quite evident. The special character of these people is a direct result of protracted isolation.

There seem to be on the other hand a limited number of places, not particularly isolated geographically and in developed areas such as England and Scandinavia, which, by virtue of the original or outstanding characteristics of their inhabitants or some freak of local nature, cannot but be regarded as very special both in regard to their own view of the world and their impact on the normal people in surrounding districts. Such places are usually villages of a modest size with a clannish local population bound together by a strong or incomprehensible dialect. It is questionable if one can ever really understand what produces one of these rare enclaves, or if the circumstances are similar in each case, but it would appear that other basic ingredients are clear-cut borders, a sufficiency of farmers, a supply of local stone or wood to build the village houses, a fair share of poverty, adequate facilities for drinking and brawling, a solid core of die-hard Christians and a general, unswerving acceptance of a score of local superstitions.

                    *   *   *   *   *   *   *   *

The Pennines are sometimes described by geographers as the backbone of England. A northern chain of hills, they divide Lancashire and Yorkshire, which is as good a reason for existing as any uplands ever had. On the western side they begin to peter out as you approach Manchester, but twenty miles further on they have a last fling before the flat, fertile plain towards Liverpool and the sea. This final, dogged ridge of land, intersected by brooks and streams and dotted with woods and spinneys, goes by the name of Billinge Hill. On the top of the hill stands a square, yellowish-grey stone house with no windows and only one door. The huge stone blocks of which the house is constructed are covered with names and dates, chiselled and carved by the local people and by others who have made the climb. Some of the dates are very old. There is always an air of history about Billinge Hill. The official name on the map is Billinge Beacon and, as the name indicates, the hill was one in the chain of beacons which were to spread the news of the approach of the Spanish Armada in the days of Francis Drake. In later years, bonfires on the hill signified coronations, the turn of the century, or simply November the Fifth. To-day the bonfires are few and the hill is frequented at night mainly by old men and their old dogs. It is at its best when dark clouds scurry across the moon and shapes come and go in the shadowy half-light. Quiet voices carry far down the stone slopes and the night wind chases scraps of paper round the grey house. The air is bracing and pure and at half past ten the old men steal quietly along the top of the quarry and take a rugged strength down with them to the village.

The old village was gaunt, grey and simple. The main street runs down the side of the hill with an ancient Protestant Church at the top, a Methodist Chapel halfway down and Catholic Birchley Chapel at the bottom. Main Street is about one mile long and all the churches and houses were built of the same yellowish-grey stone, hewn out of the quarry up on the hill. The houses were old and quaint and had a touch of the heroic about them.

But more interesting still are the people of the village. The first thing you notice about them is that they all think back instead of forward and you are won over by their old-fashionedness. They are not uninterested in who you are but they are more concerned with who your grandfather was and where he came from. People live to a very great age in Billinge and those who die in their seventies are said to have been cut off in their youth. When you talk to an old Billinger you are, basically, not communicating with a person belonging to this modern era. If he dilutes his dialect enough for you to understand him you will encounter great ingenuousness, warmth and immediate brotherliness, but you must remember that you are dealing with a man whose thoughts and way of looking at things are fundamentally different from your own. He believes in a twelve-foot ghost with curly hair, bloodstained planks in a stone cottage and a pack of savage hell-hounds which run up and down London Fields on stormy nights, baying "Pader, pader, pa-a-a-der". For him, Carr Mill Dam has no bottom and one day it might provide a watery solution to his troubles. Ask this man for a clothes-line and he will go pale and shiver, though he will lend it to you just the same. Though he will not discuss it with you, he has not forgotten the buried treasure, which must be somewhere in the village, but has never been found.

In the last decades Billinge has started to change and strangers are moving in, but for one hundred years it had a way of life and a philosophy all of its own. The Billingers I wish to describe date from 1860 or so until a short time ago. During this period they had a language of their own, customs of their own and names of their own. Tazzle, Thunger, Ducky, Linnet, Bacco Dick and Hairy Man were real people who were never known, from the cradle to the grave, by any other name. Theirs was the world of the Traddle Holes and Poverty Land, of the village stocks and the all-important smithy. If they didn't go to work they would sit round the Maypole on Church Brow and stage their cock-fights while they ate local toffee called Swaggering Dick. Often drunk and frequently profane, they feared no-one but God, the Devil and half a dozen Billinge ghosts. They were a rough, clannish, independent lot with their own turn of phrase and humour. They will not figure much in the history books, for they were a closed community. Let these few lines then suffice to record some of their words and scenes. This account should be written now, for the days and folks of which I write are almost gone, and will soon be gone forever. Some places can adapt to the Space Age and become part of it. Billinge is not one of them.

CHAPTER ONE

Billinge and the Anglo-Saxons

In pre-historical times Billinge, like Wigan and St. Helens, was a heavily-wooded area about which we know very little. The primeval forests, once flanking the sandstone ridges of Billinge Hill on all sides, vanished thousands of years ago and laid the deposits for the rich coal seams which were to be opened up in earnest in the 17th century.

It was not the wealth of coal nor the riches of the local sandstone, however, that led to Billinge's being established as a community. The village owes its origins to its dominating geographical feature — the 600-foot hill itself. When Hugh Parr, in 1953, eulogized the Beacon and wrote that the village "had been plucked from its bowels of stone" he referred to the houses, churches and schools of Billinge, most of which had been constructed from the stone brought down from the quarry on the hill. We do not know what part the hill played in pre-Roman history, but it is unlikely that the heights were left unattended by the defence-minded Celts and early British. The Romans left Billinge Hill alone, contenting themselves with a fortress at Wigan (Coccium), but a few hundred years later (about 570 A.D.) waves of Angles came into Lancashire from the east (Yorkshire, Northumberland and Durham). Bagley in his "History of Lancashire" tells us that small family groups began to cross the Pennines to settle on fairly high ground and isolated sites clear of marshland. Billinge, being the last high ridge to the west before the Lancashire plain runs flat all the way to the coastal bogs at Formby and Southport, was a prime location at this time and appears to have been settled by an Angle family called "Bylla". Bagley is fairly precise in his dating of the settlement, since he points out that the three main waves of Angles were characterized by different endings to their place-names. Those founded from 570 to 590 A.D. ended in "-inga" and gave us such names as Melling, Billinge, Staining and Bryning. The second wave of Angles, (from 590-600), used the ending "-ingaham" and Whittingham, Padiham and Habergham survive from this period. After 615 the ending used was "-ingatum", giving us Warrington, Pennington, Worthington, Pilkington and Adlington.

An alternative theory is that the name 'Billinge' is derived from a word meaning 'sword' or 'edge', hence a prominent hill. In this case the name could mean 'the settlement on or near the prominent hill' and if this is the meaning, then the village could have been settled as late as the 9th century.

Was Billinge allowed to retain its Anglo-Saxon identity? A study of place-names would appear to indicate that it was, for future waves of invaders spent

5

themselves several miles short of the Billinge high land. The Danes pushed strongly from the south but were held just south of Manchester and their most northerly place-names are Knutsford, Hulme and Urmston. The Norse filtered into Lancashire in boatloads from Northern Ireland and the Isle of Man. These Vikings, however, stayed down on the plain as the names of their settlements show. Good Viking names, unchanged today, are Ormskirk, Kirkby, Skelmersdale (only 5 miles from Billinge), Kirkdale and Burscough.

After King Ethelfrith's victory for the Angles over the British at Chester in 615 the Angle population had in fact steadily increased and continued to do so until the 11th century.

What does the family name "Bylla" tell us about the early settlers of the village and their descendants? The Anglo-Saxon root "bil" signifies "gentleness". The Bishop who consecrated Billinge Chapel already saw them as "sturdy, independent, clannish people who never did anything by halves . . . . always a humorous disposition, able to give as well as take a joke." He was looking at a community which had been in unbroken occupation of Billinge for more than a thousand years. That period had seen the birth, growth and development of the English nation with all its emerging characteristics. Billinge, like thousands of other villages throughout the country, began an orderly existence as an Anglo-Saxon settlement and would develop along orthodox Anglo-Saxon lines. Unlike many other communities, however, Billinge would remain relatively undisturbed by other influences in the mainstream of English history. More than half the country was ravaged by the Danes and Vikings who for some years imposed their own beliefs, manners and customs. Later the Normans, like the Romans before them, concentrated their administration on more important centres. We have every reason to believe, therefore, that Billinge, partly owing to historical accident and partly to its isolated location, entered the modern era as a village providing one of the best examples that we can find in the north of England of a community with a continuous, relatively undisturbed Anglo-Saxon culture.

W. N. Lockie in his writings about Birchley Hall says, "Billinge became . . . . a Yorkshire village in Lancashire with the manners of Yorkshire-men . . . . so the people will stand out as Yorkshiremen exiled and established in Lancashire for centuries, for they have seen the towns and villages for miles round all come into existence." I do not know the grounds on which Mr. Lockie describes Billingers as Yorkshiremen, but it is evident that he has noticed how much they differ in character from their neighbours. (Even people from nearby Garswood, Ashton, Wigan and St. Helens regarded the old Billingers as strange beings). Mr. Lockie may, of course, be referring to the Angle migration from Yorkshire into Lancashire in the 6th century. At all events we can suppose that history's "non-interference" in Billinge after the time of the Anglo-Saxon occupation and the consequent absence of any great Danish, Viking, Norman or Celtic influence has led to the village's maintaining Anglo-Saxon traits to a greater degree than most of its Lancashire surroundings.

Can we trace any affinity between the ways of the Billingers and those of their Anglo-Saxon ancestors? Certainly in the Billinge dialect we can find many examples (but that is for another chapter). What do we know about the Angles? They came from Eastern Schleswig, not far from Flensburg, an area so cold and rainy in winter that they would not have found Yorkshire or Billinge any worse. At any rate they never returned to their homeland and England itself derived its name from this fair race. Now if you ask anyone familiar with the area how Billingers differ from other Lancastrians, he will tell you they are characterized by an old-fashioned sentimentality, especially where the family, the land, religion and patriotism are concerned; that they are clannish — vindictive or generous, according to your attitude towards the clan; that they have a persistent, coarse sense of humour, are great story-tellers (they spin out the stories) and are above all very superstitious.

The Angles came to Billinge as heathens, but not savages. Though they worshipped Woden and Thor they had a settled order of society. They were, however, extremely superstitious and believed in elves, valkyries and other supernatural beings. Story-telling was very important to them and Anglo-Saxon poetry is almost entirely narrative. Religion and patriotism are the two main impulses of their prose. The most important aspect of their social structure was the bond of kinship and the popular courts dispensed justice according to evidence placed before them by the families. Kinsmen were expected to avenge wrongs to their relatives or, alternatively, to compensate for their misdemeanours. Anglo-Saxons had a strong feeling for the land and concerned themselves with agriculture, as opposed to the Danes who were mainly interested in trade and the Norsemen, who were great warriors. Finally, Anglo-Saxon humour was rough and ready, close to the earth, at times even cruel.

Are the "old-fashioned" Billingers of this century different from the people around them because they have remained true to the ways and traditions of the original settlers? We are going back one thousand four hundred years, but an isolated village would change very slowly in the Dark Ages and not all that much more until the turn of this century. Certainly the Bishop's description of the villagers he saw well fits the old-timers still living. Not long ago a doctor tried to give an injection to an old Billinge lady who had pains in her legs. "Inject me?" she snorted, "Be off with your bloody needle. When *I* dee, I want to *be* theer!"

CHAPTER TWO

Billinge Hill

Billinge Hill is no ordinary hill. We have seen in the preceding chapter how the Anglo-Saxon invaders chose high ridges for the establishment of their settlements. The geography of Billinge is such that, whether you approach it from north, south, east or west, you have to climb up to it. The settlers must have been delighted with the location, for it completely dominates the south of Lancashire. To the east lie the Pennines themselves, seen in magnificent splendour. The views to the north, south and west are almost completely unobstructed. Blackpool Tower, roughly 30 miles to the north, stands erect on the horizon like a dark sentinel; beyond it can be seen the hills of Westmorland, Cumberland and of Scotland itself. To the west the Lancashire plain drops down to the Irish Sea, and to the south-west Snowdon and the Welsh mountains provide an impressive backdrop to Liverpool and the cleavage of the Mersey river. To the south, low-lying counties stretch out halfway to the Midlands.

The view from Billinge Hill is so breathtaking that it is difficult to find words which can do justice to the spectacle on a clear day. I have had to go back to Victorian days (indeed, to a few years before) to find prose which made a brave attempt to afford an adequate description of the beauty involved. I quote from "Billinge Bazaar, 1834" (J. Brown, Wigan):

> "The prospect on every side is so free and unbounded, the scene so extensive, and enlivened with such a variety of magnificence, that it is next to impossible for anyone to visit this place, when the clouds and mists are dispersed from the horizon by the radiant beams of the sun, and the air refreshed and enlivened by the slow and gentle breeze, without feeling the emotions expressed in the words of Dyer: "Ever charming, ever new, when will the landscape tire my view?" . . . . many a time has the sight of the beacon cheered the heart of the villager returning from a long and toilsome journey, and struck with a string, as it were, in his heart, which ceases not to vibrate till all the tender feelings being roused to an unusual degree of excitement, the pains and tediousness of the ways are beguiled and forgotten, in the joyous anticipation of the welcome he should receive".

Even allowing for the flowery nature of early 19th century prose, it is quite clear that the writer had been deeply impressed by the scenery. Moreover, he had touched on a subject which recurs constantly in any discussion of Billinge, – the bond of affection between the gaunt hill and the inhabitant. He mentions it again a few lines later:

> ". . . . the current opinion that Billinge Hill, if not the first, is yet one of the first, points of land that attract the longing sight of the returning mariner, and serves to direct him in the safest track to that haven where he wishes to be."

The writer then goes on to try to express the sudden, inescapable sense of wonder one has as one reaches the top:

> ". . . . as the approach to the hill on every side is through an extended vale, the visitor no sooner ascends its summit than the numberless objects and extensive scenes which all at once burst upon his view, incline him for a moment to believe that he has emerged as it were into a new world . . . ."

Finally, our 19th century friend concludes that his own descriptive ability falls short of the task:

> ". . . . charming and delightful scenery. To enumerate only a few of its beauties would swell the present notice far beyond the space to which it is necessarily confined; indeed, the pen of a Milton, the pencil of a Raphael, and the flowing language and animated descriptions of a Harvey, would all be required to describe them with justice, or depict them in their proper and nature colours."

Unfortunately, Milton never climbed Billinge Hill. As my own pen would also, no doubt, prove inadequate I shall resist the temptation to add to what has been written already. There is one fact, however, that leaves me profoundly impressed, and I sometimes wonder if it has received sufficient attention. It appears that in 1807 a general survey was made of the whole country and a regiment of soldiers occupied the heights around Billinge Beacon for several weeks collecting data.The officers record that no fewer than 16 counties could be seen from the top of the hill! I must confess I find this absolutely astounding, and question whether there is any other point in the British Isles from which the same number of counties is visible.

I have seen most of what can be seen from the top of the hill on clear days, but, armed with maps and my grandfather's telescope, I was able to find only 12 or 13 counties on my own. When I consulted a local geographer, however, he confirmed the findings of His Majesty's officers, naming the 16 counties as follows: Lancashire, Yorkshire, Cheshire, Anglesey, Flintshire, Caenarvonshire, Denbighshire, Merionethshire, Montgomeryshire, Westmorland, Cumberland, Kirkcudbrightshire, the Isle of Man, Derbyshire, Staffordshire and Shropshire.

The Beacon owes its dominance, and its incredible views, to the fact that the surrounding countryside slopes downwards on all sides. When we consider what an extensive area of England, Wales and Scotland can be seen from this point, it is evident that in Billinge Hill we have a remarkable geographical phenomenon. It is not to be wondered that its presence has ruled the destiny of its community and that the stone from its loins has lent a calm, grey unity to the surrounding villages.

*   *   *   *   *   *   *   *

Though the present house on top of Billinge Hill was erected as late as the middle of the 18th century, about the same time as the Rivington and Hartshead beacons, it is possible that there may have been earlier constructions, since the beacon warning system has been in use in England on an organized basis since the 12th century.

Beacons were used in Ancient Greece – in Aeschylus's "Agamemnon" we read:
"It is the beacon fire on Ida's crest
By flaming convoys that hath brought the news. . . "
The word came into English from Anglo-Saxon (A-S. *beacnian, beacen* = beckon = give a sign) and it can be supposed that the undulating nature of British topography, with its numerous hills and downs, as opposed to mountains, favoured the development of this system of communication at an early stage. Certainly it was in full use at the time of the threatened invasions of 1213, 1217 and 1264 and a coastguard had also been organized. In 1403, by Act of Parliament, Commissioners were appointed to supervise the preparation of beacons. No one can erect a beacon without Royal permission and the roads and

showed promise as a scholar, reading anything he could lay his hands on from the age of ten. On the other hand, times were hard and Hugh found that his miner's wages were insufficient to feed his large family. It was necessary for some of the children to labour in the fields for sixpence or ninepence a day. Their schooling was neglected, for each child had to be sent to work as soon as he or she was able to be put to some simple task. In James' case, however, no harm was done, since he had already become a voracious reader and in the long,

Gentleman Jim

dark nights he went on to educate himself. Ellen, too, got a job in the Sandwash at the top of Long Fold. This was a large sand pit owned by a man named Sammy Stock. Ellen washed and riddled the sand, loading it into carts. It was back-breaking work for a woman, but it brought in a few shillings a week. The outdoor work tanned her skin and the sand ruined her hands, but the fresh air and regular toil toughened her body and she lived till she was 82.

In 1871 Hugh Parr was killed down the mine by a fall of rock at the age of 56. Ellen and the children still living at home moved out of the big house and occupied the labourer's cottage. James had married Susannah Anderton in 1862 and lived in another of the Long Fold cottages. He was a God-fearing, unbending man and proved no less fertile than his father. From his seed sprang the next generation of Billinge Parrs, most of whom lived until the 1950s. The Family Bible records: Mary Ann, born 1863. Jonathan, 1864. James, 1865. Ruth, 1867. Elizabeth, 1869. Caroline, 1871. Hugh, 1873. Wilhelmina, 1874. Samuel, 1876. Phoebe Ellen, 1879. Joseph, 1883 and Gordon, 1885.

James Parr, who worked as a checkweighman in a local colliery, had been particularly fortunate in his choice of a wife. Susannah Anderton was a big-hearted, generous woman, always ready to look after the sick and needy, but could be tough as nails when she had her back to the wall. There was no improvement in the family's economic situation under James' leadership and Susannah, like Ellen before her, betook herself to the Sandwash to earn the extra shillings which made the difference between poverty and dignity. She had the broad, handsome, high-cheekboned face and well-made body of the Andertons and for two or three years she was a familiar figure among those who toiled in the sand pit. Passers-by would stop and watch her work, for her movements were quick and graceful and strong.

* * * * * * * *

The sturdy, stone cottage in which James, Susannah and their large family lived was built after the manner of all the others in Long Fold: downstairs it had a front place, a back place and a kitchen. Upstairs were two bedrooms. It was far too small for the family, but it was quaint and cosy and it had a pleasant garden at the back, sloping steeply upwards towards London Fields. In the garden there grew red currants, white currants and gooseberries as well as a profusion of flowers such as Canterbury Bells, lilacs, jasmine, lilies of the valley, snowdrops, crocuses, daffodils, orange lilies and ladslove.

Susannah kept a clean house. In the parlour was a green plush sofa for visitors, a square walnut table and two large mahogany rocking chairs; the gentleman's chair was slightly bigger than the lady's. Against one wall was a walnut organ and on the other side a mahogany chest of drawers with an oil painting of Susannah over it. Another wall contained two built-in china cabinets, holding a selection of wedgwood, plates, mugs and glasses. Red and green matting covered the floor and full-length white lace curtains draped the window. There was also a yellow blind, as was the fashion at the time. Over the fireplace were two more paintings of young women. One was called "Sally in our Alley", the other "Black-eyed Susan".

A Parr beauty

The back place, or living-dining room, had a large, round dining table surrounded by rush-bottomed Billinge chairs. The table, like many at the time, had two levels – the polished top and a lower board, like a shelf, within easy reach of small children. The cat used to play between the two levels and stick its paw up through a hole, the size of a penny piece, in the centre of the table. On one wall was a shelf-and-drawer complex in black oak, holding the crockery and cutlery in daily use. A huge seven-drawer dresser and two more rocking-chairs completed the furnishing. The old-fashioned fireplace had gleaming brasses and a red-brick "crow" upon which one placed three pans. Most of the cooking was done in cooking pots, the oven being used for puddings, pies and cakes. To make more room for pots and kettles, a four-barred "luby" could be hooked onto the front of the hob.

In the centre of the hearth was a brass plate called a "duster" or 'tricket" which was taken off every morning in order to remove the old ashes. Cleaning out the "hess" was followed by the whitening of the hearth area with chalk and mops. A brass fender fenced off this area. Every Friday morning the whole fireplace had to be blackened and polished up. This was known as "black-leading the grate". At the same time, all the brass parts of the fireplace would be polished as well as all the other brasses such as candlesticks, brass cups and ashtrays, pokers, fire-tongs and shovel and even brass horses. Friday was also the day for cleaning the windows, changing the lace curtains and print cushions and covers and for whitening (with rubbing-stones) doorsteps, gatesteps and flags (pavement). The cornish, or mantelpiece, was lined with an array of pewter jugs and tea-pots, candlesticks, large tin canisters for tea and coffee and family pictures in silver, leather and brass frames. All these objects were dusted and cleaned. On top of the chest of drawers was a white linen cover with crochet work round the edges. The Family Bible lay in the centre of the linen cover and had a lace cover of its own. This was also changed every Friday. Friday was quite a day.

James Parr was a tall, gaunt man with deep-set blue eyes, auburn hair and a long beard. He always wore a long, black tail-coat and favoured starched white shirts. He was well-read, wrote in a beautiful hand and had a gift for finding the right words. From the time of his marriage until his death he was known in the village as "Gentleman Jim".

In the 1880s, as Superintendent of the Methodist Sunday School, Jim was the leader of the Nonconformist community. Father Powell headed the Roman Catholics and Canon St. George was the Vicar of Billinge Church. Town Clerk was William Darlington. These four prominent figures exercised great influence in Billinge in the last two decades of the 19th century. They were consulted on all matters of importance, since many people in the village could neither read nor write. Most of the grown-ups had received little education and their children were not receiving much more. Poverty was such that boys of ten and eleven were given menial tasks down the pit and might spend no more than two or three years at Billinge School before dropping learning forever.

Down Long Fold, Jim Parr did the writing for everybody. He filled out documents, drew up wills, wrote rent contracts, protests, eulogies and even love letters for people. If anyone received a note or letter, they took it along to Jim to read, asking him to write the reply. Because of his eloquent turn of phrase, he was often asked to speak out for them as well. If they were sick or if one of their relatives was dying, he was asked to go to the bedside and pray. This he did willingly, regularly and sonorously. All in all, and in his part of the village, Jim knew what was going on.

In those days Billinge was a very isolated community. The borders of the village were clearly defined and of course there were no buses or trams at the time. From Long Fold it was 5 miles on foot to Wigan and 4 miles to St. Helens. The two doctors who visited Billinge at the time – Dr. Bayman and Dr. Henderson – used to come twice a week on horseback. There were horses and carts, wagonettes and other similar conveyances, but most of the time people went where they were going on foot.

Preachers at the Methodist Chapel were generally outsiders. Jim Parr used to correspond with various speakers, who would come to preach from as far as Southport, Ormskirk and Skelmersdale. Some of them used to walk through the night to get to Billinge for the Sunday morning. Whatever the rigours of the journey, they were assured of two good meals in the Parr house, as well as a

Long Fold

steadfast and intent congregation. Occasionally, a preacher could not be arranged, and on those Sundays Jim, or one of the other Sunday School teachers, would deliver the sermon.

One Sunday afternoon, in the middle of the summer, there was a knock at the front door of Jim's house. One of the children went to answer it and opened the door to a stranger who appeared to be in his middle thirties. It was a hot summer's day and the caller was streaming with perspiration and panting quite heavily. He said he did not know anyone in the area and asked if he could be given a cup of tea. Susannah invited him in and said he was welcome to stay for tea. He readily accepted the invitation and Jim offered him the sofa and entered into conversation with him. The newcomer, who was wearing good clothes and carrying a fine, leather brief-case, proved to be a man of considerable learning. He and Jim discussed politics, religion and books. He had an engaging manner and before tea was over he was on good terms with every member of the family. He ate a hearty meal and relaxed visibly as time wore on. Jim asked him if he had anything particular to do that evening and when the man said that he had not, Jim suggested that he might come along to Chapel and speak, as there was no preacher scheduled for that day. The stranger readily agreed to do this and when it was time for the evening service he accompanied the older members of the family up the lane, clutching his brief-case in his right hand. Indeed he proved to be an excellent speaker and the congregation was delighted over Jim's idea. After the service the new-found preacher spent half an hour with some of the children, giving them sweets and jolly words. He then conversed with several church members and left only in the late evening, after charming all those who lingered on and heartily pumping their hands as he took leave. Jim asked him to stay the night, but he said that he really must be on his way. It was a dark night and at the bottom of the chapel steps he slipped away up the hill in the darkness before any of them could prevail upon him to change his mind.

The next day the police were looking for a strange man with a brief-case. He was a robber and a murderer and had arrived in Billinge fresh from the scene of his latest crime. The Billingers were never able to find out if the police eventually caught up with him.

CHAPTER FOUR

Jake Lancaster's Schooldays

Jake Lancaster was born in the year 1861 in Sally's Gap in the Ince district of Wigan. He had no recollection of his father, who died when he was two, and very little of his mother who passed away shortly after the birth of his younger brother Tom a few months later. Jake's elder brother Johnny was put in the care of relations in Ince and he and his brother Tom came to live with their Aunt Sarah in the village of Garswood, separated from Billinge by Turpin's Fields.

Sarah was a big, bony, grey-haired widow of forty-five of taciturn Lancashire stock with no children of her own. Her husband, a quiet, unassuming miner, had escaped from nondescription in a roof fall some years earlier and Sarah secretly welcomed the opportunity of livening up her empty existence by taking in her orphaned nephews. Although she had never had any experience in bringing up children, she was a hard-working, dutiful woman and it was her good fortune that neither of the boys turned out to be unduly troublesome. Tom was a contented, obedient child, sleeping at night and giggling and eating his way through the day. Jake was more independent and changeable, defiant in his rage when crossed, but was also of regular eating and sleeping habits and developed an early respect for Sarah's no-nonsense discipline and cool nerves. He was also very fond of his brother and often helped his aunt to take care of Tom, so that by the time Jake was approaching seven there was harmony in the house. Sarah drew a few shillings a week compensation money and supplemented her small income by taking in washing, though customers were hard to find, in those hard times. Theirs was a house without argument, imagination, laughter, love or money. Sarah washed and sewed, cooked monotonous, tasteless meals, and always made ends meet. The boys grew up on chips, black puddings, brawn, tea porridge, fatty cakes, bacon, cheese and sausages. Special treats were sugar butties, scones, Eccles cakes and bread and butter pudding. Tea and water were the only drinks.

The boys wore corduroy or woollen jackets, corduroy breeches just below the knee, long woollen stockings and clogs. They had one change of clothing as well as a white shirt and stiff collar for Sundays. Their only belongings were a wooden rocking-horse, a tin of marbles, a boat and a toy cannon. They played, ran and fought with all the other little boys in Garswood, threw snowballs, paddled and lit fires according to the season. Later on they were shown how to fish and this was a great luxury of their boyhood. They never realised that they were poor, for the other boys had little more than they, and they enjoyed the day-to-day routine which Sarah had organised for them. Their great delights were a 3-inch cockey (tiddler), a sago pudding, combing Uncle Billy's thinning hair two hours for a halfpenny, smashing Billinge conkers with Garswood conkers and rolling around together in the dead leaves in the fall.

Jake and Sarah had few emotions and self-pity was not one of them. From an early age he displayed a sturdy independence, like that of his aunt, but with an added touch of masculine belligerence. Tom was more dependent on others and particularly on Jake, whom he admired and remained devoted to throughout his long life. Having no father to imitate, Tom did everything that Jake did. If Jake drank three cups of tea, Tom would drink three cups. If Jake decided to stay away from school, Tom could not be dragged there by wild horses. Should Jake spit at a dog, Tom would show it no mercy. If Jake belted anyone, which happened quite often, Tom would belt them harder.

Robert Lancaster, their father, had not been a local man. In an age of developing industrial relations he had been a Miner's Agent and had worked and travelled in many parts of the country. Marriage had brought him to Wigan, but his work obliged him to journey constantly, so that his wanderings and his early death caused him to be a vague and rather mysterious figure in later years. There were no pictures of him, but he was known to have been an eloquent speaker who represented the miners successfully and to the best of his ability. Presentations had been made to him by groups of miners up and down the country, but neither Jake nor Tom ever came into possession of these medals, or certificates, or whatever they may have been. The only family heirloom they had was a water-colour of their grandfather which Sarah kept in the bottom drawer of one of her cupboards, under clean sheets. The painting was about ten inches by six and depicted the head and trunk of a handsome man of around thirty-five, immaculate in Royal Blue coat, pale grey waistcoat and claret scarf. He had light brown hair worn rather long and with a clear parting. His eyes were well apart, distinctly grey and the intensity of the level gaze was quite incredible in a water-colour. The man might have been a lord or aristocrat. His place of repose under the sheets in an old cupboard in a pitman's home seemed a little incongruous, even to Jake.

With no parental guidance, and little control from their aging aunt as the years passed, Jake and Tom were to shape their own lives and in their own manner. Going down a Billinge mine at the age of nine, they worked there without any real break for sixty-five years. They thus became prototypes of the Lancashire miner, moulded by their work and their fellow pitmen, toughened by the hardships of their profession, versed in Billinge and Garswood lore and beliefs, cutting coal for Victorians, Edwardians, for Englishmen at war and finally outliving Old King George himself. But in 1868 they were still two small boys who could neither read nor write. Sarah, who knew that their only future was down the pit, decided that they had better have some form of education anyway. Jake was already seven and Tom almost five when their aunt told them that the following Monday they would begin school. They had no inclination to do so and protested strongly, but Jake saw Sarah's resolve and agreed in the end, so he set off on the appointed day with brother Tom in his wake and rebellion in his heart.

*   *   *   *   *   *   *   *

Jake Lancaster's schooldays were brief and stormy. Mr. Crompton, the headmaster, normally enjoyed the few minutes of ceremony in enrolling a new pupil. He would put his arms around the boy's shoulders, say a few wise words to the mother, put his pen to paper with a flourish, talk a little dialect to show that he understood the local people, shepherd the woman to the door and tell her that her son would be made to work hard but that he thought that he would be all right. He had no such illusions about Jake. On that particular Monday he was having a quiet cup of tea in his study about half past nine when the door half opened and a pair of frowning brows appeared round it.

"I have our Tom outside". Jake always frowned when he had to think.

"Who?" asked the Head.

"Our Tom" said Jake.

"And who are you and what are you doing here?"

"He's only four" said Jake

"Look here, you'd better get out, bring your Tom, whoever he is, but first learn to knock and show your manners."

"I'll fotch him." The brows disappeared.

There was a loud hammering on the door.

"Come in." barked the Head.

There was another hammering.

"Come in, confound you." screeched Crompton, and the boys stumped in.

"Why did you knock twice?"

"It was our Tom the second time." said Jake.

"Well?"

"We have to start today, Aunt Sarah says."

"Here? You mean a big lad like you hasn't started school yet?"

"Aunt Sarah says it's now or never."

"Well, I don't know, my boy."

"If you're full, it's aw reet, we'll go". Jake was losing patience.

"Yes." said Tom.

"Follow me", said the Head, "it's Miss Pigot's class for you."

He ushered the boys down a gloomy corridor.

*   *   *   *   *   *   *   *

They were put behind a two seater desk on the front row right under Miss

Pigot's nose and sat quietly observing the scene for three-quarters of an hour until playtime. Miss Pigot was an ageless spinster with a pince nez and twenty years' experience. By the time the bell went she felt she had sized the brothers up. They kept their heads perfectly still, but their eyes were constantly roving from side to side, missing nothing. To Miss Pigot this indicated a rebellious nature and she felt she was in for a tough time. She did not know how tough.

When the boys burst into the yard for playtime, it was only natural that Jake and Tom were subjected to close scrutiny by all the others. They all wore corduroy clothes, heavy clogs, long grey stockings with elastic garters and braces under their jackets. Their heads were close-cropped or even shaven and most boys had fringes, in some cases nearly down to the eye-brows. They were sons of miners, farm hands and mill workers, plain, rather pale, but hardy, and speaking a fearful dialect. They were all aged from 5 to 9, as the senior boys had a separate playground over the wall. Some of the boys knew Jake and Tom and winked at them and told the others who they were.

After the first stages of the scrutiny were over, a biggish nine-year-old in a green jacket swaggered up to Jake and looked him up and down. The other boys went quiet as Green Jacket stuck his thumbs behind his braces, tilted his head slightly backwards and addressed Jake from under his fringe:

"I'm Waggy. I'm t' Cock."

Jake knew that he meant that he was the Cock of the Yard. It was a proud title and Jake came as near to showing respect as was possible for him. He nodded silently. Waggy did a little parade from Jake to Tom and back again to Jake. He stuck his thumbs even deeper and looked first right, then left.

"If anybody touches thee, tell me. Jus'tell me. I'll hommer 'um for thee."

Jake pondered this over and frowned. Tom looked at Jake and then glowered at the crowd.

"What dost mean, touch me?" asked Jake. "Noan o'them lot had better lay honds on me."

Waggy looked incredulous, his eyes widening.

"But what about Salt? Suppose Salt belts thee?"

Jake glared at the surrounding boys.

"I can thump any o'yon lot, Salt an'pepper an aw."

Salt lost no time in coming forward. He was the second best man in the yard and he was anxious to prove it. He was vicious rather than big and had the most accomplished squint Jake had ever set eyes on. He came straight to the point:

"Dost wanna scrap?"

"Ah." replied Jake.

"Tha wants a scrap wi'me?"

"Ah."

"Con't see this?" A dry fist was brandished under Jake's nose.

"Ah."

"Tha'll feel it, never mind see it."

"Go on, then."

"Tha wants t'get 'urt, dosto?"

"Ah."

"I'll hit thee once, tha'll bounce twice."

"Go on, then."

Salt let fly. He had been in a hundred fights and he knew the value of speed. For a boy it was remarkable how he could use both hands, almost like a real boxer. Jake took half a dozen blows to the face before he could find his balance. Salt, nevertheless, was feeling uneasy. One of the thumps on Jake's ear had been a real humdinger — the sort that made most boys back off, or at least hold their ear. Jake just stood there without advancing or retreating, trunk leaning slightly forward, both hands held low leaving his face unprotected, frowning intently at the other's squint. Salt moved in fast for the second attack and thumped Jake hard again over the ear. Jake, however, had not stepped back and his right fist cracked against Salt's nose, which at once spurted blood all over the boys' attire.

Waggy stepped in with an authoritative air. He put the palm of his hand on Jake's chest and pushed him back a little.

"Stop till his nose is dry. Get thi hanky, Salt."

Salt pulled out a stinking grey rag and started dabbing tenderly at his nose. But Jake wasn't having any truces. He pushed Waggy aside in an unfriendly manner, went up to Salt and belted him again on the nose as he was trying to dry it. Salt was aghast at this infringment of the rules. He felt outraged, hurt and not a little scared. His nose ached horribly, he was only eight, and he felt there was every justification for kicking Jake. He lashed out at Jake's shins with his right foot, only to miss by inches and see his clog go sailing away across the yard. Jake took a step forward, stamped as hard as he could on poor Salt's stockinged foot and the fight was over.

Salt was sent home to have his foot dressed, Jake and Tom were escorted to Sarah's in disgrace, and the next day Waggy kept as far away from Jake as he could during both playtimes. By Wednesday it was generally accepted that Jake was the new Cock and the yard then settled down to its usual games.

* * * * * * * *

Jake went to school for two years. He attended more frequently in the morning than in the afternoon, when Tom and he used to go fishing. Miss Pigot did not mind when they went fishing and used to discuss fish and ponds and rivers in Nature Study lessons any morning when the weather was promising. The Head objected strongly to any form of truancy and made a terrible fuss. First he reported them to Sarah, who beat them with a leather strap and that made no difference. Then he shouted at them and ridiculed them and caned them and that made no difference. Whenever he asked them where they had been, they told him they had been fishing. Finally he got sick of it and stopped asking them.

None of the teachers quite knew how to deal with them. They could not be classified. In the first place, it was obvious that they were both intelligent. It was not long before they could read and write as well, if not better than any of the others and they hardly ever made a mistake in Arithmetic. They showed a certain interest in Nature Study, but none at all in History, Geography, Religious Instruction, Music, Woodwork and Painting. As far as their conduct in class was concerned, it could not be said that they were disobedient or insolent. They sat still, they never cribbed and they did not fiddle with things under their desk lid. They always looked their teacher in the eye. And yet there was something — an unspoken questioning of the system — a dry hint of insubordination in Jake's apparently straightforward answers. Whenever Miss Pigot turned her back to the class she could feel Jake's eyes boring into her and she felt unsure of herself, at times even ridiculous. She found Jake's frown too mature — it made her feel gawky and spinsterish. Not that she could not handle boys as a rule. She could be strict enough and was not averse to letting them have one behind the ear. After she had tried this once with Jake she had decided it was not the way to handle him. He had just stared at her coldly and wordlessly for half an hour or so. Then he had an accident with an ink bottle and the classroom floor was stained dark blue for the next twenty years.

By the time he left school Jake could read and write as well as he ever needed to. He remained an uneducated man throughout his life, reading nothing but newspapers and writing no more than half a dozen letters a year. And yet the instruction he had received was essential to his independent character. He was never known to spell a word wrongly, or to make an error of addition, subtraction, multiplication or division. He never tried to pronounce a word with which he was unfamiliar and he never made a fool of himself before better-read people. In his two year contest with Crompton and Miss Pigot he had implemented that rugged self-reliance which had proved such an enigma to his teachers. Furthermore, and even more surprising in view of his classroom attitudes, he had somehow sensed the vital importance of learning *per se* and in later years compelled his sons to submit to years of study which he himself would have given the widest of berths.

CHAPTER FIVE

Billinge Names

Billinge was famous even in the decade after the Great War for its habit of using nicknames instead of real names, which would often be disregarded completely and fall into disuse. Due to the subsequent influx of foreigners, this custom is less apparent than it was. There was a well-known story of a man coming from St Helens and walking up Long Fold and stopping this Billinger to ask him:

"Excuse me, I am looking for a man called James Cunliffe, can you tell me where he lives in the village?"

"No, ah don't know anybody by that name."

"Well, they tell me he is sometimes known as Jem Paddy."

"Oh, Christ, it's me tha wants!"

I never quite knew whether I ought to believe this tale, until, one day I was going through old copies of the WIGAN OBSERVER, when I came across the following article which appeared in February, 1860:

"On Wednesday the inhabitants of Billinge were roused from their accustomed state of propriety by a wedding procession, the most remarkable perhaps, of any which has ever entered the village. A sinker named Peter Houghton having come to the conclusion to take to himself a wife, considered it unworthy of his position as a sinker to have the rite celebrated without the addition of some small ceremonies of his own, by which the event could be remembered. With the consent of his "lady love", Miss Mary Winstanley, he therefore obtained promises of attendance from twelve of his friends, and these in addition to the bridesmaid and bridesman, formed in procession, and, preceded by another friend "discoorsin" sweet music from a cornopean, took the village by storm as they passed to church. The fourteen men were attired in sinkers' dress, with the addition of "white chokers" and clean shirts. This was a decided novelty, and perhaps attracted as much attention as aught else connected with the proceedings. Before entering the church the conduct of the party was very good, and in the edifice itself their behaviour was exemplary, but the pair having been made one, the friends rejoiced at the occurrence in the rather uproarious manner. On leaving the church the procession was formed, the musician leading the way to most of the public houses in the district, at each of which happiness was wished to the pair in language which grew more indistinct, yet more enthusiastic, as the peregrinations were continued. At one house the assembled crowd were entertained by a dance at the front – in order, we should suppose, to prove that the "light fantastic toe" is ofttimes to be found in a sinker's clog – to the great edification and amusement of those who witnessed it. But the party began to be desirous of something more substantial, so they passed on to the "Who'd have thought it?" public house, where dinner was provided by the landlord and despatched by the guests who afterwards spent an evening much to their own gratification.

We have been favoured with a list of the parties who immortalised themselves on the occasion, and *as by their real names they would, perhaps, be unknown to our Billinge readers,* we append the terms by which they will in general be recognized: John Hurst (Hairy Man) and Mary Barton, bridesman and bridesmaid; James Forster (Red Chocket), Thomas Mather (Touch), Frank Winstanley (Collop), John Forster (Foot), James Barton (Wellington), Richard Forster (Engine Dick), John Winstanley (Jack Sly), James Palmer (Nosey), John Gaskell (Rascal), Edward Bradbury (Moss Bank Tippler), George Burrows (Shrow), Richard Mather, the musician (Why, Why, Sugar Tub or Old Pam)."

In this restrained, Victorian account, we have to marvel at the sentence I have put in italics. Here a Wigan reporter is actually confirming that Billingers did not know each others' real names. It sounds incredible, for all the people in the procession were Billingers. Yet a Billinger would probably have no idea who John Hurst and James Barton were. The naming habit was so strong that once someone had acquired their Billinge name they were stuck with it till they died. It makes you wonder how some of the 1860 names had arisen. Nosey, Jack Sly and Rascal present no problem, but what did one have to do to merit a title such as Wellington, Touch, or Why, Why, Sugar Tub?

* * * * * * * *

Moss Bank

CHAPTER SIX

The Pit

The year 1870 is important in European history on account of the outbreak of the Franco-Prussian War and the emergence of Bismarck as the Strong Man of the continent. The Wigan area was less affected by these events as by a dreadful series of pit disasters which had occurred during 1869. Two explosions at the Queen's Pit had killed 83 men; 37 more had died at Highbrook's Colliery; 26 had perished at Low Hall, Platt Bridge and 11 others at three other local pits.

Jake, who knew nothing of the War and had never heard of Bismarck, turned nine in 1870 and went down the pit.

He had been looking forward to it for some time. In those days it was the normal thing for boys from poor families to start working from the age of ten or eleven and if you were big for your age or sturdy enough, then nine would do. Waggy had been down the mine already for nearly a year and Jake was getting irritated at the sight of his black face, billy-can and superior airs. Salt, too, had started at the cotton mill, a less glamorous place to be sure, but even he was bringing home his four shillings a week while Jake was still having History and Music stuffed into him.

Finally the day arrived when Jake was due for his first morning shift. He and Tom went to bed at nine o'clock on the Sunday night in preparation and they had not seemed to sleep long before they heard a metallic rattle on the window panes. They woke up in consternation and Tom, nearer to the window, opened it and stuck out a sleepy head. Below him in the street he saw Cedric Cutts, the knocker-up. In his right hand he held the long stick with the leaded end with which he tapped on the miners' windows to wake them up in time for the shift. He was nobody's friend and he knew it. The only thing he liked about his job was that he always won. They might curse, shout or sneer all they liked. But they always got up. Cedric knew how they felt. He hated getting up himself.

"Where's Jake?"

"He's i'bed."

"Get him out then, you little bugger."

"Jake, there's a mon down 'ere wants thee."

Jake poked out a distrustful head. Cedric addressed him:

"It's half past four and mighty draughty."

"But I thought we only started at six."

"Aye, but that's on the coal-face, me lad, and thar not theer yet. Edgar said he'll pick thee up i'ten minutes and take thee."

Edgar Ferris was a miner living two doors away. Jake nodded.

"Aw reet, I'll be theer."

Cedric gloated over the reply for a moment, turned on his heel like a matador who has just seen the bull go down from his swordthrust, and strode off into the black morning.

Jake scampered quietly downstairs and grabbed his working-clothes off the rocking-chair. Vest, pit-drawers, patched trousers, woollen stockings, clogs and jacket with the elbows out. Tom watched him miserably. Here was Jake off to the pit with a brand new tommy-tin and four bacon sandwiches while he, Tom, had to go to school again. Not for long, mind you. Only two years — that was all.

Jake was trying to be matter-of-fact. He gulped down the glass of water Sarah had left on the table and stuffed his bacon sandwiches into his tommy-tin. Licking a greasy finger, he realised how hungry he was. He had had his supper too early. He took out one of the sandwiches and broke off a third for Tom. They both wolfed down the food and Tom wiped his greasy fingers on his pyjamas as he followed Jake out to the door. It was January and, when Jake opened the door, a biting wind blew round Tom's bare feet and cut through the pyjamas. His teeth chattered but he stuck it out on the doorstep with Jake until Edgar clattered and clanked along a few minutes later.

As Jake and Edgar melted away into the darkness, Tom turned his back in disgust and re-entered his home. He gave the door a vicious bang, waking up Sarah and all the neighbours on both sides.

*   *   *   *   *   *   *

It was half an hour's walk to the pit-head in Billinge and Edgar took the opportunity of enlightening Jake a little about the work which awaited him.

"Thi fust day today, Jake?"

"Ah."

"Hoggs says as they are starting thee off as a lasher-on. Tha'll be aw reet, tha'll be wi'me and me drawer on this shift, we'll keep an eye on thee."

Jake knew that Hoggs was some sort of under-manager, but he did not know what a lasher-on was. He decided to find out a little more.

"What does a lasher-on do?"

"Well, tha helps t'drawer to get tubs up to t'shunt and then tha gets 'em on to the main line. Then tha lashes 'em on — tha couples 'em up. When t'pony comes and tha has 'em all coupled up, tha goes with the thrutchers and does a bit o' thrutchin thisell. When yo get 'em up to t'pit-eye, the runners-in will take 'em off yo, then tha takes th'empty tubs back when they've finished with 'em. Dost follow me?"

Jake shook his head.

"Never mind, tha'll see what I mean when we get started."

And that was how it was. First they got into the cage with three other miners.

Jake noticed how white their faces were at the beginning of the shift; they seemed to be ailing. He remembered that he had not washed. Not much point in it anyway. His stomach gripped him as the cage descended at speed, but soon they seemed to slow down and stop and then start to climb again. He wondered what they were going up again for. Perhaps they had forgotten to take somebody. After a while the cage came to a halt and everybody got out. The air was warm and blankety and Jake realised that they were down after all. He could have sworn that they had been about to emerge at the top. He looked about him and noticed that there were rails leading right up to the shaft. Edgar told him that this place was the pit-eye. The two black-faced men who nodded a greeting to the new arrivals were the runners-in. Their job was to put full tubs of coal into the cage for winding to the surface. Jake's group left the runners-in behind them and passed through a huge brattice door into a stuffy chamber about ten feet square. Inside there waited a door-minder who carefully put the first brattice door to before opening a second one at the other end of the chamber and letting them out. Jake felt the hot air waft into him. He gathered that the chamber had something to do with ventilation. Now they were on the

Old miners

main line and, swinging their lamps, the miners tramped off down the long tunnel.

It was half an hour's walk to the coal face. Jake walked behind Edgar down the middle of the rails, peering from side to side in the dim, flickering light. Here there was plenty of height and width, the roof being supported by numerous sturdy props and closely-packed black dirt on the sides. The slope flattened out for a few hundred yards and then dipped more steeply than before. They crunched onwards for what seemed an age, until the main tunnel finally came to an end and the single track of rail split up into several tracks, which disappeared through narrow openings in the walls in different directions.

There were a number of empty tubs on some of these lines and Edgar told Jake that they would soon be filling them. The place where the converging tracks joined the main one was the shunt and here most of the miners took off their coats and hung them up with their tommy-tins on nails in nearby props. Edgar signalled to one of the other men — his drawer — and, bending a little, told Jake to follow them down one of the side-tunnels. Jake obediently pushed his tub after them, as yet with no need to bend, but seeing very little. They went on for five minutes or so, the roof gradually getting lower, until even Jake had to stoop and the tub would hardly pass. The two full-grown men were now bent double and a few moments later they went down on their hands and knees and began to crawl. Jake saw that Edgar held his right arm with the lamp stretched out stiffly in front of him, dragging himself along on his left elbow. The drawer shouted back to Jake to leave his tub where it was, practically jammed against the roof in any case, and follow them so he would be able to see what was happening up front. Jake abandoned his tub, squeezing around the side of it so he could follow the drawer, who was fast disappearing with the light. Dirt from the packed wall dislodged and trickled down Jake's neck as he squeezed through and by the time he had done ten yards on his hands and knees he felt every inch a miner. He had left his lamp back at the shunt and he could see very little apart from the clogs and posterior of the drawer. It was a queer experience burrowing along like that in the dark and he was suprised how soon he became tired.

Suddenly there was a slight widening and he saw Edgar's lamp find the black glint of coal. Jake was used to seeing coal nearly every day, but for some reason he was impressed by the sight of it now. This coal had something different about it. It looked confident and at home. It had not been shovelled around yet. Jake would have been content to sit down beside it and examine it a short while in the lamplight. Perhaps stroke some of the shiny parts. Edgar, however, had different ideas. Near the face lay a wicked-looking pick and a heavy shovel. Edgar took the pick himself and gave the shovel to the drawer who backed away to give him working room. Edgar hooked his lamp into the dirt on one side and wriggled around until he could let fly at the coal. The drawer informed Jake that they had only 22 inches to work in and it was one of the lowest roofs they had seen for some months. Edgar could not even swing from his knees, but was compelled to lie full length on his stomach and swing his pick laterally. Hampered in this manner, an unaccustomed worker would hardly have been able to hit the coal at all.

When he was hooking from right to left, Edgar managed to get astonishing power behind his blows and the coal came crashing down in huge lumps. When he hooked from left to right he was unable to get the same force behind it and often had to prise the lumps out. After he had hacked his way through several feet of coal, Edgar was obliged to wriggle on top of the broken heap in order to get another crack at the face. Lying on top of the black rubble, he first picked up several large pieces from under his face and chest and passed them back to the drawer. Then he wriggled a little further forward into the hole he had made and commenced to kick back the rest of the rubble, like a dog making a hole at the bottom of the garden to bury his bone in.

Soon he had cleared himself enough space to be able to resume coal-cutting and the drawer got busy with the shovel, piling the coal up as far back as he could. Jake was sent back to fetch the tub and bring it down to the pile of broken coal, so they could fill it. To do this, they took three or four planks out of the front of the tub to enable them to get the coal in, since the top was scraping the roof. The drawer used the shovel and Jake picked up medium-sized lumps in his hands and heaved them in after the shovelfuls. The air was filled with the fine dust and Jake coughed from time to time. He did not feel tired now that he had no crawling to do but he soon found that handling coal led to his hands getting covered in cuts and bruises. Gradually he began to feel his hands less and less and the cuts more and more, but he knew that he had not been so happy for months.

When the tub was full, it was Jake's turn to push it back to the shunt and put it on the main line for the pony to fetch. The drawer came back with him, pushing alongside. He showed him where to place the tub on the line and how to keep it in position using wedges, called scotches, rammed under the wheels. After that they went back to see how Edgar was getting on, taking with them another empty tub. Edgar, meanwhile, had brought down another impressive heap of rubble and was sitting on it drinking cold tea. Jake and the drawer had brought their tommy-tins in the empty tub and the three of them squatted in a triangle, silently eating their bacon, cheese, bread and coal-dust. Jake enjoyed it. Edgar gave him a swig of cold, bitter tea and told him to remember to bring his own the next day. Jake wondered how he was going to brew it so bitter. They went back to work.

Jake had to take back the second tub on his own. At first he could not budge it, but once the drawer had given him a start he found that by leaning right forward, getting his feet firmly dug in and his head right down and pushing for all he was worth without letting up for a second, he could just manage to keep it on the move. There was a slight up-gradient and the only time he let up for a moment to try and get a better foot-hold the tub stalled on him and he had to suffer the humiliation of calling for the drawer to come and help him get a second start. On the third tub he made no mistake, and kept on scuffling whether his feet slipped or not.

After another dose of tea, Edgar gathered his forces for a fourth and final tub's worth and rested while the drawer loaded it up. He was still a bit short, so Edgar went back to it for another ten minutes and Jake and the drawer scraped the floor clean to make the tub up. By this time they were all tired, particularly Edgar, stripped to the waist and gleaming with sweat. Jake took the tub back and the two men followed slowly, bringing lamps, clothes and tommy-tins with them.

The pony was waiting at the shunt together with the pony-boy — a lad two or three years older than Jake — and another youth whose function it was to help push the tubs up the slope. Such workers are called thrutchers. Jake lashed on his tubs in the manner he had been shown and the pony-boy led off. Jake and the thrutcher lined up behind the back tub and pushed. The pony was in good shape and Jake did not find the thrutching too hard, although it seemed an incredibly long way back to the shaft. There runners-in took over and Jake had done for the day. He waited for Edgar and the drawer to come up and they entered the cage together. By the time they emerged from the pit-head it was half past four and dark. Jake realised that he would not see daylight again until the following Sunday morning.

*   *   *   *   *   *   *   *

Jake stood with the drawer, watching as the four tubs were weighed and Edgar Ferris's number tabs stuck on them. Edgar stood aloofly at a distance, finishing off the dregs of his tea. He knew pit boys liked to walk home with the miners and he waited for Jake to join him before setting off home, the drawer with them. As they turned out of the pit yard they saw Tom standing by the entrance, holding a rod and line and a jar full of tiddlers. Jake turned to Edgar:

"I'll be waitin' at your gate tomorrow mornin'." He nodded to the drawer and went off with Tom in the dark.

"Independent little bugger" growled Edgar to the drawer.

"Aye, but did you see how he pushed them tubs?"

"I seed him. He'll do, I reckon."

*   *   *   *   *   *   *   *

For the next ten years Jake learned his trade, ten to twelve hours a day and six days a week. Going to bed every night at nine and sleeping all Sunday morning as well meant that his social life was non-existent. Apart from a Sunday afternoon walk or fishing expedition with Tom, the pit was his whole life.

Around the pit revolved the hopes, ambitions, disappointments and drama of his youth. On the whole, he was very happy. Down the mine he suffered no setbacks. It was generally recognised early on that he could work the back off anybody his own age and in the years that followed he was constantly in the thick of it. He skipped soft jobs such as leading ponies and minding doors and when he had collected enough scars on his hands lashing-on and helping drawers, he passed straight on to serious thrutching on two-scotch slopes where strength and stamina were needed and where he soon got his nose broken when a tub came back on him. He did not bother to have his nose seen to until the end of the shift and the amount of coal dust which got under the broken skin left him with a long blue scar down the bridge — the envy of his brother Tom for years, until he, too, got a bigger one over the left eye-brow when somebody caught him a glancer with a pick.

When he turned fourteen, Jake had a year as a runner-in with more responsibility, but there was too little action and soon he was down in the workings again as a packer. Packers would go round in groups of three or four, packing into holes in the walls shovelfuls of coal dust lying loose on the floor. Good hard packing made the mine so much safer. It was a hard and monotonous job and the worst of all for getting coal dust in the lungs. From packing he went on to datelling. Datellers usually came down on the afternoon shift with the purpose of making the roof safe after the excavations of the morning. They pack, put up pit props, clear the floor and have the workings in shape for the next shift. While he was a dateller Jake covered a lot of ground down several mines in the Billinge area and saw many of the various aspects of mining. He saw how much coal could be got when the roof was high enough and how incredibly difficult working could be in twenty inches. He saw dry and hot workings where miners had to be constantly drinking and he saw others so damp that the men were continually rained on. He learned to watch out for gas and to listen for the creak of props indicating an imminent roof fall. He learned how to shield himself from dropping coal and where to run when the lot came down. He saw men killed by tubs and learned to keep off the track on a steep gradient. During this time he grew and hardened, taking knocks without complaining, and when he turned seventeen the boss put him straight on the coal face as a miner, confident that he would soon be filling tubs faster than any other man he had.

It took Jake ten days to learn how to handle the pick to his best advantage and after that he began to turn out coal like a machine. The first three drawers they put to work with him could not stand the pace and were all but buried under the pile of coal. Finally they found him a strong and experienced drawer named Hitchen, who had been a good coal-getter himself in his younger days. Hitchen was glad to team up with Jake when the latter announced that he was willing to go halves with his drawer when they paid him for the coal he had hewn. There were two possible arrangements between a miner and his drawer. Either the miner could pay him a flat rate per shift and take the rest himself, or he could go half and half on what they earned. Greedy miners usually made a flat guarantee and then worked like horses to make their own money, although this policy could backfire if the workings were difficult and they did not get enough coal. A hard-working miner with a good output naturally benefited by paying a guarantee instead of sharing. Jake, however, having decided it was no use paying a man a guarantee and then burying him, stuck to his arrangement with Hitchen, who was undoubtedly the fastest drawer in the pit. The result was that before Jake was eighteen the pair of them had broken all records for getting coal that the pit had bothered to keep and they consistently took home pay packets twice as thick as those of their colleagues.

*   *   *   *   *   *   *   *

Tom, who went down the pit on his tenth birthday, followed largely in Jake's footsteps. While they were boys, Jake was always ahead of Tom in jobs and pay, but the younger brother did not mind as long as he was getting dirty every day. They always worked on the same shift and very often in the same part of the mine. When he was eighteen, Tom was promoted to the face and from then on the two brothers hewed coal side by side whenever the face was wide enough for more than one man to work at.

Tom was the only miner in the pit who could rival his brother in output. When they were working together he would match Jake tub for tub and swing for swing, though Jake generally brought down bigger lumps through better aiming and would usually be three or four minutes ahead on each tub. In build, they were somewhat different. Although they were both of medium height, Jake was noticeably broader in the shoulders but with the narrow waist and slim hips of an athlete. Tom was not so broad and slightly round-shouldered, with a thicker waist and heavier legs. His strength lay in his huge bones which were apparently unbreakable and which made him quite a heavy man. When fully clothed he appeared, with his narrow, bony face and round shoulders, a lighter man than Jake, who had broad cheekbones, strong neck and ruddier countenance, but in reality Tom was a stone heavier than his brother. Armed with a pick, he displayed brute strength and his special hard swings had a sound all of their own. Jake could swing viciously, too, but he achieved his results more by his athlete's timing and mobility. From a difficult horizontal position he could uncoil like a spring and hit the coal just where he wanted to. He put all his strength into his blows but he was crafty in their distribution and he was one of the few miners who could swing equally well in both directions. He never tried to put out more tubs than Tom and employed the three minutes he might have gained kicking back broken coal to help his drawer. They both made good money and their drawers, too, were happy.

CHAPTER SEVEN

Our Nell's Jack

In the year 1879, England was hit by the Big Frost and Carr Mill Dam, near Billinge, froze over for four whole months. It was a big year for Billinge, for it is the only time on record that a Billinger rocketed to national fame.

Jack Hill, who was later to become the licensee of the "Brown Cow" Inn at the top of the Rant, was then a young man of nineteen. Born on the 20th of October, 1860, he had been a speedy skater since boyhood and at the time of the Frost he was currently being proclaimed champion skater of all Lancashire. This claim was disputed by many, but it was true that Jack had never been beaten since growing to man's stature. In 1879 these controversies were to be settled beyond all doubt.

Carr Mill Dam is a deep and treacherous stretch of water both in summer and winter, but at the time of the Big Frost the ice was so thick that it was quite safe for large numbers of people to go on it without fear of any kind of accident. Shops, coffee-waggons and toffee-stalls were set up on the ice and skating matches were held nearly every day in front of thousands of spectators. People flocked in from Wigan, St. Helens, Preston, Liverpool and Southport and contestants and their supporters soon began to arrive from other counties. Such was the wintry splendour of the scene and the excitement of the competition that it was not long before important skating matches involving very high stakes were being promoted. In the thick of this rivalry, betting, argument and prize-winning was the young local hero skating under his Billinge nickname of Our Nell's Jack, taking on all comers from the many corners of England, and still the fastest man on the ice.

In the first two or three weeks, Jack cleaned up all the local opposition, which consisted of the best skaters from the South Lancs coalfield. Some of these he beat by half the length of the course.

In the second month, his claim to the Lancashire title was put to the test as he encountered local champions from Southport, Formby, Kendal, Nelson and so on. Some of these men were bigger than Jack and all of them wore fancier outfits, but none of them was able to finish within yards of him.

Excitement mounted as he was matched with the renowned Jacky Highcock from Windermere, who, it was reputed, had never been bested. That day nobody would bet on Our Nell's Jack except Billingers. Highcock got off to a good start and at one stage was leading by sufficient a gap to wave to some of his admirers, but Jack clenched his fists tight and overhauled him in the second half of their tilt to skate in with five yards to spare and his Lancashire title now recognized by all.

In the third month, they produced champions from all corners of the realm. Jack beat the Midlands champion with fifteen yards to spare and the champion of East Anglia by nearly thirty. He thrashed the champions of Cheshire and Derbyshire on the same day and skated past the Cumberland Number One after he had fallen on his nose at the start.

For every victory Jack chalked up, he received a gleaming cup or trophy, which increased in size and splendour as the stakes and gate money went up. People would pack the saloon at the "Brown Cow" after the day's events to see the trophies, which were on display behind the bar. Business had never been so good, for not only were strangers attracted by the exhibition of the fine cups, but the Billingers soon were rolling in money from their betting activities and they were not slow to buy drinks for the losers as well as for their friends and themselves.

By now, Billingers could size up a visiting skater like other men size up a boxing prospect or an up-and-coming racehorse. They would observe him as he put on his skates and fastened up his tunic, quietly assess litheness of movement and visible muscle, watch him practise on the ice before the match and finally decide for themselves the odds they would give or take. Most of them put their money on Jack and he rewarded their faith in him by winning consistently. All the big names finished behind him – Mannion, Gee, Brookfield, Gaffney, Daft Duck, Balmer, the West Leigh crack – counting only the big matches Jack won 22 victories in a row and still the ice on Carr Mill Dam held up the shops, the stalls and the crowds.

People began to realise that the young lad never would be beaten. But there was one man he had not met. The champion of Lincolnshire was a formidable skater with the enigmatic name of Fish Smart. Though he had not been up to Lancashire, Fish Smart had never been beaten on ice and he claimed to be champion of All England. By this time, Our Nell's Jack's fame had spread as far afield as London itself and gaming and betting men both in the North and in the South began to get interested in staging a match between the two champions.

Fish Smart was an excellent and experienced skater who had actually written a book on skating and had even competed with foreigners abroad. It was inconceivable that he could be beaten by this young Billinge novice. There were some who argued that it would be no real match and that it would not be worth while for Smart to make the journey up North. By the time Jack had won 22 matches straight and Smart's backers were forced to accept the challenge, the ice in the South was getting soft. There was one obvious venue for the match, where large crowds, heavy betting and thick ice could all be guaranteed – Carr Mill Dam.

And so it was. Fish Smart and his managers were met by a brass band at Wigan station and driven in style by pony and trap to Billinge. A special lunch was laid on at the "Brown Cow" during which it was observed that Fish was a short, stocky figure in his late twenties with thick, black hair, dark complexion and beady, intelligent eyes. He had a trim waist and strong, muscular calves.

The next day, December 28th, 1879, saw the ice black with people. Fish and Jack had each had a twenty-minute work-out on the ice and were stripping down to their racing tunics. Bets had been placed hours before. One woman had bought flour and baked bread the previous day to sell and raise money for her stake. A farmer had sold two of his pigs to increase his betting capital and Emily Baines, the landlady of the "George and Dragon" had bet a horse and trap on the result. Large sums of southern money put on Fish Smart half an hour before the start of the race made the Billingers wonder if they had been made fools of.

The match was over four hundred yards. A dark cloud passed over the wintry sun and, as the shadow spread quickly over the ice, the sharp crack of the pistol sent the two champions sprinting away. Jack had won the toss for choice of sides, but Fish, like Highcock before him, had faster reflexes than Jack and was two yards ahead after the first few seconds. This was the only advantage he was able to gain, however, and the gap neither widened nor narrowed as Jack matched him lunge for lunge, with five hundred Billingers screaming at him in the dialect he knew so well.

At the halfway mark he clenched his fists in the old, familiar way and pulled up to the shoulder of the Lincoln champion. Smart, however, had been waiting for the psychological moment when the Billinger, having exhausted himself by making up those two vital yards, could be crushed by a sudden counter-sprint on the part of his opponent. For a moment Fish glanced sideways at Jack, noted the lad's contorted face and bursting lungs, then suddenly put his head down and made his own supreme effort, mustering up all the speed that his hardened body and smooth technique afforded him. Jack lost a yard, then another; Billingers choked with disappointment as the gap widened and Jack seemed to lose his rhythm.

The Billinge skater, with the pulverized ice from Smart's skates showering and cutting his face, felt for the first time that winter the humiliation of being behind. The stream of ice, however, meant that he was still within striking distance, so he pressed his head even lower and kept his eyes glued to Smart's flashing heels as they entered the last stretch. Imperceptibly, Jack edged towards his rival and then the crowd shouted hoarsely as daylight could no longer be seen between the two men. Some say that Fish had made his bid five seconds too soon and flagged in the last few yards. Others say that Jack just skated past him in the frenzy normal to any Billinger who was about to be humiliated by a stranger in front of five hundred of his fellow villagers. At any rate, he won by six inches to a foot, which gave him 23 straight victories in 1879. Billinge, for the first and only time in its history, had a Champion of England.

The ice broke soon afterwards and in following years was much thinner and unsuitable for big matches. Fish Smart never came again.

CHAPTER EIGHT

The Pub

Jake was twenty-two before he ever tasted beer. Like most Wiganers he was a prodigious tea drinker, often consuming up to twenty-five cups a day. Sarah had once read an advertisement in the newspaper:

> "USE TRAVANCORE TEAS and get presents such as Brass Fenders, Swing Mirrors, Over Mantels, Marble Clocks, Copper Kettles, Coal Vases, Bronze Figures, Britannia Metal and Silver Plated Teapots, Counterpanes, Pillow Casing and So On."

So for years they drank the produce of Travancore, as strong as Sarah could brew it. Tom would put in one third milk and four spoonfuls of sugar and it still tasted of nothing but tea. On the morning shift Jake "scalded" his tea in a big, cracked mug, drinking it as hot as he could bear, so he would be fortified against the cold, rain or sleet on his way to the pit. When he had drained his mug there would be two inches of swollen tea grains left in the bottom.

The older miners were mostly confirmed beer drinkers and many of the pit-boys were egged on by their elders to start drinking while they were still under age. Jake had often heard his workmates boast about how many pints they had downed the previous Saturday, but was rarely teased on account of his own abstinence, it being well known that he flew into a fit of black temper if anyone made fun of him or his brother. It came as a great surprise to Tom when, one Saturday evening after tea, Jake picked up his cloth cap and said they were going round to the pub for a drink. They were dressed up in their own way – each wore a baggy, dark blue serge suit and had a spotted scarf covering the collarless shirt-neck. A peaked cloth cap and shiny, ankle-length black boots completed the attire. They walked along the row of terraced houses, tightly-laced boots squeaking on the cobbles, hands thrust hard into coat pockets, shoulders slightly hunched, head back and chin well in, nodding a curt howdo to the neighbours leaning over their front gates.

They headed up the hill towards Billinge, for everyone knew that three of the finest pubs in the land surrounded Billinge Church and many of their fellow miners were sure to be revelling there that night. Hitchen had told Jake that one of these public houses, the "Old House at Home", was the cosiest for miles around, with a roaring fire in the Snug, copper kettles on the mantelpiece and all the good company you could wish for. Like most miners, Jake loved coal fires and he considered this would be as good a place as any for Tom and himself to try some ale.

It was a cold, clear winter's night and the three quarters of a mile of steep gradient from Simms Lane End to Church Brow made a pleasant, invigorating pull. They could see the lights of St. Helens over Carr Mill Dam two miles to their left and the black shape of Billinge Hill was just discernible in the starlight half a mile to their right. The air was distinctly colder and fresher as they climbed and they quickened their pace as they saw the welcoming lamps of the Old House at Home directly in front of them for the last four hundred yards.

They crossed the cobbled yard and went in through the open doorway. Hands still thrust deep in their pockets, they edged their way through two low-beamed front rooms which reeked of ale as the occupants stood clinking their glasses, talking animatedly and occasionally spilling beer on the counter and wooden floors. Beyond was the Snug with its stone fireplace and scrubbed wooden tables, around which sat dozens of pleasure seekers, arguing, drinking and playing dominoes. They were mostly pitmen having their Saturday night fling and the air was filled with shouts, singing and blue tobacco smoke. Jake and Tom found a small table a few paces from the bar and sat down under the disapproving eyes of Queen Victoria. Jake lit a cigarette, waited till there was a space at the bar and then walked over and ordered two pints of beer. He carried them inexpertly back to the table, spilling not a little in the process. Their entry had not gone unnoticed by the crowd of domino players, some of whom had been on the night shift with the brothers on the Friday. They nudged each other under the table, ceased to chatter for a moment and stared curiously at Jake and Tom. Jake raised his eyes a little and glared at them briefly.

"Evenin'" he snapped.

"Evenin' Jake. Evenin' Tom" they chorused back.

When this conversation had come to an end Jake closed his fist round the handle of his tankard and started drinking. He did not put it down until it was empty. Tom followed suit. Jake meditated for a moment and frowned at Tom, who took the hint and hurriedly shuffled over to the bar and ordered two more pints. The domino gang resumed their game, continuing to throw glances towards the brothers between turns. Jake and Tom drank their second pint in silence. Tom fished out of his pocket a crumpled packet of cigarettes and morosely offered one to Jake. Just as Jake's frown indicated that he was in a thoughtful mood, Tom had a special thinking expression of his own. It was one of utter dejection. Not that he was really dejected; often he was merely wondering what Jake was thinking. Both men had retained their boyish habit of keeping their heads very still in public, letting their eyes rove around, Jake in the manner of a sergeant major distastefully surveying a slovenly parade, Tom like a caged wild animal looking for a chance to escape.

On this occasion they were both thinking of the same thing. They did not feel drunk yet. Tom was rather relieved. Jake, somewhat deceived, belched quietly. He found it pleasantly bitter. Suddenly they were hailed from the doorway of an adjoining room. Jake looked up and saw standing before him one of his fellow face-workers, Big Jem Parr, eldest son of Gentleman James Parr. The big Billinger was accompanied by another villager called Main Root, whose real name could have been anything.

"Sithee, look what wind's blown in. Howdo Jake, how art doin' lad? Mind if we sit dehn wi' yo'? Siddehn, Root, ah'll fotch t'drinks. Worreryavin' lads?"

Jake hesitated briefly and then motioned them to sit down. They would have beer. Jem was quickly back with four pints and soon it was Jake's turn again. After that it was Main Root and then Tom: the rota had been established. Jem Parr was no older than Tom, but he already had a great reputation as a drinker. He was the only one of the Parrs who took drinking seriously and from an early age had done so as if he had to make up for the lack of interest shown by the rest of the family. His father had done all he could to dissuade him, but in vain. Big Jem was a coal hewer in the Lancaster mould with a savage working tempo and

The "Olde House at Home"

fierce appetites to match. He could eat like a horse, sing like an angel, chase girls with the best of them and put away fifteen pints on Saturday nights. Jake liked this boisterous Long Folder who not only could put out his tubs but be the life and soul of a party with his ribald humour, hearty singing and anachronistic mode of expression. After the first few pints Big Jem's fine, square features took on a ruddy glow and his thick moustache bristled with good temper as he drank people's health, thumped pals on the back and whispered racy titbits in their ears. He was pleased to see Jake and Tom, whom he welcomed as future drinking partners and he set a brisk pace to see how they would take it.

By the time Tom went for his sixth pint, he was not sure whether it was the seventh or the eighth. Somehow he managed to get all the re-filled tankards back on the table, giving himself the one from which he had spilled most. He was peering through a gap in the fog and could see only four beers and Jem Parr's moustache. Everything Jem said seemed terribly important now. Jake was aware that Main Root had gone for the seventh. Did he have to go for the next round? He had better remember always to follow Root. Go and get them pints Jake. It was like treading on feathers. I wonder if I'm drunk. I wonder if our Tom is. He's quiet though, if he is. He's said nowt for half an hour. I'm not drunk, am I hell. I can shift more coal than Big Jem and I can shift more beer too if I have to. Fleckin' Billinger. Thinks he can get me and our Tom stewed. Humph. Not me and our Tom. Not me, anyroad. And not our Tom, noather. Our Tom's aw reet. Our Tom can shift beer.

After the tenth pint, Tom staggered outside and was sick on the cobbles against the old mounting-stone. He went back in feeling weak and inferior, but found that the fog had dispersed in the meantime. Big Jem and Jake were on their thirteenth, Main Root having missed a round sitting quietly with his twelfth. Jake was finding it hard to sit on his stool without keeping his left forearm on the table and was in a black temper. He noticed that he was three inches behind Jem and he hurriedly inclined his tankard to make up the deficit. He spluttered a little but it all went down. Jem pranced off for the next round and soon was back with two new, gleaming, froth-topped tankards, Tom and Root having withdrawn. Jake was getting uneasy. He could still walk and he could still count and he did not feel sick. But he had ceased to be thirsty. It was getting it to go down that was the trouble. He had an alarming thought: suppose he was full? He felt full. Suppose he started brimming over? Jem did not favver full. Anyway, he thought he could manage one more after this.

The fourteenth pint seemed like a gallon to Jake. He appeared to have a whole sea inside him and the waves kept breaking against the back of his glottis. When he had a bit of low tide, he would pour in another inch or two. Jem's blue eyes were riveted on him, a mischievous smile creasing his rosy cheeks. Jake kept his lids lowered, standing guard over his beer-level and nodding or grunting assent at Jem's pleasantries. Main Root gazed at the table top out of an inobtrusive coma and Tom took his eyes off Jem's face only to see how Jake was getting on with his beer.

Jake lurched to his feet. He tramped deliberately to the bar and swayed imperceptibly on his elbow while he waited for his pints. His voice had sounded very distant when he had ordered and he was a little surprised to see that the barman had heard him. He paid for the drinks, turned and steered for the back of Tom's cap. Then he was halfway through the beer and decided he could not finish it. He raised the tankard for another attempt and let the beer wash against his open lips, but it ran out again. He put the tankard down and hoped that nobody had noticed. Jake's had enough, thought Big Jem.

"Time, gentlemen; time and take your corners." The landlord said the same thing every night. Jem looked like a punter whose horse had finished fourth in the Irish Sweep; Jake acquired sudden thirst and craft. His eyes on Jem's empty tankard, he took a deep breath and demolished the damning five fingers of ale. Jem tried unsuccessfully to order more beer and the domino games drew to their logical conclusions amid a dismal collecting of empty glasses. More men were smoking now and some were already making their exit. Main Root was on his feet ready to embark on his nightly ritual of half a mile of fresh air, good neets and the old woman. Big Jem, already losing his edginess at Jake's having bought the last round, shepherded Tom to the door, his arm protectively round his shoulders. Jake brought up the rear, cursing his cigarette which tasted like burning tea leaves and concentrating on keeping his equilibrium, physical and mental.

* * * * * * *

For a man who is drunk or half drunk, a change of air is dangerous. You can sit for hours in a Rudesheim wine cellar or a Spanish bodega and keep calm, cool and clear-headed. It is when you go out in the sun that it hits you. In a public house it is the other way round. The stuffy, smoky, beery atmosphere of a Billinge pub daddies you along in relative sobriety until the unfriendly hour of ten. By this time you are so conditioned that when you make your exit the good, clean, cold air of a starry night might be the lethal clime of a far-off planet. In a matter of seconds the degree of your intoxication can double.

That is what happened to Jake. By the time Big Jem and Main Root had taken their leave and headed down Main Street, Tom was less drunk than his brother. Not that he was sober, for his head reeled and the stars seemed to dazzle him, but some of his weakness had left him and he felt better than he had done for several hours. He was a stronger and more aggressive Tom. Jake, on the other hand, had his first experience of double vision, buildings leaned dangerously out of the vertical and the flagstones under his feet moved back and forth as he staggered forward. He was bearing a grudge, against whom he was not sure. Neither was he sure of the way home. The road seemed dark now, black as pitch. What had Parr said about going down Long Fold in the dark? It would be black as the Divvil's Nutting Bag. What's a Nutting Bag, Jem? I don't know, Jake – nothing: it's just black, that's all. These Billingers. They used funny words and then didn't know what they meant. Where's our Tom? Hey, Tom, come here. Who are aw them folk singing in front of t'pub? Listen to 'em wailing away. Tell 'em to shut up. Howd yer din, will yo! Yo and all yer brass tranklements at this time o'neet. What dost say, Tom? I don't care if they are t'Salvation Army, they'll save nobody makin' a din like that. Look at them buckets on their yeds. Harken him, cawin' me brother. I'm not thi brother, Tom's me brother. Stop wavin' thi drumstick at me, or ah'll take it off thee and belt thee across chops with it.

In his lifetime, Sergeant Ramsbottom had known his share of humiliation. With a nickname like Sheep's Arse you did not have much of a chance. It was like starting off on the wrong foot. He suffered from warts and obesity by the time he was fourteen, wore glasses and was going bald at the age of twenty and proposed no fewer than six times before he was accepted. Deep down he felt that if he had been endowed with a little more physical attractiveness and a more dashing name he had it in him to lead men. The Army, the Navy and the Football Club turned him down successively, but the Salvation Army welcomed him with open arms. After several years in their ranks he was feeling much less frustrated. He had peaked cap and uniform, three stripes and a big drum. He never did any actual preaching, but he would announce hymns, deliver notices and now and then read the Lesson. And when he played in the band he was leading men. His drum was his pride and joy – the symbol of his

The "Stork"

indispensability. It lent him an air of pomp and splendour and clothed in
joviality his increasing corpulence. Above all, you did not have to be musical to
play it. The big drum was resonant, military and stately. Even among drunken
miners it commanded attention. Their eyes would widen, they would stop and
listen, their cloth caps often doing a little swagger in time with the beat.
Sergeant Simon Ramsbottom commanded their respect. And now this monster
with the spotted scarf had snatched away one of his drumsticks.

The sergeant was not sure what he ought to do. As a Soldier for Christ he
supposed he should fight his battle and get the drumstick back. As a practising
Christian his duty was to win the man over with humility and a kind word. He
approached Jake, his face twitching as he struggled with himself. Jake promptly
beat him over the head with the drumstick, as he had promised. It became clear
to Ramsbottom that he would have to fight his battle. It was also clear that he
would lose it. He was afraid to take his drum off in case Jake should think it was
a challenge and take his jacket off. He decided to summon up all his authority
and shout down at the man. Wrenching his peaked cap up again, he
straightened his back, went red in the face, put his right forearm on top of the
drum and swung it round in a menacing arc across his padded stomach.
Pointing majestically down the street with his remaining drumstick he
thundered:

"Begone with you, you insolent ragamuffin!"

Jake took a running kick at the drum and put his foot right through one side of
it. His foot got stuck inside and he clutched wildly at the top of the drum to keep
his balance, resulting in his falling over backwards and bringing the instrument
crashing to the ground. The sergeant went over the top of his drum like a
captain going down with his ship.

Tom had some difficulty getting Jake out from under the drum and
Ramsbottom's prone fifteen stone. Afterwards the drumsticks were returned to
their rightful owner and a badly-winded Jake was led quietly home by his
disconsolate brother, already firm in his resolve never to set foot again in a
public house. On the Monday morning Jake went to Wigan and bought a fine
new drum for the Salvation Army, an organization which, when he was sober,
he admired for their good work. During the following week of afternoon shifts
the two brothers re-attacked the coal face with renewed vigour and the old-
timers said they had never seen two men shift so much coal.

*   *   *   *   *   *   *   *

Jake and Tom got drunk every Saturday night after that for the next three
years. With the prodigious thirst common among miners they drank their way
through all the pubs of Billinge, Garswood, Ashton, Bryn and even as far afield
as Ince, Hindley, Parbold and Appley Bridge. As their control increased, so did

their capacity, so that anything from fifteen to seventeen pints was regarded as a normal evening's drinking. They met miners, mill hands and factory workers from all over the Wigan district and they tried and tested all the local beers and ales available. They could be good company among their friends, but Jake was an easy man to cross after the tenth pint and frequently clashed with strangers as closing time approached. As their consumption increased, the Lancaster brothers seemed to cause a row in almost every pub that they drank in. And yet they were never unpopular men. Their drunken brawling had a righteousness about it. They would not pick on anyone outright; the quiet, meek and defenceless had nothing to fear from them. But let there be a bigmouth present, a boaster, a moody waiter or an officious barkeeper and the fur would fly. Jake with quantities of beer inside him regarded ill temper as his own private prerogative. In this he would permit no competition. He would snarl a pile of insults on the head of anybody who had upset the general peace, but if they said one word back in defence he would thump them till the police arrived.

On the surface at least, Tom was much less belligerent. Beer warmed him inside and he rarely disagreed with anybody. He would often buy an extra round out of the goodness of his heart. But his expansiveness would be curbed by his brother's growing wrath. If Jake had "fixed" on somebody, a change would become apparent in Tom's manner. He would glare around until he had found the culprit and then he would fairly seethe. He would glower at the offender and then look meaningfully at Jake, like a dog asking his master's permission to go and wolf the prey. Tom would willingly have been Jake's bodyguard if Jake had needed one.

It was not unknown for Jake to throw darts at barkeepers who had upset him and kick over tables with half a dozen full pints on them. He never used anything but his fists to beat anyone with and in this respect the brothers never had any serious trouble with the police, who hustled them off the premises roughly enough but always remained on first name terms with them. The tough Lancashire bobbies, broken in on the slums of Merseyside, had an almost fatherly affection for the Lancasters, for they knew that with them there would be no broken beer bottles or knives or knees in the groin. You just had to get them out on the street and stand around them for a bit and pretty soon they would all smoke a cigarette and there would be no need even to take them to the station. When a decent interval of time had elapsed, the brothers would go back to the pub where they had figured in the disturbance and pay for anything they had broken. You could not ask for more than that in those days.

CHAPTER NINE

The Thing on the Stile

In the 1880s Billinge was steeped in superstition and there was no-one among the villagers who did not believe in supernatural phenomena of one kind or another. Even a family of Christians like the Parrs, orthodox in their belief that God made the world, accepted without a struggle such ungodlike manifestations as the hell-hounds in London Fields and the twelve-foot ghost near the Dungeon. People from Wigan or St. Helens used to make fun of the Billingers in this respect, but a shrug of the shoulders was all they would get in reply. They were outsiders – they were not from Billinge – so how could they know? So there were no hell-hounds; but on rough nights the Billingers had heard them. What would be out there in the black night's wind baying "Pader, pa-a-der!", happen cows or horses? So there was no ghost; but Bacco Dick and Linnet and Neddy Red and Hugh Parr had seen him and talked to him and felt his cold breath and run before him.

People in a closed community have a common background and a uniformity in their manners, feelings, beliefs and prejudices. They tend to think alike and react alike, especially when outside elements are introduced, for they view things in the context of their own experience and with reference to their particular world. Billinge was the world. It was a place where a single crow meant death and would send a Billinger scurrying to find another one, for two in the same neighbourhood meant good luck or a wedding. You may think well or ill of crows as you wish, but do not expect a Billinger to act naturally or relax if there is a lone crow hovering around. When Mary Ann and Tet were girls, if they had the misfortune to break anything in the house, they quickly smashed another two objects of lesser importance so that they could get on with their work, for Billingers always broke things in threes. There were a score of such minor beliefs, but more basic than these was the general acceptance in the village of the fact that the world was not what it seemed to be on the surface and that dreams and other happenings of nature were symbols or omens of present reality and things to come. If a Billinger dreamt about somebody, he would go and see him the next day and tell him about the dream. The other was sure to listen carefully and the two of them would make their interpretation. A thunderstorm, a fallen tree or a lame calf would not pass unnoticed in those days, for each had great importance for those who had eyes to see.

People in a small, isolated village tend to look at a stranger, a fresh event or a phenomenon of nature with closer scrutiny than would the city-dweller in his busier surroundings. Examination of things and personalities is slower and calmer and there is a deliberate consideration of all the different aspects. A simple thing can have many meanings read into it, when there is time to think about it. In our rapidly-moving world we tend to think three-dimensionally: a stone is a stone; it has length and width and height. The Billingers always thought five-dimensionally; for them the stone also had its niche in time and its context in their lives. These fourth and fifth dimensions of time and significance affected the way in which Billingers thought about everything. If a cock crowed at dawn, (and Billinge was full of cocks) you got out of bed and started making breakfast. If a cock crowed in the middle of the night you got out of bed, went out to the back and killed it at once. Thousands of cocks were despatched in this manner, for only by acting promptly could you forestall death in the house.

A sudden gust of wind through the house may be one thing to you, but it was quite another to a Billinger. Were these villagers over-fanciful? You may say that a spade is a spade and a chair is a chair, but a scientist will tell you that they are whirling masses of molecules and not as solid as they seem. What does the man in the street to-day, lamentably weak in his powers of observation, know about the true reality of the universe? Did these clannish villagers, living close to the soil and to each other, contemplating their trees and flowers and animals and birds, matured through poverty and suffering and death, develop a certain collective insight into the nature of reality? The few who are still alive from the period of which I write retain this sixth sense, or ability to think in extra dimensions, in a remarkable manner. I have seen an old Billinger introduced to a room full of strangers in the 1960s in a far-off part of the world and in a completely different social ambience. At the end of the evening, when we were alone, the Billinger told me which people were rich and which ones pretended to be, who was in good health and who had had pneumonia or growths or other maladies, who was honest and who was not, who was sleeping with whom, who had been disappointed in love, which persons would do well and which would fare badly, whom one could believe and whom one had to take with a pinch of salt. Flattery, sincerity, strengths and weaknesses had all been recorded in computer-like fashion. From my acquaintance with those present, I was able to verify that most of the observations had been right on the nail. The conclusions had been reached quickly and effortlessly. Was it simply a question of remarkable power of observation or was the villager psychic?

One of these old-timers will never laugh at you if you tell him that something strange or unnatural has happened to you. He will show great interest and try to get in on it himself. Gentleman Jim was once pestered by an old man called Hucko who lived alone in an old stone cottage at the Rant. Hucko claimed that three or four times a week he was almost blown out of bed by cold gusts of wind through the bedroom. The house had a reputation of being somewhat ghostly and Gentleman Jim did not doubt for a moment that the man was telling the truth. He promised Hucko he would come and spend the night with him to investigate. The first night he stayed there nothing happened. On the second night there was no disturbance either. On the third night the bedclothes were blown off suddenly at half past two in the morning. Jim got out of bed and put the light on. He examined the doors and windows and found them all shut tight. He put the light off again and ten minutes later there was another gust of wind. Jim gripped the bedclothes tightly and they flapped like a huge flag for the best part of a minute before the squall ceased. He put the light on again and he and Hucko got down on their knees while Jim prayed to the Almighty. There were no more gusts that night and Jim went home satisfied that he had done his best. Hucko still had trouble with the gusts of wind, however, and they continued till the day he died, though he said Gentleman Jim's prayers had calmed things down just a wee bit. No other measures were taken. The Billingers just accepted the fact that if you lived in Hucko's house you got your bedclothes blown off three times a week. It was just something you had to put up with. Apart from that, it was a perfectly good house.

There was a farm-house behind the Cockshut which had a blood-stained plank in the floor. Fifty years earlier, the farmer had fallen in love with his milkmaid. They had had a whirlwind, passionate affair, ending in a lovers' quarrel. The maid threatened to tell the farmer's wife of their adultery and it is said that he murdered her by cutting her throat. The bloodstains on the floor were scrubbed away, but in a few days the wood took on a reddish-brown hue. A new plank was put in, but still the stains returned. They were still there in 1910, for Hugh Parr went to see them. The farm workers told him that when the wheat was high they often saw the milkmaid striding along, her pail under her arm. She never came near enough to be spoken to, but they had all seen her.

Billingers were not afraid of the dark, but there were times when they would simply refuse to go down a dark lane, not because of the blackness but because they suddenly felt that something evil lay in wait for them. Tet, one of the biggest and toughest women in the village, feared no man or woman, but when she suspected the Devil was around the corner wild horses could not drag her round it. Most Billingers had this sense of foreboding from time to time and no amount of persuasion would allay their fears when it came upon them. The men were no braver than the women. There was one person in Billinge, however, who had never been known to be afraid. This was Mary Ann, the eldest of the Parr daughters. Physically strong, she had a mental toughness and courage exceeded by no-one in the village. She walked the dark lanes and lonely woods with confidence, either alone or dragging her sisters after her. God watched over her, to be sure, but if the Devil had one night got in her way she would have known how to handle him.

One winter's night the three sisters had been to Garswood to look at the body of a young cousin who had died two days previously. There had been a lot of sobbing and moaning and as the girls were walking home through Mulks

Wood, Tet and Caroline were distinctly jumpy. There was no moon and the path was barely visible as Mary Ann felt her way forward. It was windy and the trees and bushes rustled and swayed. In the middle of the wood there were two stone steps, familiar to the villagers, and Mary Ann, either because her religious fervour had been aroused or in order to test the nerve of her sisters, knelt down on the stone and proposed they all pray. Tet and Caroline had no stomach for a prayer meeting just then, and the stones were cold, but they were too scared to leave Moll. As they shivered in the night wind the sound of Mary Ann's raised voice disturbed some night creature and there was a sudden howl from the bushes nearby. Tet shouted "T'wood's full of boggarts!" and ran pell-mell all the way home, followed by young Caroline a few yards behind. Mary Ann finished her meeting and walked home at a slow, scornful pace, just to show the boggarts whom they were dealing with.

But Moll's turn was to come. A year later she and Tet were employed at Pilkington's glass works in St. Helens. They started work at eight and this necessitated leaving Billinge at six o'clock in the morning. Bridget Conroy, a close friend of Mary Ann, made up the trio and every morning the three girls walked down through the Dam Slacks, past Tinsley's Farm, through the Top Two Gates and then across Sefton's fields towards St. Helens. In winter the mornings were pitch black and they often had to brave driving rain or snow. The path through these fields was intersected by three big hedges, and there were three stiles to clamber over. They knew the route well and had no difficulty with the stiles, even in the dark.

One morning, as they entered Sefton's fields, the first half light of dawn revealed a thick grey fog rolling across the meadows from the dam. It was a damp, clammy fog and visibility was quickly reduced to zero. They navigated the first stile in due course, but had difficulty in keeping to the path, continually losing it, finding it again and stumbling forward, straining their eyes to follow the faintly discernible track. They cussed and swore in the usual village fashion, but somewhere between the first and second stiles Tet got one of her presentiments of evil lying in wait for her. She grabbed the others by the arm and refused to budge another inch. Now Bridget Conroy was a stout-hearted young woman and level-headed enough, but being a Billinger and Irish at the same time she was afflicted by a double set of superstitious beliefs sufficiently deep-rooted to make her heed a warning such as this. Tet, moreover, though not eloquent by nature, had such a sepulchral tone on such occasions that she could strike terror in the hearts of all around her. The awful thing that was ahead was so horrible that it could not be expressed in words or encompassed by an ordinary mortal's imagination. The extent of the nearby evil was reflected solely in her shuddering frame, her transfixed stare, her desperate, gasping breath. Bridget wavered, and then shivered. Mary Ann strained her eyes through the gloom ahead and tugged impatiently.

"What the hell art frickent on, Tet? It's only a bit o' fog."

"Oh, Christ, Moll, they're waitin' for us. I'm not gooin'!"

"Pull thee knickers up, you soft bugger. Take her other arm, Bridget."

"I'll not budge. Yo cawn't make me!"

But they made her. Bridget was comforted by Mary Ann's confident manner and, conquering her own hesitation and fear, she helped her friend to get Tet moving again. Tet continued to swear and admonish them, but only had half her heart in the tug o' war as she was terrified of being left alone. Mary Ann was worried about arriving late for work, for she knew how obstinate her sister could be. After ten minutes of arguing, quarrelling and further losing one's way, they saw the second hedge loom up out of the mist and approached the second stile. For some reason it looked unwontedly black and menacing. Tet lurched to a halt and shrieked:

"Look at the stile!"

From a distance of five or six yards, in the fog, it presented only a blurred outline; but one thing was sure: it was different. Fog billowed over it and it was lost from view, momentarily. Mary Ann swallowed hard and edged forward. She could hear Bridget groaning behind her:

"Holymarymotherofgod . . . ."

The wind touched Mary Ann's face and she could half see the stile again. The branches of the tall hedge swayed and swished. Her foot hit against the first step of the stile. She jumped nervously, for she could see a black shape on top of the stile. A fallen tree? A drunk? An animal? It did not move. She still could not see more than a yard ahead and the shapes of Tet and Bridget had disappeared in the fog behind her. She took the step up and groped forward. Her outstretched hand touched a cold, clammy, but solid object. Reassured a trifle, she ran both hands along it. Suddenly the fog rolled over and off it and she saw it clearly. It was a coffin.

She fell off the stile, picked herself up and ran. First she crashed into Bridget Conroy, who was clutching Tet. The Irishwoman was aghast at seeing Mary Ann run away from anything.

"Sweet Jesus, what is it, Moll?"

"A coffin!" shouted Mary Ann, running on into the fog, anywhere, away from the sinister stile. Her defences were down, her cool brain for once befuddled and unable to function. Her reasoning had carried her in relative calm as far as the stile, but there it had broken down. How had Tet been right and she wrong? The utter illogic of the whole situation simply routed her. She wanted to flee from this foggy Hades, this unreal, half-lit, clammy underworld and get back to familiar houses and streets and faces where she could pause and think and work things out properly, and then she would be all right again.

They had lost the path and splashed through puddles in hollows and tore their stockings on gorse and bramble. They now had no bearings at all, but kept running until their breath came in short, choking gasps and their knees trembled and caused them to stumble in riggots. Then hoarse cries came out of the fog behind them. They heard splashes and squelches and the blanketed thud of approaching feet. Terrified, they set off again in flight, willy-nilly, at a tangent from their original course – if they had had one. The sounds of pursuit abated and then took on again and soon eerie shouts of "Parr!" and scuffling feet appeared to be all round them, though hidden behind the veil of fog. Suddenly two rough-looking men came charging into their midst. They were unshaven strangers and they grabbed Mary Ann and Tet by the arms and pinioned them. As they fought and Bridget screamed helplessly, the happenings of the morning were explained.

The two men were coffin makers from St. Helens. They had been bringing an empty coffin to Billinge on order from someone in Main Street and they had put it on the stile to have a rest. Hearing the voices of the Parr girls (whom, it seemed, they knew slightly) coming through the fog, they had decided to play a trick on them. They hid in the hedge nearby and watched events take their due course. On seeing the girls flee in panic, they took pity on them and had chased them for ten minutes across the meadows to offer their explanations and, it is hoped, their apologies.

The girls were two hours late for work, for they had to go back home and revive themselves with hot tea. They were not fired, for they told of the trick that had been played on them and the foreman excused them readily. Mary Ann was never known to falter again, though afterwards she was slower to pounce on Tet whenever the latter indulged in her gloomy premonitions. Forty years later, when Mary Ann was at death's door, she was to show that her own sense of foreboding was as strong and as accurate as anybody's. But that is a story for another chapter.

CHAPTER TEN

Conversion

In the summer of 1886 Jake and Tom went on a wagonette trip to Southport organized by the "Labour in Vain" public house at the bottom of Main Street in Billinge. It was common for pubs to arrange these outings, which generally lasted the whole day. Big Jem had signed them up for it during a drinking bout a few weeks earlier. Neither Jake nor Tom had seen the sea and as the day of the outing approached, their interest grew. Jem had been regularly on such excursions and gave them glowing accounts not only of the Southport sands, but of the various watering places that they would call at en route. When the brothers returned home from the morning shift on the Friday they cleaned their best pair of boots, got Sarah to starch and iron their shirts and tried on their new cloth caps again in the mirror over the sideboard.

They were due to depart at seven the following morning from Slack Farm, across the road from the "Labour in Vain". Getting up early was part of their daily routine and, with habitual miners' punctuality, they reached the bottom of Main Street at exactly seven o'clock. The horses, driver and wagonette were there, as well as Big Jem and his younger brother Hugh, a smiling, clear-eyed boy of thirteen. The others were still to come and it was not until a quarter to eight that the Billinge contingent was complete, the last arrivals being women with their small children. There were about thirty people in all, mostly miners and farmers with their younger womenfolk. Leading the party was Gentleman James Parr, himself a miner now in his mid-forties, accompanied by his sons Jem and Hugh and two of his teenage daughters, Tet and Caroline.

The sun was shining, the air was cool and scented and everyone was in fine spirits as they clambered aboard, jammed tightly against each other on the hard, wooden benches. A crack of the whip and the two fine chestnut horses tossed their manes and headed down Rainford Road towards Ormskirk and the sea. At least half the people were from Long Fold and the conversation was lively and unbroken. The Long Folders are the Andalusians of Billinge: give them the sun, a clear blue sky, a wagonette and an open road and they will tell you that two and two makes five, even though they know that it really makes six. The boisterous chatter and rapidity of the exchanges left Jake and Tom somewhat bewildered. They were reticent by nature and by training, for Sarah's was a quiet, matter-of-fact house, designed for the sober business of living, where conversation was restrained and imagination hardly rampant. Tom listened in wonderment as the Long Folders shouted and sang, praised and accused, laughed and gesticulated, quipped with the driver and cursed the horses, joked and mimed and opened conversations with total strangers over hedgerows and fences along the route. He noticed with amazement how Billingers comported themselves in exactly the same way wherever they went, just as if they had never left the village. They were quite different from the people in Garswood or Simms Lane End, who were diffident and retiring on first contact and did not care to reveal their true nature until they had an inkling of what other people thought of them. Billingers did not seem to care a jot about the opinions of strangers and took their own little world around with them as they travelled.

Jake, tight-lipped and wary by nature, sat in awe at the naturalness of the villagers. When they had had their fill of shouting at workers in the fields, they all faced inwards and began to tell Billinge tales. Jake heard how Bacco Saul had drowned himself at the second attempt in Carr Mill Dam and how Phil Yallick had caught Saul's scarf when he was fishing for perch. How Nellie Dumplin had been so frightened by a twelve foot man wearing a white hat she had met in Mulks Wood she had had a miscarriage and how Linnet had been bitten in the leg by a luminous Hell-Hound in the quarry. Even to-day dog-slaver used to ooze out of the scar in damp weather. After that Big Jem led them all singing "Early One Morning", "How Should I Your True Love Know?", "The British Grenadiers" and "D'ye ken John Peel".

As they were winding up the last song, they pulled up in front of the "Wheatsheaf" near Rainford, where they were due for refreshments. Here Big Jem was in the habit of singing an appropriate solo before entering and he did not fail his admirers on this occasion:

> *"I passed by your window*
> *When the morning was red,*
> *The dew of the rosebud,*
> *The lark overhead,*
> *And ho, I sang softly,*
> *Though no one could hear,*
> *To bid you good morning,*
> *Good morning, my dear."*

Refreshments consisted of a glass of whisky or brandy for the grown-ups and port wine topped up with hot water and sugar for the children. They were soon on the road again and Jake found himself squeezed between the two Parr girls, Tet and Caroline. Caroline was about fifteen, pretty and feminine. Her father was sitting next to her and she spent most of the trip chatting to Gentleman Jim and her brother Hugh. The three of them looked very much alike. Tet was a much sturdier girl of seventeen and was a female version of Big Jem. Sleeves rolled up to reveal powerful forearms, she sang, shouted, waved her arms, bounced up and down like a rubber ball and swore like a trooper when she thought her father could not hear her. She was employed at the glassworks in

St. Helens, but she knew all about the pit through her brother and father and she gave Jake her opinions on various mining operations and on several pitmen too. Jake nodded and grunted his way to Ormskirk, where they clattered into the big yard behind the "Morris Dancers". It was full of horses, wagonettes and day-trippers. Breakfast awaited them and they tucked in to biletam butties (boiled ham sandwiches) with mustard on. Jake noticed that Tet ate more than he did and he supposed that this accounted for her great energy.

Again they boarded the wagonette and completed the last lap to arrive at Southport just after noon. They alighted quite near the beach and the company split up into groups of four or five, each with differing ideas as how best to spend the day. Gentleman Jim was to show some monuments to his son Hugh and one or two of the others. Most of the women headed with the children for the stalls and amusements and other groups decided to start off on the sands. It was announced that they would all meet at half past four and have tea in the same café. Big Jem, Jake and Tom made a beeline for the nearest pub and drank two quick pints each. The brothers were by now quite anxious to see the sea and they followed Jem down to the sands and looked for it. Low tide at Southport is not quite the same spectacle as rough water at Blackpool or New Brighton and although the sea was not quite so far out as it is today, they still had to walk a long way over the sand until they actually got their feet into the water. With breeches rolled up to their knees, carrying boots and stockings under their arms, Jake and Tom paddled along happily behind Jem, breathing in the tang of salt, iodine and shrimps, squinting at the sunlight on the waveless surface, enjoying the light breeze, the hustling donkeys and the huge expanse of sand.

Jem was the one who decided how long they paddled, for he had done it before and knew what he was about. After half an hour or so they came out of the water, feet numb with cold and forearms aching from carrying their boots. Sitting down on drier sand, they rubbed their toes and dried their feet on their crumpled breeches. The sun ducked momentarily behind the clouds and Tom sneezed as the beach turned grey. Quickly they put on their thick stockings and walked on to the nearest tea stall. After steaming mugs of hot tea they went from stall to stall and bought each other the sea-side delicacies – cockles and mussels, clams and whelks, shrimps and oysters. The Garswood men picked gingerly at first, but Big Jem ate everything with gusto and ordered the same again and it was not long before Jake and Tom realised how hungry the sea air had made them and they bought more bags of everything and ate till they had stomach-ache.

They passed the day pleasantly enough, walking up and down the promenade and sands, looking at the shops and restaurants in Lord Street ("the finest street in England") and smoking a few cigarettes on benches in the parks. Big Jem knew how to relax on an occasion like this and he had a whale of a time insulting the local shopkeepers and waiters and then winking at them to show he was only kidding. He bought sweets for children he had never seen before, flirted openly with flower girls and had them in and out of all the antique shops trying to find a teapot for his mother. Jake and Tom were not used to entering shops and then leaving without buying anything and they wondered how Jem got away with it without offending the proprietors.

The party reassembled at the appointed time and, after a brief discussion, decided to limit their refreshment to tea and cakes, since it was unanimously agreed that they should make a stop on the way home at a well-known chipshop approximately midway between Southport and Billinge. Half an hour later they were homeward bound, excitedly discussing their different experiences and comparing souvenirs and other purchases they had made. In those days, when a bag of shrimps cost three-ha'pence, you could get a lovely brooch for twopence, a necklace for fourpence and a fine pendant and locket for sixpence. Jake was shown a whole array of clasps, pins, ear-rings, marble ashtrays, leather purses, combs, mirrors and spoons. Many of these articles bore the name "Southport" as did a large assortment of cups and saucers, jugs and commemorative plates destined for the numerous Welsh dressers in the Billingers' possession. Gentleman Jim had bought a plaque for the wall of his parlour. It said simply: THY FATHER KNOWETH. His son Hugh had purchased another one for his mother Susannah: WHAT IS HOME WITHOUT A MOTHER? But the bargain of the day, in Jake's eyes, was the teapot eventually secured by Big Jem. It was what they called in those days a barge teapot. Made of glazed earthenware, it was dark brown in colour, adorned with primrose flowers and green leaves, but what interested Jake most was its size. Squat and heavy, it held all of six pints. It was an appropriate present for Susannah, who had her seven surviving children all living at home. Jake resolved to look for a similar teapot for Sarah, Tom and himself.

The chip-shop was thronged with rosy-cheeked customers, most of them elated through having spent the day by the sea and one more ravenous than the next. Jem and Tom volunteered to queue up on behalf of their party and thirty minutes passed before the feast arrived: bags of fish and chips, barm cakes with pork and onion stuffing – what a repast!

It was almost dark when they resumed their journey and soon the moon rose and stars winked down at them as they jogged and swayed along the bumpy roads. It was pleasantly cool and some of the women and girls put shawls around their shoulders; the men turned up the collars of their jackets and smoked contentedly.

A mile out of Skelmersdale, one of the wheels came off. This was not an uncommon occurrence, for if care was not taken to apply sufficient grease something would catch fire, the weight of thirty people would drive bolts or axles through weakened woodwork and a wheel would suddenly stick out at a angle or drop off altogether. In this instance they heard the shrill grind of metal against metal and seconds later an ear-splitting crack as the left rear wheel jammed, skidded a few yards and flew off into the ditch. The back of the wagonette sagged sickeningly, they veered wildly to the right and the horses were hurriedly pulled to a halt. Nobody was hurt, but they were all in for a long wait while the driver set off to the nearest wheelwright. The repairs might take several hours and Gentleman Jim decided to go on ahead and return to Billinge on foot with news of the accident. In this manner he would allay any fears on the part of Susannah or others, that any graver consequence had befallen the members of the expedition.

Jake and Tom offered to accompany him and they eventually set off together with the boy Hugh, leaving Big Jem and the other men to keep up the spirits of the women and children, who could not be expected to cover eight or nine miles under the weight of their various purchases. It was an ideal night for walking and they strode briskly along the country lanes, four abreast as they chatted, occasionally giving way to passing wagonettes. The brothers listened with respect to Gentleman Jim for they knew that the latter, though now only a checkweighman, had been an adventurer in his youth and had actually visited the United States of America and spent a year travelling around that vast country. It was the first time that Jake had conversed at length with a man of Parr's background and learning. First they talked about mining and their common acquaintances, for they had sometimes worked in the same pits. The mine was Jake's whole life and he knew it intimately, but he realised as they talked that Gentleman Jim, though a miner by profession, was hardly one by inclination. Parr was interested in his work and did it well, but he saw the local pits and indeed the whole mining industry as a passing phase of the Industrial Revolution, a temporary, troublesome and menial activity which, in the name of progress, sentenced thousands of 19th century Englishmen to meaningless toil in conditions worse than those endured by the slaves of the Pharaohs. He was not so concerned with political reform, for he supported no party, but he questioned the whole concept of excessive industrialization and deplored the evils and ugliness that it had brought with it.

He had a wider vision of a better, more old-fashioned England, where the modern sciences would be applied to agriculture and the traditional crafts, where Englishmen could stay close to the soil on better farms and fields, cling to their solid, stone houses and churches and cathedrals, keep their boats and their woodland and animal life, and adhere to the old values, which urban encroachment seemed to destroy. Jake, to whom all these ideas were completely new, could not help feeling the essential Englishness of this Billinger who took it for granted that the rural beauty of the countryside through which they were passing was his by right of birth and must not be destroyed. Gentleman Jim quoted freely from the most English of the poets – Spencer, Milton, Pope and Tennyson, now and then going to Keats or Shelley for a description of Nature.

Jake, now out of his depth, now again picking up the thread, found that his interest grew as his own ideas began to form. He had never really considered the question of beauty versus ugliness, nor had he ever stopped to think what might be good for England, for he had never travelled and did not think internationally, but he knew what Parr meant about factories and mills producing a race of men which differed from those people who enjoyed more space and dignity of environment as they made their living. He felt that miners – face workers at least – were different again, for the all-out nature of their toil had to make them a special breed.

Jake and Tom were astonished to hear Gentleman Jim say that he had known their father, inasmuch as he had attended meetings of the Miners' Association at which Robert Lancaster had spoken. He had only been a youth in his teens, but he remembered the eloquence and forthright character of the man, how he had completely gained the confidence of his audience, how he had been warmly applauded on concluding his remarks. As he listened to this account, Jake marvelled at his father's talent. He and Tom were simple pitmen, gruff and inarticulate because that was their way of life. Would he be able in some way to pass on that talent to his own sons? He suddenly felt that it was important to do so, without really knowing why.

They talked for a while about public speakers and preachers and the churches. Gentleman Jim, in his capacity as Sunday School Superintendent, was used to attending meetings of various kinds and had heard all the best ministers in South Lancashire. He was a great believer in the power of the spoken word and felt keenly the responsibility of his generation to instruct young people in the old ways and to guide them through the period of decay and dissipation that inevitably lay ahead. He was a Puritan, without compromise, except in the way he put across his ideas. Jake, who rarely compromised himself, liked Parr's unswerving attack on the evils of the age (laziness, slovenliness, dirt, greed, dancing, drinking, ungodliness and actresses) and his loyal defence of the good and true. His eldest son Jem drank and never went to church, his daughters Tet and Moll swore like cavalrymen, even young Hugh, his spiritual heir, would grow up with a twinkle in his eye and put over the Scriptures in his own humorous, give-and-take style far removed from his father's; but Gentleman Jim continued along the path which tradition and his forbears had chosen for him. In an age of transition he led from the front, with little doubt in his mind that the Devil would take the hindmost, and if any around him did fall by the wayside they could not say that they had not been warned.

In spite of his complete intransigence, Parr never offended a listener, for he had the secret of depersonalizing the whole conversation. He must have been well aware of the fact that he was talking to two men whose way of life differed sharply from his own, but he discussed the conflict between Good and Evil as if he were speaking to fellow preachers. He took them into his confidence and respected their background and family, their rough and ready manner, their noble bearing, their record of honest toil and their ability to listen.

It seemed they were soon in Billinge. They topped the crest of Rainford Road in bright moonlight and followed the highway down past the "Brown Cow" and Slack Farm as far as the humid doors of the "Labour in Vain". There Gentleman Jim and his son took their leave, quietly shaking hands and turning right down Long Fold. The brothers tramped on in silence up Main Street, now a deserted, straggling silver ribbon of road leading up towards the Hill. Billinge is a place where night asserts itself, bringing with it a sense of order and finality. It is a time when the natural elements take over and a man on the streets creates tension, as if there were things about that his eyes were not meant to see. Tom glanced uneasily over the churchyard wall and glimpsed row upon row of watchful tombstones – a silent legion of black silhouettes ready to pounce upon lonely sinners. It was one o'clock as they headed over Turpin Fields.

$$ * \quad * \quad * \quad * \quad * \quad * \quad * $$

About a month later, Jake Lancaster went to church for the first time, accompanied by his brother Tom. It has never been clear what led him to make this decision, but once made, it was irreversible. It was characteristic of Jake that he would ponder a matter over for days, or even weeks, without consulting anyone else or seeking advice. Then he would suddenly announce a new course of action, a change, or a policy to be followed, and after that nothing would budge him. Tom did not learn of the new plan until half an hour before the service began. Jake told him to hurry up and put his suit on as they were going to chapel, and that was it. It was a short walk down Victoria Road to the Independent Methodist Chapel at Downall Green, where a Mr Short from Appley Bridge was scheduled to take the Morning Service, commencing at 11 a.m.

Independent Methodist churches have no resident minister, so that preachers are planned on a rota system. Speakers fell into three main categories. Firstly, there were the professional ministers who would visit on loan from other Nonconformist churches. They were properly attired, college educated and proper in their convictions. They had an authentic sameness about them. Not afraid to look the Devil in the eye, they could handle him quietly and they were aware of certain contradictions in the scriptures, for which college had given them all the right answers. They were doctors armed with the right drugs. Only occasionally did they tell their patients what was wrong with them.

The second category consisted of the well to do local preachers who were often prominent men in the area. They were successful laymen who were determined to be successful preachers. More natural in speech than the ministers, they told up-to-date parables which rang true. They could walk and talk with God, but their feet were firmly on the ground. They gave credit to the Lord for their prosperity and were humble before Him, but they let it be known that they got on well with Him.

The third category of preachers was less well-to-do. These men worked in offices and mills and down the pit, and had had to educate themselves. Many of these preachers were Hot Gospellers and poverty was not the only cross they embraced. They did not gild themselves over, for they were wallowing in sin and they knew it. They looked down into their vulnerable souls and produced one misdemeanour after another before the eyes of an awe-struck congregation. Soon the people of the congregation began to look into their own souls and they found out they were as bad as the preacher. Altogether it was a rather dismal procedure, though it served to keep everybody fully awake. Probably to-day it would be called some sort of shock therapy.

Jonas Moore had been Sunday School Superintendent for twenty-five years. Nobody is indispensable, but with Jonas it was a near thing. Basically humble, he belonged to that class of people who shun leadership, limelight or even credit, and at the same time manage to run the whole show. One sometimes wonders what are the real ambitions of people who deliberately spend their lives playing second fiddle. No amount of persuasion can induce them to play first fiddle, but there is mutiny if they are asked to play third. They are the bosuns, the sergeants, the secretaries, the curates, the vice-chairmen, the sidekicks of this world, the St. Peters or the Beezlebubs of the next. They want to hold the reins of power, but they will not ride the horse. They collect influence as others collect stamps. They catalogue their own rights, press slowly and patiently forward, with few setbacks, because they never aim too high. They are capable of great faith and loyalty and can sicken you with it. They can construct but not create and their mediocrity grates all the more for being organized and efficient.

Jonas had never been Chapel President, Vice-President, Secretary or Treasurer, but he had the Sunday School, which was what he wanted. Give him the young ones while they were malleable and he would see that they learned the right things. The President, Vice-President, Secretary and Treasurer were all Jonas's former pupils. Jonas had groomed them for stardom. When they asked him for advice, he gave it willingly. He helped the Treasurer with his books and the Secretary with his Plans. The President consulted him on matters of church history and precedent and the Vice President was always coming to him asking for odd jobs. Jonas reported to them on the progress of the children and told them who the Promising Young Men were. He was the authority on heating, plumbing, repairs and interior decoration and knew more about subsidence than a geologist. He called all the visiting local preachers by their first name and he had known most of their fathers. If the preacher failed to turn up, Jonas could conduct a makeshift service and he could knock four tunes out of the organ when the organist had a bad back. His place was on the front row at the right near the door to the vestry, so that he could nip out and fetch another glass of water for Hot Gospellers when Satan was having the Book thrown at him.

* * * * * * * *

Tom followed Jake into chapel like a lamb going to the slaughter. He hoped desperately they would sit on the back row, but Jake marched down to the front and they sat across from Jonas. The congregation stared at them curiously until the preacher entered with Jonas and climbed the six steps up to the pulpit. He was a stranger to Downall Green and he did a preliminary shuffle with the two Bibles and Hymn Book while the congregation sized him up and he them. Three rows of children, half a dozen adolescents, seven grown-ups, the organist and Jonas. Not so sparkling at all. Certainly not enough to put on a show. Better talk to the children this morning and hope that there would be enough adults to warrant a performance tonight. Wonder where I'm having dinner. Could do with a nice bit of lamb and mint sauce. Give them a long Lesson, throw in an extra hymn, amuse the kids for twenty minutes and finish at ten to twelve. Don't overdo the kid stuff, though, or they'll have you coming to Sunday School in the afternoon. No good missing your snooze.

The service went with a swing and Jonas thoroughly approved. The new man could certainly hold kids. Jonas mentally planned him twice annually for the next five years. Pity he was going to Hortons for dinner. He would get Agnes Horton's grisle pie. Everybody did. He hoped he was not expecting lamb or pork. Might not want to be planned again after the Pie. Horrible thought, and such a reemer with kids, too. Maybe he could ask him to come to the School in the afternoon and give a little talk. Obviously fond of kids. He was probably just hoping he would be asked. Jonas resolved to let him come.

The preacher eyed the clock. Two hymns, the Lord's Prayer, intro to the kids gone, and it was only twenty past eleven. Watch it, or you'll be finishing at twenty to. Spin out the Lesson a bit – better still, get one of the congregation to come out and read it. Never failed. Sound pedagogy, too. He benignly inspected the front row.

"How about one of our fine young gentlemen on the front row coming out to read the Lesson for us?"

He beamed at Jake and Tom. Tom shuddered. Jake looked as interested as a stone statue. Jonas was apprehensive. The preacher decided they needed encouragement and became more jovial. He centred his attention on the fine young man in the grey suit and crooked an inviting finger at him.

"Why, you there, son, – I've no doubt you can read the Lesson better than preachers for miles around, and it wouldn't be the first time you'd done it, would it?"

Tom wanted to shake his head and nod at the same time. Blood pounded in his ears and he felt his collar sticky with sweat. Incapable of replying he sat there transfixed, like a rabbit in the glare of a car's headlamps.

Jonas knew how to deal with it. His cracked voice broke the silence:

"Maud wants to read the Lesson this morning, Mr Short. That is, if you would see fit to let her."

Maud wasted no time in getting to her feet. She always wanted to read the Lesson. The preacher forgot about Tom and transferred his joviality to Maud. A fine young girl, even if she did look like a blue stocking. He beckoned her up to the pulpit and she read the Lesson so fast he could have kicked her all over chapel. He finished at eighteen minutes to twelve and saw Jonas sneak a backward glance at the clock as they sang the last hymn.

                    *   *   *   *   *   *   *   *

Jonas buttonholed Jake and Tom in their pew before Amen had been fully squeezed out of the organ. He knew who they were and something of their reputation and had resolved to get to them before the preacher or anybody else did. He asked them directly if they intended to join the church. Jake replied in the affirmative and Tom nodded agreement. Jonas tried to sum them up. He made a note of Jake's level frown and broad shoulders, of Tom's air of compliance and self-consciousness. Jonas could evaluate. Jake had decided to accept the Lord, but he was not sure if the Lord had decided to accept him. There was nothing whimsical about the boys' appearance in chapel. He bet they would stay the course. Still, no use making a fuss just yet. Let them show up for a few weeks first and then go through the formalities. See how they make out and take them under your wing later, if they behave. Get them in School and keep your eye on them for a while.

"I'm glad to hear it, my lads. What about coming to Sunday School at two and we'll have a talk. I have a nice Young Men's Bible Class and they'll be right pleased to see you."

CHAPTER 11

Aches and Pains

I had to come and see you, Doctor, I've had a sore throat and ear-ache for over a week.

Sit down, Hugh, and let me take a look at you. Does it hurt when I press here behind your ears?

Aye, it does.

Tell me, do you have a headache when you wake up in the morning?

I do, Doctor

Do you get short of breath, Hugh, when you are lifting something heavy?

Yes.

Do you ever lose your balance?

Aye, especially lately.

Is there a yellow coating on your tongue?

Yes, Doctor.

I wonder what the hell it can be, Hugh?

*   *   *   *   *   *   *   *

I'm sorry to tell you, Jack, you'll never be able to work again.

Thank God for that!

*   *   *   *   *   *   *   *

Billinge Beacon rises 600 feet above sea level and many of the inhabitants of the village live at an altitude of 300 feet or more. The air at that height, though hardly thin, is fresh and pure and there is no local heavy industry to pollute the atmosphere. At the end of the nineteenth century, the average Billinger was strong and healthy. He would spend his youth constantly walking and running, fetching and carrying, lifting and labouring. He was exposed to the sun, wind and rain, the smell of the fields and soil and the familiar night air. Incessant physical and outdoor activity gave him a huge appetite, village food was wholesome and the women knew how to cook. Life expectancy was not short.

But even Billingers could fall ill now and then. More often than not, they were just out of sorts. In those days there was no hospital in Billinge and the doctors who visited on horseback were not always readily available. It is only to be expected, therefore, that Billingers, like others in isolated communities, had their own remedies for various types of indispositions. There were three ways of effecting a cure. Firstly, you could take one of the popular medicines so extravagantly advertised in the local and national press. Secondly you could doctor yourself according to one of the "scientific" recipes which everybody wrote down and followed on a do-it-yourself basis. Thirdly, you could apply the old-fashioned, old wives', drastic village remedy, which would cure you quick or finish you off altogether.

The front pages of the newspapers of the 1880s were heavy with advertising for medicines, tablets, ointments and prescriptions of all kinds. Here are some examples of the magical cures offered in the local press to the good people of Billinge between the years 1880 and 1893:

MELLIN'S FOOD

HC, AGED 7 MONTHS (SEE PHOTO) CROSSED THE ATLANTIC, LANDING THE DAY HE WAS THREE WEEKS OLD, HAVING LIVED THE WHOLE TIME ON MELLIN'S FOOD, AND NEVER WAS "SICK OR SORRY". (FOR CHILDREN AFTER WEANING, THE AGED AND DYSPEPTIC)

THE AFRICAN HAIR RESTORER

NEVER KNOWN TO FAIL IN RESTORING HAIR IN 8 OR 10 DAYS.IT PROMOTES GROWTH AND PREVENTS ITS FALLING OFF, ERADICATING DANDRUFF AND PROVIDING VITALITY TO THEIR ROOTS. IF PROPERLY APPLIED, IT NEVER FAILS, BUT IT SHOULD BE WELL SHAKEN BEFORE USING.

THOMPSON'S HERBAL EMPORIUM

HERBAL SPECIALIST. QUICK CURES IN ALL AILMENTS. THE ONLY ACKNOWLEDGED PERFECT BAD LEG DOCTOR IN ENGLAND

DO NOT UNTIMELY DIE! FENNINGS FEVER CURER

BOWEL COMPLAINTS CURED WITH ONE DOSE	
TYPHUS OR LOW FEVER CURED WITH	2 DOSES
DIPHTHERIA CURED WITH	3 DOSES
SCARLET FEVER CURED WITH	4 DOSES
CHOLERA CURED WITH	5 DOSES
INFLUENZA CURED WITH	6 DOSES

SOLD IN BOTTLES AT 1s-1d EACH
WITH FULL DIRECTIONS IN CHEMISTS

WHELPTON'S VEGETABLE PURIFYING PILLS

WHEN THE TONGUE IS COATED, THE HEAD HEAVY AND ACHING, AN OFFENSIVE TASTE IN THE MOUTH, THE APPETITE POOR AND THE SPIRITS DULL

GEORGE'S PILE AND GRAVEL PILLS

SAD BUT TRUE — ABOUT 3 OF EVERY 4 OF THE ADULT POPULATION OF THIS COUNTRY SUFFER, MORE OR LESS, FROM PILES OR GRAVEL, OR BOTH, IN SOME FORM.

ABSOLUTELY PAINLESS EXTRACTIONS!

BY AID OF NITROUS OXIDE, GAS OR CHLOROFORM. THE MOST TIMID NEED NOT FEAR TAKING IT UNDER OUR CARE. OUR DENTIST CAN GIVE HUNDREDS OF REFERENCES TO PERSONS HE HAS INSERTED TEETH FOR.

DODDS KIDNEY PILLS

DID YOU KNOW THAT THE SUM OF £154, 480, 934 WAS SPENT IN THE UNITED KINGDOM ON ALCHOLIC LIQUORS?

and finally this modest gem:

CHLORODYNE

EFFECTIVELY CHECKS THOSE TOO FATAL DISEASES — DIPHTHERIA, FEVER, CROUP AND AGUE. ACTS LIKE A CHARM IN DIARRHOEA AND IS THE ONLY SPECIFIC IN CHOLERA AND DYSENTERY. IS THE ONLY PALLIATIVE IN GOUT, CANCER, TOOTHACHE AND MENINGITIS. CAUTION: BEWARE OF PIRACY AND IMITATIONS!

In spite of these advances in medicine, Billinge was not over its troubles in 1899, as the Medical Report for the area in the "Wigan Observer" shows us. The Medical Officer, Dr Mather, gives the following statistics:
Area of Billinge — 4,591 acres.
Deaths during 1899 — 65.
17 infants under 1 year
7 children 1-5 years
18 persons 5-60 years
23 over 60 years of age.

There were 23 cases of infectious disease reported, representing an increase over 1898. It is pointed out that most of the infectious cases originated on the borders of the district, implying that diseases came from outside.

Enteric fever was up, due to bad drains, etc.

Scarlet fever was also up on 1898, as was Erysipelas (inflammation of the skin and swelling of membranes, ofter referred to as "the Rose" or "St. Anthony's Fire".)

Diarrhoea — 9 people died, as against none in 1898. This was due to the low level of ground water and the high temperature of the earth recorded in August and September. Mainly among children 1-5 years.

Bronchitis, pneumonia and pleurisy were all going down.

Influenza had been severe during the year, but not killing.

Phthisis (pulmonary consumption) — 1 death.

*   *   *   *   *   *   *   *

But all was not lost. If you were not cured by the widely advertised commercial medicines, then you could make your own. As the new century dawned, cheap, paper-back publications divulged age-old recipes for simple but infallible medicinal mixtures. Billingers tried them by the score:

For "troublesome, hacking coughs" two fine syrups could be made in the warmth of your own home:

Horehound Syrup. Infuse half a pound of white horehound in half a gallon of boiling water for 2 hours. Express the liquor, strain and add sugar to taste. One tablespoonful is a dose.

Linseed Syrup. Add 2 tablespoonfuls of linseed to 2 breakfastcupfuls of water and simmer very gently for 3 hours. Then strain, and only one cupful should remain. Stir into this till thoroughly dissolved a quarter of a pound of sugar candy and add 4 tablespoonfuls of white vinegar. Stir all well together and allow to cool. Bottle and keep well corked. One teaspoonful effects the cure.

Cases of ringworm, eruptions or ulcers could be rapidly disposed of by

Tar Ointment. Melt together, stirring until thick, one ounce beeswax and two and a half ounces of tar. Daub on thickly.

Cure for Drunkenness. 5 and a half drachms of peppermint water, half a drachm spirits of nutmeg, 5 grains of magnesia, 2 and a half grains sulphate of iron. The mixture, which acts as a tonic and a stimulant, prevents the prostration which usually follows a sudden cessation of drinking. To begin with, 10 drops on a lump of sugar twice a day is sufficient and may be increased gradually to 2 teaspoonfuls.

For rheumatism sufferers, salavation was at hand:

Embrocation for Rheumatism. 2 wineglassfuls of turpentine, 3 ounces soft soap, 1 ounce liquid ammonia, 2 and a half ounces strong acetic acid, 25 ounces boiling water. Dissolve the ammonia in the boiling water, add the soft soap, and stir well, then add the other ingredients, stirring constantly. An egg will improve the recipe. Keep in well-corked bottles marked "poison" and shake well before using. Do not forget to wash the wineglasses.

The insect population of Billinge (exact figures unknown) also came under severe attack at this time. It was dealt with as follows:

Fleas   Oil of pennyroyal is a quick means of riddance.

Lice   Wash body and clothes in a strong solution of pearl-ash and finish them off with carbolic soap.

Black Beetles   Sprinkle a mixture of borax and powdered lump sugar every night for a week or 10 days, sweeping away all remains daily.

Ants   Use carbolic acid, tobacco-water, or a strong solution of spirits of wine and water. Pour into the holes for several days running and persist until the insects are destroyed.

Bugs   These unpleasant creatures may be successfully eliminated by making a paste of one pennyworth of alum and boiling water and applying to all infected parts. Fill up crevices with equal parts of flour and alum to seal their fate!

Rats and mice (Billinge heaved with them at the end of the 19th century) were due to fare no better. This was what was in store for them:

Poison for rats and mice.   Grind one ounce of nux vomica into a fine powder and mix with margarine or lard into a paste, then divide into small balls. Wrap up in paper and place in the rats' holes. It kills the pests, but only sickens cats, dogs and children, who may be cured by a spoonful of oil.

*   *   *   *   *   *   *   *

When recipes, prescriptions and nationally advertised brands of medicine failed, Billingers fell back on their own cures. Diarrhoea, for instance, would certainly cease if you took a glass of Indian Brandy mixed with warm water, followed a few hours later by blackcurrant tea.

The opposite condition was not regarded as serious:

"How's thi bowels, Bill?"

"Oh, shut up!"

"So is mine, it must be t'cowd weather."

In Billinge you were not constipated. You were CAUSTIVE BOUND. There were two remedies — both infallible. One was to boil cenopod leaves and then drink the water. A fancier method was to put cenopods straight in your tea. The other remedy - even more drastic - was jollop. Jollop was a brown powder you generally put in coffee; results were guaranteed. The word became a verb in the local dialect ("I'll jollop thee.")

Stomach pains required a few drops of oil of peppermint in warm water. For toothache or severe pains in any part of the body, relief could be obtained with a few drops of "lodnum" (laudanum). This remedy, which became very popular at the end of the 19th century, could be obtained only on a doctor's prescription and came in little white bottles marked "POISON". The way to take it was to pour a few drops into a large lump of sugar morning and evening. It made you sleep all day and achieved its popularity largely through its addictive qualities.

Leeches were just the thing for fits, strokes and blood pressure. Some of the older people kept them at home in glass jars.

Broken bones would soon knit together again if you bathed them in comfrey — a tall, rough-leaved ditch-plant which everybody in Billinge grew in their gardens. After bathing one wrapped the broken limb in the big, green comfrey leaves and put a bandage round it.

In those days it was quite normal to see Billingers walking about with a bandage steeped in vinegar tied round their forehead. That was how you cured a headache.

For bad cuts, abrasions and bleeding parts you needed a spider's web. Bandages were all right, but if the bleeding persisted, find a big, sticky, silvery spider's web and apply it directly to the wound, resting on the bare skin. The flow of blood would cease forthwith.

For those whose delicate stomachs turned at the thought of a spider's web, there was worse to come if they were unlucky enough to develop a weak bladder. In Billinge you could pee against anybody's wall, but if your visits were too frequent you would have to cure your ailment with the proper medicine: the juice of a stewed mouse. Little boys who wet their beds excessively would be treated in this way. The moggie would be boiled in a small pan over the fire and the juice would be left to simmer, adding salt and pepper according to taste. There seems to be good evidence that youngsters who were made to drink this particular beverage never wetted their beds again.

* * * * * * * *

Finally, there is the story of the new doctor who arrived in Billinge just a decade or two ago. On his first surgery night the first six people to come in were all over eighty, none of them with anything more serious than rheumatism or housemaid's knee. When the seventh – an eighty-seven-year-old – came in for a bottle for his slight cough, the doctor commented on the longevity and good health of the people of the village. The old man stared at him in disbelief for a moment, then replied:

"If you think we are healthy now, you should have seen 'em in the old days."

"The old days?"

"Aye. We're a bunch of weaklings compared with what *they* were."

"Really?"

"Well, you've seen Billinge churchyard, haven't you?"

"Yes I have."

"Full of graves, isn't it?"

"Well, yes, but . . ."

"Do you know how they started it off?"

"No."

"They had to SHOOT 'em."

CHAPTER TWELVE

The Chapels

In those days the chapels were well-organized. Morning Service was at eleven and Evening Service at six. Sunday School began at 9.30 in the morning and again at two in the afternoon. Children up to the age of sixteen went to both sessions of Sunday School and were required to stay on for the Morning Service. Fully-fledged members over thirty were normally expected to put in appearances at both Services. People between the ages of sixteen and thirty were expected by Jonas to turn up at all four meetings. He considered that those in this age group knew enough about the Scriptures to get something out of what the ministers had to say, but not sufficient to warrant their slipping out of Sunday School with an incomplete education.

After Jake and Tom had put in their first attendance at Sunday School, it was clear to Jonas that there was a lot of ground to be made up. He had had them alone for half an hour and subjected them to the little tests he always tried out on new pupils. Many people starting to go to church for the first time remembered quite a lot of what they had learnt during Religious Instruction at school; others remembered nothing at all. Jake and Tom recalled something, but they had fifteen years of coal dust and thousands of pints of beer to think back through; it was too much for Miss Pigot's thin voice to penetrate.

"Now Jacob, I am going to ask you and your brother Thomas a few questions about the Bible to see how much you have remembered of what you learnt at school. Don't worry if you are not sure of the answers – just try. It doesn't matter a jot if you are wrong."

Tom was thinking it was the first time that anybody had ever called him Thomas. It made him feel more religious. The test began:

"Now, Thomas, what do you remember about God making the World?"

Tom looked sad and started chewing his nails.

"Come on, my lad, don't be afraid to try. How long did it take Him?"

"Oh, er . . . . six days."

"Excellent. And what did He do then?"

"He took Sunday off."

Jonas smiled, for he knew the lad was sincere.

"And what did He put in the world at the beginning?"

Tom shook his head quickly:

"I don't know."

Jonas turned to Jake:

"Jacob, do you know?"

Jake never admitted not knowing anything in his life. Nor would he pretend to know everything. When he did not know something, he would just keep quiet. Now he had to speak. He frowned hard at Jonas before replying:
"I reckon he must have put a lot of coal in it."
Jonas felt that his geology did not go back that far. He pushed on:
"Thomas, which characters do you remember out of the Old Testament?"
"Er . . . . Jesus Christ."
"The life of Jesus is related in the second part of the Bible – the New Testament. Think of those people who lived many years before."
"I can't remember their names."
"Come on: just one. Try."
"Oliver Cromwell."
Jonas swallowed.
"Well, he was a sort of Methodist, but he wasn't in the Old Testament. Jacob, which characters do you recall?"
"Abraham."
"Correct. What can you tell me about Abraham?"
"He used to keep sheep and kill 'em."
"What did he kill them for?"
"He used to sell the meat."
"Really? To whom?"
"The nomads."
"Did they tell you that at school?"
"Tom and me missed some lessons."
"What else do you remember about the Old Testament?"
"Moses."
"What did he do?"
"He crossed the Red Sea in a basket."
Jonas smiled again and Jake looked at him stonily.
"Thomas, whom do you remember out of the New Testament?"
"Jesus Christ."
"Where was He born?"
"Lazarus."
"You mean Nazareth. It was Bethlehem, anyway. What do you know about His life?"
"He was a fisherman."
"Go on, what else did He do?"
"He used to walk around a lot and make speeches and give people fish and bread."
"How was He different from other men?"
"He could do miracles. He turned water into beer."
"Wine. Did Jesus have any companions?"

"Yes. He persuaded twelve other fishermen to leave their wives and go after Him. They followed him everywhere to watch him do miracles."

"Do you remember the Last Supper?"

"I think one of the twelve men betrayed him while they were eating, but I don't remember his name."

"Do you remember, Jacob?"

"Barabbas."

"Well, he wasn't far away."

Jonas eyed the pair of them. Rough diamonds, that's what they were. Too big for morning School, though; get them in the Young Men's Class in the afternoon and it will sink in in time. Let them come to both Services, too, and make real chapel-goers out of them. They won't understand what is going on for the first year, but neither does half the congregation, anyway. Two more fine young men for Jonas on the front row. Not half packing them in these days. Look at those shoulders; these were the men for carrying the banner next Walking Day. We'll show the Baptists.

"Well, that has given me a rough idea of what you need. Now we had better be getting along to the Young Men. Every week you will hear these tales from the Bible told in a simple and refreshing way. Don't forget that these were real people we are talking about and the things they said and did are still said and done to-day. That is why the Bible remains the great Book it is: it rings true. Human nature does not change much and I sometimes doubt if it changes at all. You will find men in the Bible who remind you of men you know down the pit and you might even find yourselves, too. Don't forget: religion isn't something you dip into on Sundays and leave in chapel here at half past seven at night. It is something you have to carry around with you. If you come and see God here on Sundays, He comes and sees you down the pit on week-days. Don't forget the Lord and the Lord won't forget you."

It was the note Jonas liked to finish on and he was pleased at the reverent way in which they had listened to him. Tom was picturing God going down in the cage, not needing a lamp on account of his luminosity and Jake was wondering if drinking would have to go.

*   *   *   *   *   *   *   *

In the months that followed, Jake and Tom became regular chapel-goers and much of their time was spent consolidating their position within the church. There are several tales told about the time when the brothers were being broken in, some no doubt exaggerated, others in which one can detect a clear ring of truth. The boys were consistent in pursuit of their distant goal of respectability, but it was not roses, roses all the way. It must be said for Jonas that he covered up for them for all he was worth.

Every now and then, Jake would fly off the handle about something or other. The discipline to which he submitted, though self-imposed, was, in the long run, a strain. He missed his drinking and his drunken outbursts of wrath, for which there was no place in church. He found a substitute: righteous temper. Certain things would get on his nerves. One of these was the hymn-singing of Ernie Appleby, who occupied the pew behind the brothers and sang in Jake's ear. Jake was not musical and never had been. Ernie was musical and knew it, but he had the most grating voice in creation and did not know it. He could pitch his notes and knew the tune and words of every hymn in the Independent Methodist Hymnbook. If some preacher picked a little-known tune, he would sing half a beat faster and steer the congregation all the way through it. He had the courage of his voice. It was insufferable. Jake stood it for a few Sundays because he was new. One evening he turned on Ernie in the middle of the second hymn and told him in vicious undertones to shut up or he would strangle him after the service. The threat was audible to most of the congregation including Jonas, who smiled at the preacher, hoping he was deaf. Ernie mouthed his way through the remaining hymns and on the following Sunday changed pews to one nearer the door. From then on he sang as before, but led the congregation from the rear.

Then there was the walking day incident. Jake and Tom had been enlisted to carry the banner at the head of the procession. In blue, silver and gold, it depicted a compassionate-faced Jesus looking down from a hillock on an assembly of youths, maidens and sheep. The caption read: WE ARE HIS LAMBS. Jake had been reluctant to take on the job and had agreed only on Jonas's gentle insistence that the boys were the age when they should gradually assume more and more responsibilities; furthermore the banner could be near unmanageable on a windy day if the bearers were not men of some strength.

It was blowing hard as they led the column along Victoria Road and preoccupation with their swirling task had somewhat quietened Jake's misgivings, when he heard the voices of some of his former drinking cronies among the onlookers. Crowds of people, church-goers and church-haters alike, usually turned out to watch church processions. In the nineteenth century free entertainment was rarely foregone. There was an ominous snigger from one of the pitmen when he saw Tom and Jake under their banner. Jake's face darkened and his black eyes flashed in the man's direction. His friend in the crowd, however, was far from sober and failed to resist the temptation to take a dig at the brothers:

"Well now, hasn't their mother turned them out nice to-day!"

Jake and Tom looked each other in the eye and for a moment the column faltered, then they picked up their step again.

"Look at Jake the Lamb!"

Jake walked over to Tom with flaring nostrils and, pulling his pole out of its holster, rammed it into Tom's left fist.

"Just hang on to this a minute, Tom."

Tom staggered round in little circles to keep the banner in business while Jake turned to look for his friend. But Jonas had rushed up breathlessly to retrieve the situation. He grabbed Jake by the arm. By now he had learnt something about the way Jake should be handled and his advice was shrewd and succinct:

"After!" he whispered fiercely in the ear of his banner-bearer.

Jake's eyes narrowed for a moment, his glance sweeping the column now frozen in its tracks, awaiting his next move. The wind and the banner were getting the better of Tom, who was on the verge of toppling like a stricken stockyard steer. Jake recovered his pole and the procession moved on again, Jonas dabbing the back of his neck with a big white handkerchief.

*   *   *   *   *   *   *

Jake had always been contemptuous of girls. he could never quite figure out why they were in the world at all. They were soft, brainless and, he suspected, hysterical. He had seen girls cry for nothing at all and he had an idea they did it when they wanted to get something. He steered clear of them. So did Tom.

At school they had been separated from the girls and there were none in the mine. Down the pit, though, they soon learned the facts of life. The miners seldom discussed women, but they employed a formidable vocabulary of four and five-letter words dealing with the chief ingredients of sexual experience. At first the boys strained their ears and their heads to make sense of it all. When they had done so Tom was embarrassed, Jake simply neutral. His work was his passion and his love. His social evenings in the pubs had supplied him with additional fuel for his misogyny. Half the women he saw were bleary-eyed, drunken hags. There were others who appeared at the pub doors with rolling pins and yanked or drove their husbands home. Jake had never been in contact with a marriageable woman of his own age until he began to go to chapel.

Over a hundred women were full members. Many of these were no longer young. There was a large and influential group of middle-aged and elderly ladies who had reached that time in life when there was everything to be gained and absolutely nothing to be lost in dedicating their days to Jesus. They attended chapel ruthlessly, narrowed down their pleasures and kept an eagle eye on everybody within range. They were outspoken in their views, sang hymns wholeheartedly and decided a great deal of church policy in the Wednesday night Women's Class. There were times when Jonas had to tread warily. They were tough customers.

There was a smaller group of younger women who had recently got married or were hoping to. For them, Jesus was only half the story, even in church, and they were tractable beings. The young wives were cheerful and helpful and served tea at church socials. They flirted harmlessly with each others' husbands and a few of the bachelors too. They liked their fun, enjoyed dancing and games and the socials were lively and warming because of their presence. The single girls were a mixed lot: schoolgirls, blue stockings, mill girls, shop-girls. Some of them had been to Grammar School and had their little, respected cliques; some were comfortably-off in clean, well-pressed clothes; most of them were rosy-cheeked, well-scrubbed and working class. They were simple, friendly, chattering, unmarried and hopeful. Many of the ways open to most women to attract men were barred to them by the rules and customs of the church.

Bachelors over twenty-five were fussed over by all the women, young and old. Jake and Tom were prize exhibits. The old ladies surrounded them swiftly and jealously at the end of the service and fell over themselves to squeeze in their little compliment. How well Tom's hymn singing was coming along. Poor Jake had a cut hand and no proper dressing on it. The preacher last week had told them how those two young men had drunk in every word. Tom has a hair on his collar, brush it off for him. Had the sun been in their eyes through the stained glass window? Aren't they looking well?

Tom was shy and blushing, coughing behind his fist and exuding his own variety of charm. He had not been mothered for some time and he enjoyed it. His heart yearned towards some of the old ladies and he stuttered at them gratefully. Jake stood his ground with a sheepish grin, adopted to disguise his boredom. He wanted to be off but he could see no way of achieving this without appearing rude. He suspected that Tom was having a good time and was in no hurry to leave. At least it was better to be encircled by fussing old ladies than by tittering young ones. The unmarried girls – no match for the old ones in such a contest – stood respectfully at a distance and admired the boys' broad shoulders from halfway down the aisle. They occasionally ventured smiles, especially at Tom, who was the more likely of the two to return them. They never dared intrude upon the old ladies' prerogatives and by and large they were gracefully retiring.

It was this retiring disposition of some of the better-looking girls that made Jake somewhat modify his attitude towards them. He knew that some of the old women looked upon him and Tom as their own private property, but he had expected some of the more daring spinsters to make advances, which he was only too eager to rebuff. He was well aware that his brother would surrender unconditionally to the first girl who so much as pouted her lips at him. He told himself that if this happened, he would have to give Tom a good talking to. As time went by, the brothers got to know all the girls by their Christian names. There were socials to attend and church outings to go on, choir practices to endure and plays and walking days to organize. Tom was dragged into everything and offered no resistance apart from that deriving from his natural shyness. He found that these activities were fun for him and secretly he enjoyed them more than drinking. He was of a willing nature and let himself be put upon. Jake took part also to some extent, but he was cautious. He would carry the banner and take the collection, but there was to be no dancing, no parts in plays and no reading Lessons. Choir practices he would go to, but he would not sing. At church socials he drank countless pints of tea. Gradually he began to have short conversations with girls:

"Hello Jake, are you enjoying the social?"

"It's too hot."

"What are you drinking tea for, then?"

"Hot tea makes you cold, cold beer makes your blood tingle. Don't ask me why – that's just the way it is. I should know, I've drunk enoo' o'both."

"Is it true that you used to be a big drinker before you started coming to chapel, Jake?"

"There's big drinkers and there's big drinkers. You'd better ask Tom about that. Ah'm a big tay-drinker. Fotch me another cup and don't ask so many questions."

"Don't you ever dance, Jake?"

"Not to piano music."

"What sort of music do you dance to?"

"I can do a clog-dance. Do you know what that is?"

"No, what is it?"

"I can't show you in here. Why do you ask so many questions?"

"Mr Moore says your choir-singing is coming along fine."

"There must be something wrong with his ears. I don't sing."

"Why do you go to choir practice if you don't sing?"

"I go to keep Tom company. It's my brother that sings. Jonas thinks it's me. He's wrong, I just stand next to him. It wouldn't make any difference if I did sing, they all sing out of tune to start with. Choirs like these, people don't go to listen to. They go to watch. That's why you have to have enough men there to make them look nice and solid in the back rows. That's what I'm for. I makes 'em solid."

"Do you ever go for walks, Jake?"

" I walk a mile and a half to the coal face every morning and a mile and a half back to the cage every night. I reckon that's enough walkin' for anybody."

"Don't you ever go for walks with girls?"

"Only with Gertie."

"Gertie who?"

"Gertie's one of the pit-ponies. She has to pull tubs. You wouldn't like that."

"Oh, Jake, you're impossible."

CHAPTER THIRTEEN

Isabel

It was about this time that Jake decided to get married. He told nobody of his intention, but once he had made up his mind the matter was as good as settled. He felt that it was time, anyway. Not so long ago Sarah had made a passing remark that a strapping lad of his age should be looking round for a wife. Jake had merely grunted and gone on reading his newspaper, but afterwards he had thought about what she had said. He had learnt from experience that Sarah knew what was good for him. She was the only person who knew him to any degree and hers was the only advice he ever really listened to. Then there was the matter of his body. For several months now it had not been acting the way he told it to and he was not a little disturbed. His body had always served him well — a sturdy, versatile machine for delivering blows, moving at speed, swinging and cutting, transforming large quantities of food into great reserves of energy. He had driven it hard, with ruthless control, and he had been rewarded with efficiency and precision. But now the timing was off. There were hidden tensions and pressures; he was no longer fully in control. His stomach, temperature and appetite were no longer blind disciples of his will. He experienced new irritations, particularly in moments of leisure. His intuition told him that he needed a woman.

To say that he lusted after a woman would be to misrepresent the nature of his desire. His eight hours a day of slugging and smashing at coal took care of nearly all the pent-up energy which even his dynamic body could generate. By Friday, he would be almost tuned-up again, but then came Saturday and Sunday with the new restlessness. Week-ends did not agree with him any more. There was something missing.

It never occurred to him to pick up a loose woman and take her behind the slag-heaps. Harmony did not lie that way and in any case it did not fit in with his new way of life. In no desperate hurry, he was as yet less than enchanted by the prospects of physical contact. He tried to accustom himself to this new field of thought, without abandoning his more deeply-rooted instinct of misogyny.

It is obvious to anyone with a knowledge of human nature that the type of girl to attract Jake would be one who did not rush him. That is exactly what Isabel Webb did not do. In the first place she was incapable of doing anything in a rush even if she wanted to. Secondly, she never wanted to. She liked to play the waiting game, a strategy for which Nature had equipped her admirably. Rosy-cheeked and fair-haired, she was of medium height and well proportioned. Her limbs were clean-cut with strong, fairly large bones and a good covering of glowing Anglo-Saxon flesh. At twenty-three she showed no signs of fat, but she was solid and firm and quite a lot of woman. All her movements were slow and her leisurely step, combined with a good carriage, gave her a regal air as she walked. Her face was pleasant and open, although her usual expression was a quiet, knowing, Mona Lisa smile which she achieved by slightly turning up the corners of her mouth. She seldom showed her teeth, which were white and even, so she must have set great store by that smile. In summer her hair was the colour of golden corn at the front and the light tan she used to acquire gave her skin an exquisite hue of golden pink of unreal beauty and delicacy. It was her only outstanding feature and she sat in the sun whenever she could.

Isabel's father worked in the mill and she was the eldest of three girls. She had worked in the same mill as her father for four years up to turning twenty. When her father was promoted, with fifteen shillings a week more, he took Isabel out of the mill and since then she had helped her mother sewing at home. During her time at the mill she had been rather flighty with some of the younger hands, who were always anxious to squeeze her when the occasion arose. Thus she had acquired a certain amount of experience concerning men, but had been careful to avoid getting over-involved. Her initial curiosity satisfied, she was well content to withdraw to the seclusion of her home and make her analysis while she sewed. It was clear that she was attractive to men and that finding a husband would be no insurmountable problem. She had noticed that the more interesting and intelligent men were less susceptible to a come-on look than the dull ones. Worthwhile suitors seemed to pursue only more inaccessible goals. It paid a girl to keep herself to herself. For three years Isabel was a model of primness and was rewarded with five proposals, all of which she declined. She never spoke to Jake.

Jake did not dislike the look of her at all. She reminded him of Sarah, but was better looking and two score years younger. He did not think of her as lovely or beautiful, since these words did not feature in his active vocabulary. He thought she was clean and pleasant and smelled nice. He felt that she was ripe, though he did not think about what for. He was restless in her presence. She was the first person he had encountered who dared ignore him completely, which left him both infuriated and impressed. For months he stared right through her, their most intimate contact being when he held the collection box in front of her for her to drop a penny in. He had an idea that she was looking at him out of the corner of her eye when he was not looking at her, but he did not see how he could prove it. Her inscrutable smile was a constant source of irritation. It occurred to him that he would like to marry her and that he had not the foggiest idea how to go about it. He realised that he knew nothing about her and his inbred treadwariness warned him against premature self-commitment, but he had the working man's ability to sum up a person on sight and he had a good feeling about Isabel. She was acting a part and daring to tease him, but she was healthy, fresh and uncomplicated and if she thought she knew how to handle husband Jake, he would make her think again. She would bear strong and good-looking children and that what was what he wanted. But how the hell did you tell her?

Isabel was giving her hands-off policy an agonising reappraisal. Something had gone wrong. The man just ignored her. There he was — the strongest, toughest and manliest-looking bachelor for miles around, twenty-six years old, several hundred pounds in the bank, radiant with sex and bristling with eligibility. And here was she — twenty-three, good-looking, even if she said it herself, sound of wind and limb, a good cook and a better seamstress, knew how to dress, modest and retiring — not a man had laid as much as a finger on her for three years. Wasn't that retiring enough? What more did he want? He could never have heard any rumours from the mill; he didn't mix with mill people. And what if he had? What did he expect, a virgin? She *was* a virgin, anyway. It wasn't sure that *he* was, what with his reputation before he started going to church. Isabel experienced a little thrill as she thought of his wild days. Why did he ignore her so?

* * * * * * * *

Isabel tried new tactics. It was September and church socials had been resumed for the autumn. Some Saturday evenings there would be dancing, short talks, tea and sandwiches. A lot of chapels were against dancing but Jonas supported it. Attendance was what he was interested in and he was not going to lose his young people if he could help it. Dancing was artistic, anybody could see that. He would waltz himself. He liked to start the dancing off when the lads were a bit shy and oftener than not he would honour Isabel. He was brisk and light of foot and would swing her round and round, stiff-armed, a resolute six inches of space between them, beaming at her down both sides of his nose, occasionally casting a glance to the ceiling in the middle of a twirl. Ostensibly, his action was to start the dancing off, but if anyone ventured onto the floor before he had finished giving his little exhibition they would be grilled in Bible Class for weeks to come with questions a Cardinal would have floundered over. Isabel was aware of the compliment being paid to her and she took pains to improve her dancing, for which she had a natural bent. She also started teaching Tom.

"Tom, you haven't danced with me tonight, Don't you want to?"

This under Jake's nose.

"Well, I know I haven't, but I haven't danced with anybody. I can't dance."

"And how do you expect to learn if you don't try, silly? There's really nothing to it, when you've tried. Listen to the music: onetwothree, onetwothree, onetwothree, round and round and round and round — you just keep going, that's all. I'll follow you, come on, try."

"Ee, I don't know, I mean I think I'd make a mess of it. I have big feet. I'd only tread on your toes and spoil your nice shoes, wouldn't I, Jake?"

Jake snorted unsympathetically and drank his tea. Isabel grabbed Tom's hand impatiently and pulled him, protesting, onto the floor.

"You are coming to try, now."

Tom was as clumsy as he had promised. Dancing came to him as hard as it came to any man, but Isabel gritted her teeth and went through with it. He could only improve, that was sure. Soon he was beginning to enjoy it and after the third dance he was evidently having more fun than she was. When she could stand no more she took him back to his brother and sat between them. She talked amiably enough to Tom, affording Jake little more than a back view, now and again a fleeting profile. He could hear her, though.

"Now listen, Tom, let me tell you something: you are not as bad as you think you are. Well, I know you can't do it proper yet, but you'll learn if you keep at it. All you need is to be a bit lighter on your feet. We'll try again in a few minutes. Remember: onetwothree, onetwothree and keep going round. Once you get into it, it'll be as easy as pie. And another thing — you don't need to hold me as if I was a China doll, I won't break, you know. I mean, you can put your arm round me a bit more, not that I want to be squeezed, you understand, but I am supposed to lean back on your arm when we turn round. All you're doing now is holding my frock between your finger and thumb and if I lean back, I'll tipple over."

Tom blushed with the shame of it. Isabel smiled coyly.

"You're not afraid of putting your arm round me a bit more, are you Tom?"

Tom obviously was.

"Oh, no." he blurted, ambiguously.

"Now listen, Tom, you are to come and dance with me just any time you feel like it, do you understand? I want to teach you how to dance proper. Promise?"

"Ee, well, I don't know."

"Of course it might be that you'd rather dance with some of the other girls."

"Well, no, I...."

"Maybe you'd like Audrey to teach you."

"Oh, no, not her."

"Or Susie?"

"No, not her."

"Teresa?"

"No."

"Who then?"

"Well, none of *them.*"

"Who then?"

"Well, er....I mean, look how many times I trod on your feet."

"Of course you didn't, silly. Well, only once."
"Do you really think I can learn if I keep at it?"
"I'm sure you can."
"I bet I could never be as good as Jonas."
"You wait and see."
"Will you teach me, then?"
"All right, Tom, if you want me to."

Jake could listen to no more of it. He went off in disgust in search of more tea, the bitterness of his drink matching his thoughts. Look at him. That brother of his, just look at him. And look at her, too. You only trod on little footie wootie once, silly willie. Soon be better than Jonas, Tom would. Oh yes. Jonas would like to hear that. Not half. It would be a helluva Bible Class next week if he did. Tomsie womsie wouldn't dance with Susie wusie, would he? Or Teresa? Oh, no, they weren't fast enough for him, were they? But her. She was fast all right. His brother. Look at him. A goner already he was. Not a chance. Not a sausage. And couldn't see through her. Look at him dancin' again. Looks like a bloody pit-pony. Seen that look in his eyes? And her grinnin' at me over his shoulder. She'll not look at me now. I'll swear she grinned like a cat. She thinks she's gettin' at me, doesn't she? Playin' with him, that's what she is. Look at his face. Gormless. Disgraceful, that's what it is. Dancin' bloody marvel, our Tom is.

There was scant conversation on the way home. Tom mumbled this and that and was cold-shouldered unmercifully. As they were putting out the lights and getting into bed, his harmless remarks were cut short by Jake's verdict on the events of the evening:

"Tom, ah've no patience with thee."

Tom asked what was the matter, but Jake considered his words self-explanatory and repeated them with conviction as he snuffed the last candle:

"I've no patience with thee."

CHAPTER FOURTEEN

The Courtship

As Jake had mentally phrased it, Isabel had found a way of getting at him. He might still refrain from showing any personal interest in her and certainly there was no improvement in their relations, but he could no longer remain completely and supremely indifferent. She was under his feet. Tom was like putty in her hands. From dancing it went to singing, picnics, walks and collecting leaves. There was no doubt about it, his brother was suddenly leading a fuller life. And yet Jake was annoyed.

It was not as if there was a romance going on. She danced with Tom in full view of a respectable and self-respecting audience. The picnics were flocked to and the walks and leaf collecting were healthy if not edifying exercise. Isabel and Tom were never alone. And yet at times they might well have been, for in the midst of the crowd she would freeze the others out. She could be unobtrusively possessive and Tom would be effortlessly whisked away to the destination of her choice without anyone except Jake noticing aught amiss. When Jake wanted to say something to Tom, Isabel had taken him away. If he wished to be left alone, they were both there at his side. Jake did not quite know how to conduct himself when all three of them were together. If Tom and Isabel had been courting, then he would have known how matters stood, for he had definite views on courting couples and how they should be addressed. If Isabel had just been one of the girls whom Tom knew, then that would have been that. But this one was different. He sensed that for the time being at any rate she regarded Tom as her own property. He was not sure what she was after. She might be using Tom and parading him under his nose to make him jealous. And yet that would have been heartless and he could not envisage her as quite heartless. He could not be sure. There were times when she seemed to be genuinely fond of Tom. She was patience itself when they were on the dance floor. She had to be. She always had a welcome smile for Tom and her voice took on gentler tones when she spoke to him. She would link her arm in his or give his red ears an affectionate pinch when he was being particularly slow about something. She was often coy, but never seductive. Nobody could say she was throwing herself at him. It was all good, clean fun.

But Jake smelled a rat. She would ignore him for days and then suddenly flash him a confiding smile. He was getting sick of her confiding smiles. If they had been a little more frequently granted, he would have asked her what the hell she was grinning at, but they came so rarely and were followed by such long periods of aloofness that doubts would always creep in as to whether he had been imagining things. More than once he decided to tackle her about leading his brother round on a string. He could come straight to the point when he wanted to and he knew how he would handle her. He had often rehearsed the interview:

"Just come over here, I want a word with you."

"Yes, Jake?"

"You think you're being fly, don't you?"

"What do you mean?"

"You know thumping well what I mean."

"Oh....you mean....me and Tom?"

"I don't believe in beating around the bush, so listen here. I know that you're supposed to be one of the beauties round here and I've no doubt you can twist all these admirers of yours round your little finger. That's their funeral. I know our Tom is dafter than most of 'em and whatever he gets he deserves, but just remember this: our Tom is my brother and I have to live with him. For a start off I'm fed up to the teeth with seeing him walk round in a daze. He doesn't know what I say to him. Last Friday I asked him if he wanted bacon or cheese on his sandwiches and he said yes. Thursday he left the tea at home and we had nothing but water all the shift. He's even puttin' his coal in my tubs. He'll have me drawin' his wages next. It'll have to stop. I've seen you making eyes at me on the quiet. God-only-knows who else you're making 'em at. Well, you can make eyes at who you like, but not behind our Tom's back. I'm havin' no brother of mine bein' made a bloody fool of. Just keep on like this and I'll put the fat in the fire good and proper. I'll tell you what you are in front of all of them and you know I don't give a damn who's listening. And if that brother of mine interrupts me, I'll take him outside and knock some sense into him."

He would turn on his heel and leave her, incapable of reply.

The more Jake thought about it, the more this seemed his only course of action. He could not have Tom being led around with glazed eyes like this. People were beginning to notice it; very soon they would start laughing at him. That wouldn't do. It would reflect on him, too. After all, he was his brother. They might start thinking he was as soft as Tom was. He had better have that talk with her and put a stop to it.

And yet he was loth to start. He wished he was a little more sure that that was her game. Suppose she really liked Tom? Wouldn't she in that case make a good wife for him? After all, he had fancied her himself. But wasn't it up to the man to conquer the woman and not the other way round? Hell, Tom could conquer all right if he had to punch somebody on the nose, but now Isabel was doing the bossing. It wouldn't do — and yet — wouldn't any woman find it easy to lug Tom around like that if she had really wanted to? He wasn't exactly difficult to handle. Why should it not be Isabel to hand it out to him, at least she was God-fearing? Suppose he got somebody worse? What did he mean, worse, she wasn't too bad. He could stand a bit of her himself.

Still, Tom couldn't go on like this — he was absent-minded enough to start with, never mind in this condition. Somebody would have to talk to somebody. And then there were those looks; he couldn't have imagined them all. And Tom didn't know about them, that was sure. That wasn't fair. Did she give them to anybody else? He doubted it. Or was he being conceited? Well she couldn't be spending much time with anyone else, because she was never away from Tom. Suppose she was using Tom to get to know him (Jake) better, what was wrong with that? Deceit? Well, it was deceit, but what else could she do? He hadn't exactly egged her on, had he? He hadn't egged anybody on. All the other girls were scared of going within a pew's length of him. That was how it should be, let them keep their distance. And yet, how was he ever going to get on more intimate terms with a woman? Who wanted to be on intimate terms with them, anyway? But suppose he should want to get to know somebody a bit better? Or supposed a girl liked him — it was no crime. Could he blame her for it? How was she to go about it? Smile at him? He would have scowled back. Maybe he should pretend to be just a bit more human at times, even if he wasn't. Who said he wasn't? Maybe he was human and they a flock of bloody sheep. But to get back to this woman, what was she up to? At least she was acting different from the others. He'd talk with her. Get her on her own and talk to her like he had planned. He knew how to talk to her even if she did think she was smart.

It was not easy to get her on her own just when he wanted to. He edged around the room, tea in hand, without seeming to make any progress. She was here, there, and here again, but when he moved in on her, she was off. When he caught her she was with Tom. His eye followed her through five dances and at last she was within earshot and alone. It was Jake's chance; he cleared his throat:

"Isabel."

He cursed himself for having bungled the first line.

She ignored him.

"Isabel." Louder this time. He was aware of several heads turning round. She glanced up at him, a surprised look on her face.

"I want to talk with you." He felt twenty pairs of eyes upon him, but stubbornly watched her lips. He thought he detected a smile before she said briefly:

"All right, but you'll have to wait. I have to help with the cakes."

She was gone and he was left standing there with his speech getting cold. He watched her serve cakes behind a counter at the other end of the room and soon Tom and others had joined him. Surrounded, he gave up the idea of his interview, not without some relief. He had sat down and was relaxing with the others when suddenly she was back:

"Now, Jake, what was it you wanted to talk to me about?"

He glared at her.

"It can wait." His answer sounded unduly sinister. He wondered if the others were wondering what he had meant. He tried to appear nonchalant. Isabel drifted off, unconcerned.

It was not long, however, before she gave him the opportunity of saying what had to be said. In the days that followed she seemed to be continuously crossing his path, often alone. She cornered him one night when she was preparing refreshments for the choir. He had not been singing and had come along to pick up Tom. She offered him a scone which he grudgingly accepted. She looked him in the eye and said:

"How have you been keeping?"

It was a leading question, or might have been. They were alone and the voices of the singers could be heard indistinctly upstairs. He gave her an introductory frown:

"I told you the other night that I wanted a word with you."

"Yes, what was it going to be about?"

"Can't you guess?"

"Can I guess? Well, a girl can always guess."

"Guess then."

"I don't want to."

"Why not?"

"Well, I don't want to say it."

"You don't want to say what?"

"You'd think I was silly."

"Silly about what?"

"About what I should guess if I guessed."

Jake was losing his train of thought. He felt he was not getting anywhere.

"Guess what?" he asked hoarsely.

"What you were going to say to me."

"I was going to say...."

"Let me guess." interposed Isabel.

"Well for Christ's sake guess then and have done with it."

"Jake! How can you use such language and in church, too? You know how Jonas carries on about taking the name of Our Lord in vain. It isn't necessary, anyway. Why didn't you say "for Goodness sake?""

"For Goodness sake."

"That's a nice boy." Jake winced. She smiled shyly and looked down as she continued:

"All right, I'll guess what you wanted me for: I thought you were going to ask me to dance with you but you couldn't have been, because you won't dance with anyone and you scowl at me so much. But anyway you asked me what I thought just then, and that was what I thought."

She dropped her face even more, so that Jake could see only the golden hair and a little of her nose and cheeks and the top of her ears. She was blushing wildly and her hands were behind her back. She was clearly embarrassed at what she had said and continued to stare at the rows of empty cups. Jake felt her embarrassment like a hot wave breaking over him, leaving his own cheeks flushed and heavy. He could not decide if she was sincere or not. Why was she embarrassed? At all events his speech went sour on him. Suddenly he felt generous.

"Who says I scowl at you?"

She smiled quickly and apologetically:

"Well, don't you?"

"Maybe I do and maybe I don't, but do you think that I scowl at you particularly?"

The way he said it sounded as if a particular scowl was an honour he conferred on special people.

"Oh, no, you treat me just like everybody else." she replied hastily.

"And how do I treat everybody else?"

"Well they think you are a bit superior."

"They do, do they?"

"Well, look how polite and gentlemanly some of the other boys are, not to mention some of the nice old men. And your Tom — everybody likes him: he'll go along with anything, he will. Look how he comes to choir practice and carries things on picnics and never argues with the girls or teases any of us. I mean, you're not exactly sociable, are you?"

"Just listen to her, sociable. What do you want me to do, recite poems?"

"That's not what I say, that's what the others say — you asked me."

"And what do you say?"

"I don't say anything. I let the others talk. I can form my own opinions and keep them to myself."

Jake did not see how this could be anything but a compliment. He was pleased, too, at what she had said about the others' comments. If they liked him along with the other men, then he would start worrying. Isabel was looking at him proudly and she wondered if she was proud of him or proud of herself. He decided there were nice things about her and that he would give her time to lay off Tom before blasting her. Was he hoping she would? Why was he? Jealous of his own brother? Not a pleasant thought. Saving him from ridicule? Sounded better. Maybe a bit of both. Supposing she tried to make a fool of him too? She couldn't, he was too strong-willed. She had spirit, though. Thought he would ask her to dance and dared say so in so many words! He liked her audacity. Obviously he would have to take her in hand — Tom would never be able to handle her, that was clear.

His thoughts were interrupted by the tramp of thirsty footsteps and Isabel busied herself pouring out tea. Jake found himself surrounded by the choristers, noisily sipping the hot, fresh tea and engaged in their usual chatter. It seemed to him more inconsequential than usual and shortly he fished out his brother and they made their way home. They trudged along in silence from one gaslamp to the next, Jake more benign than he had been for some time and Tom basking in his brother's amiability. Their thoughts were both of Isabel.

*   *   *   *   *   *   *   *

Things were different after that. Jake's somewhat abortive interview had nevertheless borne fruit, though not quite of the kind he had expected. He had found out one of the things he wanted to know — she was not a little taken by him. Her words, her blushing and her meaningful looks had cleared away most of his doubts. He was not too happy about the way Tom had got into the act, but he understood now that she had been using the only method of access to him that circumstances afforded. If he were now to attempt to get something started between himself and Isabel this could be done with a minimum of effort and without attracting attention, since he, she and Tom had often been seen together by everybody in the district. Here he had been racking his brains for months trying to think up a way of getting to know her better without having to stick his neck out, and now he found her virtually sitting in his lap — or Tom's lap at any rate — and he had not so much as lifted a finger. He could swear that nobody had the least suspicion of his intentions, unless it was Isabel herself, and he could not understand how she had. It was now or never, anyway. If he wanted to show the girl that he was interested in her he would have to be nice to her whether anybody noticed it or not. He decided he would be nice to her gradually. To start off with, he would be civil for a few weeks.

Tom was delighted with the change he discerned in his brother's attitude. He shied away from unpleasantness of any kind and he was filled with relief when the tension which had existed between Jake and Isabel began to fade away. Jake was far from affable even yet, but he was getting visibly more tolerant. When Isabel joined them he began to say "Hello" instead of giving her a curt nod and he was more careful with his spitting than he had been. A keen observer would have noticed that he had changed his collar more often and that he carried white handkerchiefs in his pockets at week-ends. He smiled at Isabel at least once a month.

As time went by, she found herself spending as much time with Jake as with Tom, though she was never completely at ease with him. She always knew what Tom was thinking, but not the other. When he was apparently in the best of moods he could turn on his bad temper like a cold water tap and one seldom knew what was the cause. He seemed to sicken of people periodically and at those times no one could go near him, but she noticed that his vicious moods were less frequent when she was present. It occurred to her that she was making progress and the thought left her breathless.

Tom proved to be no problem at all. The more attention Jake paid to Isabel, the greater was his glee. Incapable of jealousy, nothing seemed to him more natural than that his brother should get to like this pretty girl who had taught him to dance and been so kind to him so consistently. Good old Jake. Pretty Isabel. They were all good friends and he had not a care in the world. Not a care had he. If you had a pretty girl being nice to you, that was good. But if you had a pretty girl whom Jake thought a lot of being nice to you, then that was really good. Dancing and singing and linking arms and whispering secrets into girls' ears: oh, they were leading the life of Reilly, him and Jake were.

Isabel did not lose one jot of her affection for Tom. If she had done, Jake would have dropped her like a ton of bricks and she was well aware of it. Her feeling for Tom was genuine. He was her younger brother, her blind disciple, her woolly lamb. With him she was protective, homely, old-fashioned and alive. Tom she could love because she understood him through and through. Jake she loved, but part of his attraction for her was that she could *not* understand him entirely. Love is a very broad word and has been bandied around by a large number of people for a very long time. We are not sure what it means, or if we are we ought not to be. Isabel would have used the word "love" to describe her feeling for Jake because she had heard it often enough and in enough different contexts for it to have acquired some meaning, however vague.

As for Jake, it was a word he had distrusted and never used. What was "love" or whatever people meant when they talked about love? Was he capable of love himself? There were some things and people he approved of and others he disapproved of and his likes and dislikes were primitively spontaneous and honest. He was no reasoner and he had no patience with people who tried to show him reason. He *knew* he was right whereas they only *proved* they were. You could prove anything if you had enough words. Words. He was no monger of words, but he could see what was in the world, too. Love honest lazy work play right wrong respectable do don't ought to might married engaged faithful unfaithful drunk sober fault conscience ministers pulpits sermons love-thy-neighbour-as-thyself clean proper credit decent indecent black sheep baa baa love always never name reputation glory hope consolation redemption blessed blasted sinners forgiveness good and bad words without number amen. His tongue was clogged up with words. They hid behind his front teeth and ambushed what he had to say. His thought was frustrated and inarticulate, until he learned to keep it to himself. His good and bad and right and wrong and gradely and daft and black and white had their own intuitive connotations. His mental self-reliance was no less than his physical.

So they might say that he was in love. What did they know about love, let alone *him* in love? In love? What did it mean? Fever? Loss of appetite? Loss of

memory? Hangover? Insomnia? Second childhood? Reawakening? In heat?
He supposed it meant so little because it meant so much. They groped around
with their short little word. So he liked her, would marry her, go to bed and
breed with her. Love, would they say? It was good and that was all he knew. It
was *his* good without grounds or any way round it. He consulted neither God,
nor Tom, nor Isabel. He had to ask her to marry him of course, but it was not as
if she had really been consulted — only asked, as it were, to witness an
agreement he had reached with himself. She said yes, which did not surprise
Jake, who had not envisaged any other answer.

					*	*	*	*	*	*	*	*

After the day had been named he courted her in the normal manner, rightly
surmising that in this way he would attract less attention. He bought the
plainest engagement ring he could find, put it on the third finger on her left
hand and never looked at it again.

Part of the business was seeing her father. Not that Isabel was all that keen on
it, but her father was. A father of three daughters has a lot to put up with and the
compensations are few. This was one of them. Have the young man on the
carpet. So you want to marry my daughter, hey? Nothing new at all, me lad, so
does half of Wigan. After her, they were. His daughter. And the prettiest of the
three. That was for sure, the others were nothing to shout about. So you think
you can make her happy, hey? And what have you got that the others haven't
got? Pitman, hey? She wouldn't have anybody, you know. Did she tell that
young Fearnley where to go or didn't she? And Rigby. Him and his bread shop.
One of the Lancaster boys, hey? Oh, he'd heard a bit about them. He'd heard
enough to want to hear some more. Which one was he? Not that it made much
difference. Jake, hey? The one with the eyebrows. Fallen for her, hey? Thought
he could make her happy, hey? Send him in, Agnes, and let me get at him. Just
send the young man in.

Jake took his cap off as he came through the parlour door. He nodded briefly
to Webb, who opened his legs a little and put his hands behind his back.

"Good evening, young man, I suppose...."

"I'm Jake Lancaster."

Jake stared at the armchair.

"Oh, sit down, will you, Mister...."

Jake sat down. Webb waited for him to speak. Jake contemplated him for a
while and then pulled out a packet of cigarettes. Webb hastened to the
mantelpiece for his own, looking round for matches. Jake lit Webb's cigarette
and gave him a meaningful squint through the flame. He produced a rare grin.
Webb thought his face would crack.

"You know what I've come about."

"Well, yes, Isabel said...."

"She's right. These things have to be talked about."

"Quite true, quite true. A father always likes to know...."

"What she's gettin'?"

"Well, its not that I don't think th...."

"I should have sent Tom."

"Tom?"

"My brother"

"Why send him?"

"Well, he could tell you what I'm like. I'm in no position to."

"Why not?"

"There's good and bad in me."

"Well, I don't suppose any of us are...."

"You understand I can't just sit here and tell you anything good."

"Why not?"

"That would be blowing my own trumpet. Our Tom can blow it harder, anyway. And then again, I can't just sit here and tell you all the bad. It would take too long."

"Oh, there's no need to run yourself down, young...."

"I'm not running myself down."

"I've always said...."

I'm making four pounds a week and I have another five hundred in the bank and nothing particular to do with it. I'm the fastest collier on the face and I can beat hell out of any fellow in the district, except maybe for my brother Tom — and he doesn't know it."

Webb was wishing he had five hundred where Jake had.

"Young man its easy for me to see...."

"I take it you have no objections."

"Objections? Well, no, I hadn't thought...."

"Then its settled." Jake was on his feet and putting out his cigarette.

"It's like I say, if Isabel is sure that she wants you, then I don't see any reason why I should have anything more to say."

"She's sure, all right." Jake reached for his cap.

"Good night, Mr Webb."

"Good night...er...Jake."

*   *   *   *   *   *   *

They were married one Saturday morning, in church, in nice weather. It was an unspectacular wedding if ever there was one. Mr Webb gave his daughter away, proudly and with apparent reluctance. Tom was best man, with red ears and white carnation. Jake looked as excited as a man waiting for a train. The preacher said some touching things and Isabel had misty eyes. She was beautiful in pink. There were about twenty people in the church and another two dozen waiting outside. Jake hated every minute of it.

CHAPTER FIFTEEN

The Andertons of Birchley Hall

On a bleak February morning in 1889, three St. Helens journalists set out on a special assignment and trudged their way to Billinge through six inches of snow. As they themselves put it, no sanguine tramway or railway promoters had ever turned a pitying eye on the inhabitants of Billinge, so that the traveller to that ancient hill-side hamlet was compelled "either to wheel it or walk it". They seem to have found the trip somewhat arduous in the wintry conditions and one of them described the venture in the following words:

> *"Three travellers with aching backs,*
> *Half buried in the snow, made tracks,*
> *Each grasping with a look seraphic,*
> *Some apparatus photographic."*

The three men were employees of the "St. Helens Lantern", at that time a fortnightly publication giving "Reflection on the Labours, Recreations and Distractions of her People". They puffed and pulled their way up Moss Bank, "with many a slip and backward slide", and at last the summit was attained. At this critical stage they discovered they had left their notebooks back in St. Helens, so they scampered after a bunch of juvenile Moss Bankites "trooping into school" and gained possession of a few "copy books", thus avoiding a painful delay in the work they had to do. Still out of breath, they paused for a short respite on top of Moss Bank, before completing the last lap into Billinge.

Birchley valley lay at their feet. To the right the waters of Carr Mill Dam gleamed between the leafless branches of the plantation of trees around it. Halfway up the opposing hill they could see the square outline of Birchley Church and, beyond, the straggling line of grey cottages to Slack Farm and the "Labour in Vain" and the crooked Main Street twisting up to the dominant silhouette of St. Aidan's at the top. The Beacon, seen at its best from this angle, crowned the cheerless February scene, still white from the previous Sunday's blizzard. In line with the Beacon, and two hundred yards to the left of Birchley Church, they could just make out the bulky shape of another building, well back from the road and mysteriously shrouded among bushes and trees to be well-nigh invisible from the highway itself. This old, imposing structure, their destination of that morning, was Birchley Hall, a Catholic stronghold steeped in

91

history and adventure. The word was out that a Protestant landowner had offered £10,000 to Lord Gerard, the owner, for Birchley Hall and Estate, on condition the Catholic schools nearby were removed elsewhere. The journalists had an appointment that very day with Father Austin Powell, the chaplain of St. Mary's Birchley, to ascertain the fate of the Hall, which had been rebuilt by Catholics in 1588, the year of the Spanish Armada, and had served as a Catholic Mission since 1645.

A crisis at Birchley was nothing new; indeed the very survival of Catholicism in the Birchley valley is a remarkable story and one which reflects credit on several generations of Billingers of all faiths. Billinge, after the days of Henry the Eighth, was traditionally Protestant. The population figures of 1717 show a total of 198 families, of which 174 were listed as Protestant, 10 Papist and 14 Dissenters. Birchley Hall itself was reconstructed at a most difficult time for English Catholics, for the Penal Laws were such that even to declare oneself a Catholic endangered livelihood and possibly life. It was under such conditions that the Anderton family of Birchley clandestinely transformed the Hall into a centre of Catholic resistance and the story of their struggle is as exciting as any modern spy drama. "Plain clothes" priests posed as farmers in the Birchley area, and in the concealed chambers of Birchley Hall, operated a secret printing press – the first Catholic Press in England since the Reformation. Things were really happening in Billinge in the days leading up to the Civil War.

Birchley Hall owes its historical importance to the dynamic, prolific Anderton family, which took it over shortly after the middle of the 16th century. The Birchley estate had belonged to the de Heton family from the 13th to the 16th century and a mill house, possibly erected around 1450, had stood on the site of the present Hall. William de Heton went to live at Birchley around 1500 and remodelled the mill-house in the early part of his residence, so that the first reference to the mill-house in 1558 describes it as being in the timbered or "Chester" style. The name Birchley is thought by some to derive from the Old Norse "bjarkar" (cf. modern Swedish "björk") meaning "birch" and Anglo-Saxon "leah" (grass-land). Dean Powell, however, pointed out that the trees surrounding Birchley were at that time mainly chestnuts and that hardly a birch-tree could be found on the estate. He considered the name derived from "Birchall-ley" since one of the tenants of the mill-house had been a Thomas Birchall.

In 1550 William de Heton the Younger was in debt to a certain Roger Wetherelt of Lincoln's Inn. By coincidence, Heton's brother-in-law, Christopher Anderton, was also a lawyer – and a very good one – at Lincoln's Inn. Anderton appears to have succeeded in purchasing Birchley around 1558, though the actual transfer of property seems to have taken place in 1581. At any rate Christopher and his son James are both credited with the rebuilding of the Hall at considerable expense, although it was likely that Christopher had obtained the estate at a bargain price, since the sovereigns of the day played shuttlecock with Catholic estates, as Dean Powell put it, and a Catholic would have to be out of his mind to start investing in land and property at that time.

The Andertons, however, were no ordinary Catholics, and Christopher not only walked the tightrope with confidence, but died a man "of many acres" in 1593. The family owned the important Lostock Estate and many others, but they did a good job on the rebuilding of Birchley, producing a fine example of an Elizabethan mansion, three-storied in Billinge stone with large gabled wings, a recessed centre and fine chimneys. James's younger brother Thurston also made his contribution and his initials "T.A." appear over the original front door opposite the date 1594. After James's death, it was the youngest brother, Roger Anderton, who took charge and who in fact really founded "the Andertons of Birchley", producing 6 sons and 4 daughters. Four of the sons became priests and three of the girls nuns.

There was no end to Roger's energy. He was a much stouter Recusant than the Andertons before him and he began to implement measures which his predecessors had up to now avoided. Both Christopher and James were good Catholics at heart, but they were not averse to "playing ball" with those who imposed the new religion. Roger, on the contrary, moved from the defensive to the offensive and it is probably in the period of apathetic Protestantism following 1595 that he involved his family and friends in the installation of the secret printing press described above.

It is worth pausing for a moment to ask oneself why a man of Roger Anderton's background and standing would suddenly begin to work against the throne and expose himself and those near to him to expropriation and perhaps death. What were his motives and how dangerous in fact was his course of action? It must be borne in mind that only a few decades previously England had been a Catholic country and the landed gentry were naturally strong supporters of the King. After the Reformation, English Catholics rejected, in varying degrees, the imposition of the new religion, but few of them wavered in their loyalty to the throne. A Catholic admiral commanded the British fleet that sailed against the Catholic Spanish Armada. Catholics stayed loyal to the Stuarts and incurred the wrath of Oliver Cromwell and the Parliamentarians. It was only natural that some of the people who demonstrated unswerving loyalty to King and Queen would also retain their loyalty to the old faith. It was a severe dilemma for conservative Lancashire and her people. Roger Anderton had to make the difficult decision for himself. He was an Englishman from a good family blessed with land, property and education. His allegiance to the throne was unquestioned. One of his sons was in fact to turn soldier and fall fighting in the Royalist Army. But was the new religion good or bad for England? As one of the most important men in Billinge, how should he use his influence? Which side should he be on?

Christopher and James had compromised, and with good reason, but Roger took the plunge. He was a courageous man, for almost everything he did was illegal. A look at some of the Penal Laws will show us what risks he was running:

A priest caught saying Mass could be imprisoned for life.

Catholics receiving education abroad forfeited their estates to the next Protestant heir.

Any son of a Protestant house who became a Catholic was not allowed to receive his inheritance.

No Catholic could acquire legal property by purchase.

No Catholic could sit in the House of Lords or Commons, neither could he sit on a Judge's Bench or practise as a lawyer.

No Catholic had a legal claim to a horse valued above £5. (That meant that any one could take away his horse by offering him that sum for it. A story is told of a Catholic gentleman who, on being offered £5 each for his carriage horses, went to the stable and shot them all).

Birchley Hall

No Catholic could carry arms.

No Catholic could teach.

Catholics would be fined for not attending the Protestant Church.

These laws were not always enforced and the Andertons had been successful skating on thin ice for several years, but rewards were offered for information leading to the conviction of Catholic offenders. Roger was well aware that one informer, for a sum of £100, could lead to disaster, financial ruin and imprisonment for all the Andertons. Nevertheless he set about organizing his underground movement. For some time the family had stayed away from the parish church and Roger paid the fines for his absence. It was natural that Catholics would hear Mass in secret and in 1618 a chapel had been added to Birchley Hall, disguised as a granary. There are now steps on the outside of the wing leading up to the chapel door, but originally it was a blank wall and the only access to the chapel was from the upper floors of the main house. The construction of a granary would appear quite normal in view of the agricultural nature of the estate and its mill-house traditions. In order to discover the religious service, Protestant spies would have first had to penetrate the main house, with it many rooms and passages and find their way to the upper floors without disturbing any of the inhabitants. It is unlikely that the Andertons would have left the route to the chapel entrance unguarded and we can safely assume that the alarm would be given. The interior of the chapel itself is striking in its simplicity and it would be a matter of seconds for the priest to gather up the sacred vessels and escape through a trap-door which is still in evidence in a small room off the sanctuary. A ladder led down to the concealed presbytery below and it is possible that further secret passages led back into the main building and even underground to Birchley Wood. It is supposed that a fire was kept lit for burning vestments and other items in an emergency and that a plan would be in operation to decoy intruders in various ways while the priest made good his escape or donned his "plain clothes" in his hiding place. Finally there would be a look-out man on the roof during Mass.

Such were the security arrangements at Birchley Hall that we have no record of any priest having been caught or arrested on the premises. A Missal and Chalice were found hidden under the trap-door, inferring that concealment was a necessity, but it would appear that the "country squires" managed to keep their aliases intact and held regular Mass while no doubt learning something about local farming in the meantime. Away from Birchley Hall, however, protection was not always so well organized. One of the priests who offered Mass at Birchley was St. Ambrose Barlow, born near Manchester in 1585. He became a Benedictine monk at Douai and returned to Lancashire after ordination. Arrested one Easter Sunday morning, just after finishing Mass, he was hanged drawn and quartered at Lancaster in 1641.

The construction of secret passages and places of concealment at Birchley had been a defensive operation, but now Roger began offensive manoeuvres. One of the difficulties faced by the Catholics of the time was that of making their views known to the people. We would say today that the government controlled the media and not only was it forbidden to print Catholic literature in England, but the importation of Catholic books from abroad was also a treasonable activity. The Jesuit press at St. Omers in France produced the books which were needed to combat the many anti-Catholic works being written, but you risked your head to get them across the Channel. Roger not only brought in books, but was almost certainly involved in importing a whole printing press from the Continent and setting it up within the bowels of Birchley. The hazards were tremendous. Apart from the problem of shipping bulky equipment, great care would have to be taken in choosing printing type, to avoid providing investigators with easy clues as to its origin. Then there was the question of choosing the operators, for printers at that time were regarded as special craftsmen and Roger would have to be sure not only of their professional competence but also of their religious convictions. We can imagine that the work was noisy and arduous and that the printers (also dressed as rural characters) would be glad to escape from their clandestine production and spend a few hours walking in the fields and, it is said, taking exercise in the caves and copses which adjoined the estate.

In spite of the many problems, "Operation Birchley" achieved many of its objectives. At least sixteen books seem to have been printed on the secret press and one Wigan authority estimates the number of books and pamphlets printed there to have been over sixty. Who were the authors? It is likely that Roger Anderton himself wrote some of the early ones, using a pseudonym, but his first cousin, Lawrence Anderton, was more active and qualified for the work and wrote under the name of John Brereley. Lawrence had graduated from Cambridge, become a Jesuit at 28 and was known as "Golden-mouthed Anderton" on account of his eloquent speeches. He resided for a while at Birchley and there is little doubt that he would be regarded as the star author in the Billinge writing team. Rome was determined to win back her lost provinces and Lancashire was one of the prizes. Lawrence Anderton was made superior of the Lancashire province in 1621 but in the same year the Birchley printing press was raided. There seem to have been some indications that the authorities suspected the existence of a secret press in Billinge as early as 1613, but the luck of the Andertons had held out for almost a decade more. The curate of St. Peter's Chapel in Newton-le-Willows stated in a 1624 publication that "there was a printing-house in Lancashire, suppressed about some three years since, where all Brereley his works, with many other Popish pamphlets were printed."

This may or may not have been the end of the Birchley press, for it is said that the incredible Roger rode out this storm and actually reactivated the printing through the 1620s. Lawrence Anderton, certainly, continued to publish works, although these may have been printed in other parts of Lancashire or even abroad. Whether the press continued to function or not, Roger still had another 20 years to go. He seems to have thrived on danger and intrigue and died of natural causes (we are not sure exactly at what age) in 1640. There were, of course, sons to follow him. James, the heir, took possession of the Hall on his father's death. The second son, also named Roger, had entered the priesthood and was educated at St. Omers. Later he went to the English College in Rome, where he was entered into the records as "Edward Poole" – another example of a Birchley alias. Two of Roger's brothers adopted the name of Shelly and another that of Stanford. Roger was ordained in 1645 at the age of 24 and in the same year came to take charge of the Birchley mission. There has been an unbroken line of priests at Birchley to the present day. They used the "granary" chapel until 1828, when a Catholic Church was finally erected on the other side of the highway.

The young Roger Anderton had not inherited the Hall, but he did inherit his father's incredible stamina. He was created Archdeacon of Lancashire in 1676 and served the mission at Birchley fifty years until his death in 1695, "leaving the sum of £200 for the maintenance of a secular priest to officiate at Birchley, on two Sundays every month". His brother James, the heir, bore no sons. His only daughter, Elizabeth, inherited the Hall and passed it on to her daughter, Mary, who had married Sir William Gerard, a well-known Catholic of the area. Thus Birchley Hall became part of the Gerard Estates and the line of the Andertons of Birchley came to an end. The close association with the Catholic Church continued however. If the succeeding priests were not actually Andertons, they were priests in the full-blooded Anderton tradition. When the Gerards rented off parts of the Hall to other families, (not always Catholic) they were careful to stipulate that the mission be allowed to function unhindered. It was the Protestant offer of 1889 to purchase the Hall outright, accompanied by the conditions stated, that had provoked the crisis which sent our three St. Helen's scribes hurrying over the fields to Dean Powell.

The priests who followed Roger Anderton in the mission continued to use aliases. Thomas Jameson was known as "Sedden" and Thomas Young as "Brooks", and so on. One of the later priests bore the spendid name of Rev. Emerick Grimbaldestone. The Rev. John Penswick built St. Mary's Birchley in 1828 and died at Garswood, in 1864 at the age of 86. During the 18th century the baronet Andertons of Lostock appeared to have kept up their connection with Birchley and one name from their line stands out in particular in this respect. This was Sir Francis Anderton (1680-1760). He seems to have visited Birchley regularly and is said to have raised fighting-cocks on the estate. Indeed Birchley and Moss Bank appear to have become a well-known centre for sport and gambling around 1730-40. The Duke of Suffolk is reputed to have matched his cocks against those of Francis Anderton in a pit in a field to the rear of the

"Black Horse". Thomas Martlew, a collector of antiques and owner of a luxurious cottage on the slopes of Moss Bank, is said to have been a good friend of Francis and gambled his valued possessions on various cock-fights.

Sir Francis was the last of the Andertons that we know had a close connection with Birchley Hall. He was clearly very different in character from his serious-minded cousins, but he was a typical Anderton in that he had tremendous energy and lived till he was eighty. We may say that with his death the story of the Andertons of Birchley comes to an end. The deeds of Christopher, James and the two Rogers are fairly well authenticated and there is little doubt that Sir Francis's activities in Billinge made a real contribution to the village's colourful history.

But the story does not quite end there. It has not been my intention in this book to write a history of Billinge, for this can be gleaned from the record books, but rather to put down all I know about the people of Billinge, their ways, their thoughts and their lore. In trying to do so, I would be wrong if I ignored gossip, or superstition or legend. And there is one legend which has been passed down from generation to generation – that of the Andertons and the Treasure.

Before devoting a few lines to this subject, I think it is time we got our shivering journalists out of the February cold and into the warmth of Birchley Hall. Dean Powell was waiting for them, surrounded by his reference books. As this famous Billinge chaplain is worth a chapter all to himself, I propose to leave the details of their interview till later in this book and go back for a while to discuss an event which may or may not have taken place sometime between 1642 and 1700.

                    *   *   *   *   *   *   *   *

The Andertons had hung on to their property and wealth partly through their own intelligence, skill and luck, partly through the independent character of Protestant Billingers, unwilling to turn informers against respected neighbours. The Civil War was to follow, however, and one version of the legend is that an Anderton buried treasure – sovereigns, jewels and pewter in the troublesome times of Cromwell. The Civil War lasted from 1642 to 1649. Another version is that one of the Andertons, in the latter part of the 17th century, married a rich Irishwoman and returned to Billinge by stagecoach, bringing with him his Irish bride and her fortune in gold and jewels. He is reputed to have stopped the coach at night outside or on the outskirts of Billinge, gone off into the darkness with the treasure and a spade and buried it good and proper. The task took him over two hours, so he is likely to have made a good job of it. He made such a good job of it that the treasure has never been seen since. His wife, who was said to be unhappy about burying the fortune in the first place, was even cooler towards him when he discovered he was unable to find it again.

Whatever truth there may be in either of these two stories, the legend of the Anderton treasure was firmly established by 1700. Joseph Anderton, the grandfather of Susannah, was born in 1790 and his grandparents had not only told him about it but had actually looked for it. Susannah (b. 1841) believed that it had been found in her lifetime and that the finders had kept quiet about it. Many Billingers in the 1880s and 90s considered it was still under the ground and it was not uncommon for old men to go off and look in the woods for it. Others said it had been buried ten miles away and it would be impossible to trace its whereabouts within such a wide radius.

The original Andertons of Anderton, Lancashire, threw out many junior houses and if you follow a curve running from Anderton through Eccleston, Mawdesley, Wrightington, Appley Bridge, Skelmersdale and Billinge, the tombstones in the churchyards along the route show the resting places of a goodly number of them who died in the 19th century. At least three Andertons emigrated to America. They were sisters – Lavinia, Phoebe and Maria – and were probably nieces of Joseph Anderton, as Susannah kept in touch with them for a while when she was a young woman. They had all gone over on the same boat sometime in the 1840s – three young, good-looking and presumably fertile girls. Phoebe, the eldest, was already a young widow and took two small sons with her. Jim Parr visited them during his American journey in the 1860s and reported that they had all got married and were doing well. One of them had married a man called Duncan Hamilton, for whom Jim had conceived a great admiration. Hamilton was said to have been the illegitimate son of a duke. He was a proud, resourceful man, not without money, and he had helped all the sisters to settle down over there. Another sister had married someone called Gee and the third a man called Speakman. Jim spoke of a fine handsome boy named John Speakman. They were in New York and Illinois and were in the hotel business. That was all we knew. Jim had no doubt related much more, but nothing had been written down and all the letters from the American Andertons had been thrown away.

About 1955 someone down Long Fold turned up an old, brown photograph which had been lying in a bottom drawer for close on 70 years. It was an imposing picture. It showed a group of approximately thirty people arranged in three rows in front of a large wooden frame house. The back row was standing, the middle row sitting and the front row squatting on the grass. Those sitting on chairs were the elder members of the family. In the dead centre sat an austere old man with an abundant white beard, side-whiskers and an aristocratic air. There could be no doubt as to who ruled the clan. This would be the redoubtable Duncan Hamilton. It was not surprising that Jim Parr had taken a liking to him. Both were tall, upright, proud-looking men with a reputation for scholarship and justice. Next to Hamilton was sitting an equally proud-looking woman with her hair done up in a severe bun, her arms folded and her chin

The pond behind Birchley Hall

jutting forward. She strongly resembled Susannah and we knew that this was either Phoebe, Lavinia or Maria. The remaining eight men and women on chairs were subjects of great controversy among us, for we had different opinions as to which ones would be the other two sisters and their husbands. About Hamilton, however, there was unanimity of opinion. On the back row there was a tall, athletic-looking youth of such extraordinary good looks that we felt this must be John Speakman, described so flatteringly by Jim Parr. He seemed to be about twenty on the photograph and had a confident, unmarried look about him. The children appeared brown, mischievous and healthy. The house was vast and solid and we wondered how many of them lived in it. All in all, they looked an impressive clan.

* * * * * * * *

In 1957 I visited the United States of America. As I have some Anderton blood in my veins, it was suggested that I try to contact the American Andertons, who would no doubt be very numerous by now, and possibly quite rich after so many years in the hotel business. One of my problems was that, in trying to locate them, I had very little information to go on. I knew that they were in New York or Illinois, that they had married men called Hamilton, Gee and Speakman, and of course I had the picture. Armed with this aging photograph and a map of the United States, I set forth on my mission. I started in New York.

At that time New York had seven and a half million people and four million telephones. I do not recall any more how many of these telephones belonged to people with the names of Hamilton, Gee and Speakman, but I once wrote the number down and was very impressed by it. I also discovered that if you ring up a New Yorker you have never met and ask him if he had a grandmother called Lavinia, you are not always taken with the seriousness you deserve and can get some very original and lively things said to you in reply.

After a while I gave up on New York and went to Illinois. There we found the Americans much more patient and understanding and when my photograph had been examined by some learned professors and wise old journalists, I was assured that the house in the picture was almost certainly in Illinois. More detective work narrowed the area down to Lasalle Country, south of Chicago, and a little further investigation found records of a Duncan Hamilton who had lived in the village of Lowell in LaSalle County. It only remained for me to drive there.

We were three in the car, for I had been touring America with an Englishman called Alex and a Swiss friend named Jean-Guy. As we drove south towards LaSalle, we often stopped and visited places of historical interest en route. This resulted in very haphazard scheduling, so that when we reached the town of

LaSalle it was already well past midnight and the streets were deserted. There was fog in patches and we did not reach the village of Lowell until two in the morning, being able to read the signposts only from close quarters with headlamps trained on them. We could make out very few houses in the village and decided to park the car inside a park which we found by the highway. Two of us would sleep in the car and Jean-Guy (whose turn it was) would spend the night in his sleeping bag on the grass. He was not too happy about this, but we decided that we could not wake anybody up at that hour, so finally he dragged out his bag, put it carefully on top of a mound, where there was less moisture, climbed in and said good night.

The night passed quickly and I woke up at six. The windows of the car were steamed over on the inside. Rubbing a transparent porthole with the sleeve of my pyjamas, I peeped out at the morning scene. We were in a cemetery and Jean-Guy was sleeping peacefully on a grave. A white mist lay close to the ground, the sun as yet being too weak to disperse it. The grass was heavy with dew and the trees visible over the hedge were leafy green and still. It was a very English scene and could have been in old Billinge. I pulled out the picture and looked at it. The old-fashioned wooden house fitted perfectly into the landscape I could see before me. A mid-western house for sure, the Americans had told me. It was probably less than a mile away. Maybe somebody on the picture was still living in it; some of the tiny children could still be alive. It was difficult for me to imagine them as mid-twentieth century Americans; the picture had too much of Merrie England about it. And yet they would certainly talk like Americans. Would they have an old-fashioned air about them, as Billingers still had? Lowell seemed just as isolated as Billinge, possibly even more so. All we had found of it so far was a graveyard. Maybe old Duncan and Phoebe and Lavinia were sleeping just a few yards away.

Duncan and his wife stared stolidly up at me from the faded brown picture. Our eyes met and for a moment we seemed to bridge those seventy years. As I stared I felt as if I had entered the picture or as if they had come out of it and we had the same grass and trees around us and were breathing the same air. The younger people were watching me expectantly.

The feeling passed. I put the picture on the back window and returned to my century, eager to get going. Pretty soon I should have the answers to many of my questions. I awakened the others. Alex was sleepy-eyed and slow, Jean-Guy full of his usual early grumpiness. At that hour they did not share my enthusiasm. They were not their relations. Alex and Jean-Guy have no sense of history.

We had some warm coffee still in our flasks and we managed to put together a few sandwiches. The sun began to melt the fog and birds twittered in the trees around us. It was a lovely morning and had all the signs of a hot day ahead. Time heals all wounds and after a while my two companions began to speak.

Alex said we were in a graveyard and Jean-Guy told us he had slept on a grave. We packed everything in the car and backed out on to the main road. There was nobody in sight and we drove on slowly until we came to the first houses. There were only ten altogether and none of them looked like the one in my picture. I was not a little disappointed; it had been pulled down, as I had feared. Still I nursed the hope that some of the inhabitants would be able to give me more information. We stopped in front of a large wooden and brick house which seemed to be the centre of the village. Climbing out, we sat down on the grass and smoked in the sun until there was some sign of life.

Our car must have attracted attention, for after half an hour or so an old gentleman in a straw hat came out of the house and asked us if we were looking for somebody. I told him my errand and showed him the picture. He shook his head. Not only did the surnames mean nothing to him, but he was sure there was no house like that still standing in the neighbourhood. He had been living there for twenty years. We tried the other houses and the only shop, but our luck was no better. None we spoke to had been residents of Lowell for more than thirty years. We walked up to the other end of the village and looked round the bend; there were no other dwellings in sight. However, when we returned to the car a youth came up to us and suggested we go and talk to Mrs Price. She was an old lady who lived in the very first house as you came in from the cemetery end. She had just got up and was leaning over the garden gate. The youth said she had been born in Lowell.

I hastened over to her – a frail old lady in her seventies. When I mentioned the names I detected a glimmer of recognition in her eyes. She stretched out her hand:

"Let me look at the picture".

She took out her spectacles, put them on and scrutinized the faces.

"That is Duncan Hamilton. There's his wife Phoebe Hamilton next to him."

"So it was Phoebe who married him. Do you know all the others?"

"I know everybody on this picture, although a lot of them died when I was still young."

"Which ones are Lavinia and Maria?"

"Who?"

"Phoebe's sisters."

"Oh, I never knew them. They didn't live in this part of the country."

"You mean they aren't in the picture at all?"

"No. They were not from Lowell."

"But who is this lady and that?"

She mentioned unfamiliar names.

"Do you see that three-year-old girl there, playing with her doll?"

"Yes"

"That's me."

You could see the likeness, when you knew.

"Who is that handsome youth? Is it John Speakman?"

"Why, so it is. Poor old John, God bless him. How did you know?"

"We heard he was good-looking."

"He's only been dead a few years. Eighty-seven he was. He was as handsome the day he died as he is on that picture. He had white hair and a silky moustache. He looked like Mark Twain."

"Mrs Price, what happened to the house?"

"What do you mean, what happened to it?"

"Well, where is it?"

"Where is it? You just came from it. That's it there."

She pointed to the house where our car stood.

"But that house has an extra wing and no porch."

"They built the brick wing after this picture was taken. The porch they took down forty years ago. Don't you recognize it now?"

"Yes. The man who lives in it told us he'd never seen it."

"Listen, young man, you ought to go and see Grace Poland. She's John Speakman's daughter. She lives in Tonica, the next village about three miles down the road."

"Are there any relations left in Lowell itself?"

"No."

Thanking Mrs Price warmly for her information, I returned to the car and took two pictures of the big house, one from close up and another from the spot where the old picture had been taken from. Then I rounded up my colleagues and we drove on for five minutes till we reached the village of Tonica, about half the size of Lowell.

Grace Poland was a small, bespectacled widow in her sixties with snow-white hair and a Lancashire face. She was a pleasant, alert old lady and soon we were chatting readily over tea and sandwiches. I showed her my photograph.

"I have one just like it in one of my drawers. My father often used to take it out and look at it."

"How many of these people in the picture are descended from the Andertons?".

"Two. Phoebe, my grandmother and John Speakman, my father."

"Who are all the others?"

"Neighbours."

"We thought you had a thriving clan over here. Where were Lavinia and Maria?"

"Maria married a Canadian and went to Canada. She died in Vancouver. Lavinia married a man called Gee, but they went to live in Indianapolis. I only saw her once when she came to visit. She was very much like my grandmother."

"What about Phoebe's second son?"

"He died on the boat on the way over. There was only John here."

"No children with Duncan?"

"No. He was getting on when he married her."

"So there are no Hamiltons around?"

"None. And no Speakmans, either. Speakman was the name of Phoebe's first husband in England."

"Did John have no sons?"

"No. I was the only child."

"What about Lavinia and Maria?"

Maria had one daughter, also called Maria, who stayed in Vancouver. Lavinia had a daughter and there is one grand-daughter. She came back to Illinois. Cousin Susie. She's a widow of about my age. She lives about ten miles from here."

"Do you mean that you are the only two left? We imagined there would be scores of you around here. We thought everybody on the picture belonged to the family. Think what thirty people might have produced in three generations."

"The only person on that picture still alive is Mrs Price."

"Do you remember Duncan Hamilton?"

"I certainly do. He was a tyrant if there ever was one. Mind you he was honest and straight and all that. He never let you forget it."

"Was Phoebe happy with him?"

"She tolerated him. She was a pretty hard nut to crack herself, you know. They were rather a strait-laced lot in my father's younger days."

"What was your father like?"

"A grand old man, you'd call him. Always had a humorous twinkle in his eye. Here, this is a picture of him a couple of years before he died."

"He's magnificent. It's incredible how much he looks like Hugh Parr, Susannah Anderton's son. Same eyes, same eyebrows, same moustache."

"My father was a full-blooded Englishman, of course."

"And you are half English and half American. You certainly look English." She took it as a compliment.

"You talk the same way as Phoebe used to."

"We're from the same village."

"Billinge, wasn't it?"

"Yes."

"Susie and I often wonder what it's like."

"It's a bit bigger than Lowell. It used to be very old-fashioned."

"Susie says you English still live in castles and mansions and all that."

"We thought you lived in hotels."

"Hotels?"

"Jim Parr thought you were in the hotel business. He must have got mixed up."

"Oh, I know, Duncan once started a boarding-house, but he gave it up. Never had any boarders. He wanted everybody to be in by ten every night and they always had to say grace before meals."

"No business man?"

"Hopeless. Too many principles, I suppose. He could afford to have them, though. He had some land and he left Phoebe three thousand dollars. She left most of it to my father and he left most of it to me. We all just had ordinary jobs – never went in for investing or that kind of thing. This house is mine."

It was small, square and wooden with a neat garden and an elaborate American kitchen.

*   *   *   *   *   *   *   *

In the afternoon we visited the graves of John Speakman and the Hamiltons and then went to see Susie. Alex stayed behind to mow the lawn and Jean-Guy went to sleep on the porch. Susie looked very much an Anderton with her expressive eyes and prominent cheek-bones. She showed us an oil painting of Lavinia, done when she was about fifty. Lavinia and Phoebe were like two peas from the same pod. We had tea at a small, round table. Susie had a kindly, thoughtful manner of speech, with a stronger mid-Western accent than Grace:

"I've always been conscious of my English blood. Of course, I was born over here and the pattern of my life and all my friends are American, but there is still some sort of nostalgia. I didn't notice it much when I was young and while I was married. Lavinia used to tell me about England a lot, but I didn't pay much attention as a little girl. It is chiefly since I have been widowed and have had only Grace here that I've thought more about my origins. When you get to a certain stage in life the future holds less for you and you begin to think more and more about the past and what older people talked to you about. When I came to live in Lowell, where Phoebe and Duncan and John are buried, it reminded me so much of the way Lavinia and Phoebe used to talk about England. We English-Americans don't stick together the same way as Italians and Jews and so on, but sometimes I feel that we keep more of the old country inside us than the others, even after two or three generations. I might be wrong."

"I think the very way you said that proves that you are right. I mean, the reserved manner you have of expressing yourself."

"You know, I'd find it interesting to go back there, just for a month or so, meet my English relatives and see the houses and fields where Lavinia grew up. And the place where the treasure was buried."

I tried not to twitch.

"You mean you know about the treasure?"

"Oh yes. The sovereigns. Lavinia loved to tell about it. How people had looked for it for generations."

"I suppose it will never be found," I said.
"But they found it."
I twitched.
"Are you sure about that?"
"I am only repeating what I have heard. But Lavinia was sure."
"But Phoebe wasn't," said Grace.
"Who found it, and where, and when?" I asked.
"I don't know who, but Lavinia said she heard the sovereigns had been unearthed soon after she came to America. It was a rich hoard."
"But not in Billinge?"
"No. It was a few miles to the north – in a field."
I asked her more questions, but that was all she knew. Even this piece of news was incredible, coming from a third generation American.
"What is Billinge like?" asked Susie.
"As I told Grace, it's an old-fashioned place, just outside an industrial area. Nearly all the inhabitants work in industry now."
"Isn't there a town nearby?"
"It's equidistant from Wigan and St. Helens. They are industrial."
"Like Chicago?"
"Chicago's bigger."
"I suppose Billinge is very different from Lowell."
"Well, it's quieter around here, but actually you look just like two Billinge ladies, chatting over your cup of tea. I don't see that the emigration of your grandmothers changed very much."
"Lavinia said that in England times were hard, but they weren't all that easy over here either."
"Some people just have an urge to travel. Just think of the challenge a new country like America would offer in Victorian days."
"My father used to say the only reason why people travelled away from home was so they could come back and talk about where they had been," said Grace. "Certainly Phoebe wanted to go back, in her old days."
We sat on for an hour, filling up the tea-cups and staring out through the open French windows over the lawn to the oaks beyond. The green was soothing and I felt very much at peace and at home.

*   *   *   *   *   *   *   *

Our story is almost at an end, but not quite. Many years later I was going through some old papers when a newspaper cutting from the "Wigan Observer" caught my eye. It referred to an interesting find which had been made on the Old Hall Estate, near Heskin, in January, 1852. One of the workmen, a James Babet, was clearing up the roots of an old ash tree in a field on

the estate, when his axe struck something hard. On examination it proved to be
a pint pewter tankard containing 200 sovereigns from the reigns of James I and
Charles I. Not so long ago I was able to visit the spot and verify the story with
the people who now live there.

Heskin is ten miles north of Billinge, as the crow flies. And who was Babet's
employer – the tenant of the Old Hall Estate in 1852? He was a well-known local
farmer named Roger Anderton.

CHAPTER SIXTEEN

Billinge St. Aidan's

We have seen how, in all probability, the present uplands of Billinge were occupied in the second half of the 6th century by heathen Anglo-Saxon tribes coming into Lancashire from the east. The Christianization of the Saxons was advanced the second half of the 7th century and the Angle church in Wigan was probably in existence a generation or so later.

The early Billinge farmers, on their high ridge overlooking the extensive valley between Billinge and Rivington, would be distant witnesses to the sweeping changes taking place in more accessible settlements. On a clear day Wigan Parish Church is often visible from parts of Billinge and the beautiful sound of its bells sometimes reaches the village on the wind. The Saxon Church would also be visible, since it was built on the site of the present parish church, which indeed contains even Roman remains. For many centuries, therefore, the people of Billinge would be able to look down on their distant parish church, to which their children had to be taken for baptism and their dead for burial, without having recourse to a place of worship of their own. This was not at all unusual in the Saxon and later periods, when many English villagers were required to cover distances far greater than the 4 miles from Billinge to Wigan to attend their parish church. Newbigging in the "History of Forest of Rossendale" tells us that the 12 miles from Rossendale to the church in Clitheroe proved so arduous in the winter season that young infants being borne to the church to be christened at that time of year were in great peril of their lives and almost starved with cold.

Shortly after 1534, the people of Billinge asked for a church of their own. This was an interesting move, since (with the single exception of Up-Holland Priory in the fourteenth century) it was the first attempt at church extension in the vast parish of Wigan. The typically independent character of the villagers was shown in the way they raised some of the funds themselves, though outsiders helped. Furthermore, the effort was made at a time of great religious unrest. Luther had been excommunicated in 1520 and Henry the Eighth had Parliament separate the English church from that of Rome in 1534. The Billingers nevertheless pushed on with their plans for their "Chapel of Ease" and they "found one priest at their own proper costs and charges to say and sing Mass, Matens, and oyr devyne Service and to minister the Sacraments". This was done with the due permission of the then Rector of Wigan (Richard Kyghley, 1534-43) and the congregation seems to have numbered around 200.

There are some things we do not know about the early Billinge Chapel. Firstly, we have no records of its size or its exact location, though there is strong evidence to suggest that it was built on the site of the present one. Secondly, it is doubtful if it was ever consecrated, as there is no trace of any dedication. It was probably quite small and poorly furnished. When the King's Commissioners visited it in 1552, they found, of things that could be plundered, only "j littil belle," though it is not unlikely that other things may have been previously removed. From the very first years of its existence, the Chapel seems to have numbered turbulent spirits among the members of the congregation. In 1539-40 the first curate had to bring an action against James Roby, the churchwarden, and others, for "wrongfully detaining" £7-0-0 which had been collected from the worshippers. This had presumably been destined to pay the curate's salary, but the money had been passed on to a certain William Heyton Esq. and it stopped there. The vicar therefore prayed the court to direct the King's most honourable letters of privy seal to Heyton and Roby to pay the £7 to the use and maintenance of the chapel. There seems for a time to have been no service on account of "lake of payment of the priest's wages ministrynge." As we have but these scanty records, we are left to wonder if it was a question of the

Billinge Church as it was built in 1718

Billingers' honesty or if they simply did not like the "ministrynge" they were getting at the time. Not long afterwards, the same persons were again sued for detaining money collected for the repairing of the ways to Billinge Chapel. Stubborn villagers showing their independence of higher authority?

Much worse was to come. In 1553, at the beginning of Queen Mary's reign, the swing to Protestantism was reversed and a proclamation was issued restoring the Roman religion. It is likely that such a decree would be greeted with opposition in many parts of the country, but few communities can have expressed their displeasure in as direct and impertinent a manner as our old Billingers. Led by a James Wynstandley of Windstandley (who may have been the then squire) a band of militant "Protestants" broke into the chapel and "neyther regardynge dutye towards god nor obedyence to the quene's maiesty" contemptuously ransacked it. Everything of value was stolen, including the newly-provided vestments, chalice and patten, surplices, chests, coffers, a cross and a cruet. They turned out the seats, took the glass out of the windows and stopped them up with boughs of trees. The chapel was filled with corn and hay and thus turned into a barn. No services at all were held until further honourable letters of privy seal had been sent to Billinge and Wynstandley had been hauled off to the Law Courts, though there is no record of his punishment having been administered (as often seems to be the case when old Billingers broke the law).

We assume that the chapel was soon fitted out again for service, but scanty records were set for several decades afterwards. By 1598, as Queen Elizabeth's reign was drawing to a close and the Reformed state of things had been established for some forty years, we have indications that Wigan would have been far from satisfied with its Billinge chapel. Most of the gentry seem to have been inclined to the Roman religion and the legal fines for absence from church were not being levied. We have seen in the preceding chapter how Christopher and James Anderton merely paid lip service to the new faith and how Roger Anderton not only defended his estate and standing in the community but in the years following 1595 actually took the offensive against Protestantism in Billinge and to a certain extent got away with it . The clannish nature of the Billingers seems to have been very much in evidence in this period. The poor rate was not collected, few Billingers received Holy Communion thrice yearly, and of those who did many could not say their Catechism. Indeed many could not say the Creed, the Lord's Prayer or the Ten Commandments. The Chapel was out of repair and the only book on view was the large Bible. The curate was "no minister", but only a "reader", that is to say, someone unlicensed to preach. We know that the minister from 1609 until 1625 was "Reader" Bolton, who presumably suffered from the same lack of qualification. Rev. D. W. Harris points out that Bolton is a man to be admired, since there is little doubt that he would be reminded of his alleged deficiency during the 16 years he stuck it out in the village. Nevertheless he seems to have done a good job, for when Bishop Bridgeman, who was also Rector of Wigan, sent his replacement in the curate, Tempest, in 1625 to take the service at Billinge, the ornery villagers promptly threw him out.

Bishop Bridgeman had the trustees on their knees before him in Wigan and Mr. Tempest went on with his good work, no doubt wishing he had been sent to a more easy-going village. Albeit, things seemed to improve for a while and in 1637 a painted glass window bearing the arms of a member of the Bankes family was put in the church, indicating that it was not being entirely neglected.

The next upheaval was soon to come and in 1645 the Nonconformists gained the upper hand. In 1646 a Puritan Minister, John Wright, was installed in Billinge and he, too, spent 16 difficult years in the village, though reputedly "a very honest, godly minister and of good lyffe and conversacon." We have records of his pay (£50 from the intruded minister at Wigan, £4 per annum from the inhabitants of Billinge and Winstanley, and a donation of 46s. 8d. per annum from Thomas Billinge) until his ejection in 1662, when Anglican church services were restored.

It is interesting to note that during the Puritan period, a suggestion was put forward that Billinge be made a separate parish. In the "Lancashire and Cheshire Church Surveys", 1649-55, we read:

"...the said Chapel is distant from Wigan four miles, and from Holland two miles and a half, and from any other church or chapel three miles. Therefore we present Billinge fit to be made a parish, and to have those parts of Winstanley next adjoining to them to be annexed to the said parish of Billinge."

These parish divisions, which were recognized, were revoked at the Restoration in 1660, although the independent Billingers were to dispute Wigan's authority over them more than 100 years later (see below).

There is very little information about Billinge chapel from 1662 until the re-building in 1718. However, the minister to follow John Wright seems to have been one John Blakeburne, who is mentioned in Roger Lowe's *Diary* on more than one occasion. Lowe went to hear him preach in February and November, 1665 and several times in 1666. We are not told so much about Mr. Blakeburne, who, it seems, lived at Blackley Hurst, but we are given an interesting detail of Billinge social life in the middle of the 17th century: "it was a cold day and at noone Humphry Cowlys house was so thronged that we could not ataine a fire to sit by but we sacrificed ourselves ore the twopenny flagon in a cold chamber, at noone there was Henry Birchall with us the younger, we had each of us a messe of pottage, we spent 3d apiece." That was December 2nd. Two weeks later Blakeburne was dead and Lowe attended his funeral in Winwick.

In 1718 our cliquish, headstrong bunch of dogged Billinge church-goers did an incredible thing: they built the finest church for miles around. A little earlier there had been a lot of church building in the diocese. e.g. Liverpool, St. Peter

(1704); Warrington, Holy Trinity (1709); Manchester, St. Ann (1712); Ashton, St. Thomas (1714 rebuilt). Prescot Tower was built in 1727 and Lowton Church in 1732. Billinge compares most favourably with any of them. It is a unique building, just as Billinge is a unique village. There is no record of the name of the architect.

It is an admirably proportioned building, modest in size, yet imposing and dominating from every angle. Good dressed stone (probably from Billinge) had been used for the exterior and the old pews were of oak, to which age lent a delightful hue. The architectural style is Renaissance, with touches of Gothic (this again was an original feature, since Gothic was in disuse at the time) and Corinthian in the fluted pilasters within the apse. Every detail of the church suggests that it was built with great care and attention. The prime mover in the construction was a man called James Scaesbrike from Liverpool. Though not a Billinger, he spent a lot of time in Billinge, since he seems to have had a brother-in-law in Winstanley – a certain Peter Rainford. Scaesbrike, who attended church on his visits to Billinge, donated £200 towards the building of the church and this was matched in 1720 by Thomas Bankes, the then squire.

The second of the Billinge registers tells us:

"This chapel of Billinge was rebuilt in the years 1717 and 1718 by Contributions, when the Right Revd. Father in God Francis Bishop of Chester by his Verbal Orders to the Revd. Humphry Walley Curate of the said Chapel did appoint Thomas Bankes of Winstanley Esq., the Revd. Mr Sam Aldersey Rector of Wigan, and the aforementioned the Revd. Mr. Walley to seat the Inhabitants of the said Chapelry who had claims to seats and forms or pews in the old Chapel, and to dispose of the rest; which order was obeyed and the seats ordered and disposed of as follows:"

The pews were numbered 1 to 49 and their allotment gives us considerable information about the make-up of the congregation at the time. Four pews were given to Thos. Bankes, Esq., for the use of his Family, and about twenty-six others for the use of his tenants. Sir Wm. Gerard, Bart., of Garswood, had one pew for his Family, possibly in acknowledgment of his ownership of Birchley Hall. Thomas Bispham, Esq., of Bispham, had two seats for his Family, likewise Mr. William Blackbourn, Gent., of Blackley Hurst. The Curate of Billinge had one pew for his Family and one for a tenant, and Lord Derby had one for a tenant. Fourteen others were allotted to different individuals who were probably small freeholders, or had some other claim to them. James Scaesbrike was given a pew behind the Bankes and Gerard families and in front of the curate. It was therefore one of the chief pews and Scaesbrike was paid a further compliment by the people of Billinge by the erection of a Record Board on the south wall of the church, praising him for his initiative during the reconstruction.

The Billingers, with the help of Scaesbrike and, of course, the unknown architect, had done their work well. Not only was the new building noteworthy on account of its architectural beauty, but it was a good example of sound, long-term planning. The population of the village in 1718 was about 900, and the rebuilt chapel was designed to hold around 200 – proportionately a more generous provision for church accommodation than that in the 1908 restoration or indeed than at the present time.

The new Chapel was built during the incumbency of Humphry Walley, (1708-48) to whom a commemorative tablet is dedicated at the east end of the church. He served from the age of 24 until his death at 65 – a lifetime devoted to his wonderful new chapel and its people. It is worth noticing that many ministers followed him in this Billinge tradition of long incumbencies (Howard St. George, of living memory, holds the record with 45 years) and we are left with the impression that the ministers of Billinge from Walley onwards must have felt a certain fascination for their rugged, anachronous congregation and their work among them on the bleak, wind-swept hill-top.

After Restoratio

By 1765 the villagers were ready for another declaration of independence –
this time a formal one. The feoffees of the chapel decided to dispute the
patronage of the Rector of Wigan who, they alleged, had deprived them of it on
the death of Mr. Walley in 1748. The plaintiffs were William Bankes, John
Gildart, Humphry Atherton, John Harper and Lawrence Pennington. (John
Gildart was the grandson of John Blackburne of Blackley Hurst). The case was
tried in the Court of Common Pleas at Lancaster, and the defendants were the
Bishop of Chester and the Rector of Wigan. The Billingers had built up a strong
case and it appears that the Attorney-General was, in fact, for the plaintiffs.
Several deeds were produced by the feoffees:
   1. One, dated 1561, by which Thomas Winstanley, Esq., conveyed the chapel
and chapel yard to certain feoffees. He was probably the survivor of earlier
feoffees, for the chapel was standing soon after 1534.
   2. One, dated 1603, by which Peter Latham, the surviving feoffee, conveyed
the chapel and chapel yard to other feoffees.
   3. One, dated 1614, by which Peter Marsh conveyed to the chapel feoffees
two closes of land in consideration of the sum of £60, most of which had come as
a legacy from "Thos. Walley *alias* Billinge." The income of this land was to be
an endowment for "a Minister or Reader," who should be yearly admitted by
the feoffees. ("Reader" Bolton had charge of the parish at this time.)
   4. One, dated 1665, by which Mr. Humphrey Cowley, the surviving feoffee,
appointed other feoffees, one of whom was "Peter Mather (if he was then and
should continue a Member of the Church of England)," and another, "William
Blackburne of Blackley Hurst within Billinge aforesaid, Gent."
   5. And finally one, dated 1754, by which John Blackbourne, only son and heir
of this William Blackburne, not only appointed six fresh trustees, but also
provided for the continuance of the trust in the future by co-option to the
number of seven.
   The plaintiffs urged that they, or rather that Mr. John Blackburne, had been
deprived of the patronage by Dr. Roger Bridgeman, Rector of Wigan, on the
death of Mr. Walley in 1748. In one of the other papers in the parish chest, a
statement by Fogg, Proctor, it is said that this Humphrey Walley, "being a man
very agreeable to the Trustees, and having an extraordinary influence over
them," was allowed to enter into possession of the trust estates, which he held to
the time of his death. Not only so, but he "some years before his death (by what
means is not known) got into his Possession the several Deeds and
writings. . .with the Privity of Mr. John Blackburn." These were lost at the
time of his death, but were found and returned by his executors five years
afterwards (1754). Mr. John Blackburn, the surviving trustee, was thus reduced
to a helpless position. Then "Doctor Bridgeman, the then Rector of Wigan,
taking advantage of the said John Blackburn and the want of the several Deeds
before mentioned, surreptiously and by false suggestions nominated the

Reverend Edward Parr Clerk as his Curate or pretended Curate to the said
Chapel of Billinge, and prevailed with the late Bishop of the Diocese of Chester
to grant him a Licence to officiate in the said Chapel. It being then out of the
power of the said John Blackburn the surviving Trustee to produce the said
Deeds or set forth the Right and Interest of the Trustees. . .and this was and is
true publick and notorious in and throughout the Parish of Wigan Chapelry of
Billinge and other places adjacent."

The case for the plaintiffs was forcibly put by the Attorney-General; the
deeds were put in; witnesses were called – Joseph Colshead and Elizabeth
Woodworth, both aged eighty, and William Derbyshire, aged seventy-seven –
to prove past appointments and payments by the trustees (e.g. "Sedgwick-
Curate, 60 years ago – paid 10/- Sunday, by Blackburn Trustee as he has heard
say"), and independence of Wigan.

But, in spite of all this, the rector won his case. He pleaded that Billinge was a
chapel of ease, exactly on the same footing with Hindley and Up-Holland, and
never a donative. He proved that the Billinge chapel wardens had always
appeared and been sworn at the bishop's visitation, and that copies of registers
had been sent to Chester; that the curates had been licensed by the bishop; that
in 1717 Mr. Walley admitted to Queen Anne's Bounty Commission that £6 was
paid yearly to him by the rector; that this was attested upon oath, and that the
certificate sets forth that the nomination of the Curate of Billinge was then in the
Rectory of Wigan. He also proved the dependance of the chapel upon the
mother church, by showing that the Curate of Billinge had time immemorially
attended at Wigan Church every Good Friday, and assisted the rector and
curate there in the duty or service of that day, and in the administration of the
Sacrament; by showing also the provision of the Sacramental Bread and Wine
by the Wigan churchwardens, the provision by them of surplices, "Cupps for
the Communicants," and Common Prayer Books, and the repairing of the
pulpit; and finally, he showed that when the chapel had been rebuilt in 1718, the
Rector of Wigan, together with the Curate of Billinge and Mr Bankes of
Winstanley, by the direction of the bishop, allotted the seats to the inhabitants.

And so the Billinge feoffees, in spite of the pains they had taken in assembling
their evidence, lost their case. This is hardly surprising if we bear in mind that
the Rector of Wigan – an ancient and loyal borough with its Charter from
Henry III – was as powerful and incumbent as could be found in the whole of
England. Moreover, his own case was strong, and the patronage has rested
quietly in his hands for the last two hundred years and more. There is no doubt
that Billingers, independent though they are, tend to face towards Wigan, and
this element in their character has applied particularly in ecclesiastical affairs.

In 1823-4 the north and south galleries were put up to accommodate the
increase in worshippers, but these detracted from the simple beauty of the
church and they were removed in the 1908 restoration. One of the greatest

living English architects, Mr. T. G. Jackson, R.A., effected the changes in the 1908 restoration and once again the Billingers showed that nothing but the best was good enough. The apse was moved eastwards and the transepts added, but scarcely a stone of the old chapel was lost and all the fine oak work has been preserved on the walls. As in the 16th and 18th centuries, part of the cost of the work was borne by the villagers themselves, 400 parishioners contributing. A sum of £4,470 had been spent by March 1908, at which time Billinge Church was given a patronal dedication for the first time in its history – to Saint Aidan, who was born about the same time Billinge was being settled by the Anglo-Saxons.

A Register Book belonging to the chapel, containing entries of baptisms, weddings and burials, quotes during the tenure of Mr. Humphry Walley the occupations of the fathers of the baptized children. I list these for the reader's interest: (1708-49)

"farmer, labourer, webster, linen weaver, collier, linen salesman, chandler, yeoman, naylor, hingemaker, jointmaker, slater, husbandman, delfman, whitesmith, shopkeeper, blacksmith, linen tradesman, miller, shoemaker, maltster, maltman, etc. (We are reminded that Malt House on Church Brow has been in existence since 1674).

Of even greater interest is the book of churchwardens' accounts, which was kept with great care from August 1770 ("payd for this Book, 3s.3d.") until Easter 1857. These show us clearly the day-to-day work of the church officials

The interior showing the old oak pews

and the tasks and problems with which they were confronted in the 18th and 19th centuries. Here are some of the entries:

1771.	Paid to Delfman and several others Fixing the Step Stone it Requiring great strength	0	1	5
1772.	For Wheeling and Clearing of all the Rubbage after Flagging was done	0	1	0
	Paid for Sacrament Bread for two years	0	1	10
1773.	For fetching Wine from Wigan	0	0	8
1774.	For 6 Bosses to kneel upon	0	6	0
	Paid John Taylor for Ale; that was had for Ringing on Holidays, and for Workpeople, as by bill.	0	12	2
1775.	Paid for Sacrament Bread	0	1	0
	To fetching Wine five times from Wigan.	0	3	4
1776.	Paid Thos Barrow for 20 Empty Wine Bottles that are Missing at 3d p.b.	0	5	0
	To Peter Yates for Straw Matts at Commn.	0	5	0
1777.	Parkinson for Weather Cock.	0	5	0
1779.	To three men for Cleaning Snow of Chapel, and cleaning Walks [Frequent similar entries.]	0	2	0
1781.	To Expenses at a Rejoicing	0	1	0
1783.	To going to the Top of the Chapel to look at Cupola, fetching Ladders, and bringing home	0	1	0
1786.	To Boards, Nails, and Work at Chapel Windows when Blowed out	0	2	6
1787.	[The Chapel was whitewashed at a total cost, with some plastering, of £4, 2s. 7d., including "allowance in Ale, a Pint a day each man, 5s 0d." and "Betty Cadmon and others cleaning Chapel twice, 2s 0d." N.B.—Men's Wages, 2s. and 1s. 10d., Apprentices', 1s. 4d. per day.]			
1788.	To 9 Baskets of Coals and carting . . . . [So others.]	0	3	0
	To 3 Journeys to John Rigbys to Receive Cash for Oat Bread [So others.]	0	2	0
1800.	A new Matt for the Communion	1	12	6
1801.	(Oct.) Paid for Ringing and Ale on Account of Peace . . . [N.B.—One Bell.]	0	12	6
1802.	Postage of a letter and ink	0	1	3
1812.	Paid James Anderton for Clerking . . . . . [This is in addition to Clerk's Salary in various items, £7, 2s. 10d.]	1	0	0
1815.	Paid for Assistance of fixing Scafforts, and also for proping the Galary	0	3	6
1817.	Expenses of Proping Galary and taking Down at Charity Sermon [This seems to have been thirsty work. The Pulpit, reading desk, clerk's desk, and some pews cost £56.]	0	8	6
1818.	Paid for Lowance when the new Pulpit was in fixing up . . [A similar entry in each of the next three years.]	0	11	4
1819.	Given to the Singers at the opening of the new School . .	0	6	6
1821.	Given to Singers [N.B.] Sun. Sc. Anniversary	0	10	6

1822.	Allowance on Repg Chapel and yard—expecting Bishop . .	0	1	9
1824.	[Pew Money received—that is, the money paid for Pews in the new Gallery amounted "inc King's Duty," to £204, 10s. 11½d. The Winstanley Rate produced £30, 14s. 9d., and the Billinge Chapel Rate, £38, 13s. 7d. The amount spent is given on the other side. £1 was paid to the architect, Mr. Warburton, for the plan, and £15, 3s. for Faculty.]			
1825.	Pd for the Large Room and Liquor at the Confirmation of Boys and Girls.	0	8	2
	Do. Journey to do.	0	4	0
1827.	Pd for repairing Pews in ye Chapel on the Bishop's Visit and Boards	0	5	6
1830.	Pd for a cork screw	0	1	10
	For an Iron Chest	14	14	0
1833.	Pd for Candle Snuffers	0	1	10

On several occasions money was paid for ringing, &c., on November 5th. Apparently, May 29th was a great day at Billinge. Year after year, from 1770 to 1814, expenses are entered:—

1770.	[1]Bowning and Adorning the Chapel on 29th May	0	1	6
1771.	May 29, Customary adorning Chapel and expenses . . .	0	1	6
1779.	To Ringing and Expenses on 29th May	0	2	6
1794.	May 29, for Ringing and Liquor.	0	2	6
1814.	May 29, Decorating the Chapel	0	3	0

The Billinge people seem to have been a loyal set, as the following entries show:—

1770-71.	For a Form of Prayer for the Queen's Delivery	0	0	8
1771-72.	Paid for a Paper for Correcting in the Prayer Book the Prayer for the Royal Family	0	0	8
1816-17.	Pd for Fixing the King's [George III.] Coat of Arms up as a Gift from Meyrick Bankes, Esqr., of Winstanley	0	10	6
1817-18.	Pd Mr. Richd Marsden for Morning Cloath Pd Jn[o]Marsden for do. and putting the Chapel in Black for Princess Charlotte's death [d. Nov. 6, 1817]	3	15	0
	Jorney and Expense to Up Holland and Wigan ro (?) the Pulpit and Reading Desk on Account of the Chapel being in Black	0	2	6
	Do. to Purchase Black Cloath, &c. &c.	0	2	6
1819-20.	Paid Richd Marsden's Bill for Black Cloath on Account of the Death of the King [George III., d. Jan. 29, 1820] . . .	14	6	9
1826-27.	Paid for Crape on D. of York's Death [d. Jan. 5, 1827] and fixing up	0	19	3

---

[1] Bowning, i.e preparing. An obsolete or archaic word (variously written), derived from the Norwegian búen, pa. pple. of búa, to get ready. The word was derived from the ppl. á, which is found in Chaucer (1386), Franklin's T., 775: "She was bown [i.e. prepared] to goon the wey forth right." Harding (1470), Chron., viii. 1: "He to paye was so readye and bowne, For his Vitayle." Ross (1768), Helenore, 93: "The Squire. . . to find her, shortly makes her bown." Sir Walter Scott revived the literary use of the word; cf. Lady of the Lake, IV. iii.; cf. Dr. Murray's New English Dictionary. It is interesting to find this old word in use at Billinge in 1770.

1830-31. Paid for Crape for Mourning on the Death of the King, &c.
   [George IV., *d.* June 26, 1830] 2 14 10
   For taking down Mourning and Cleaning 0 2 6
1837-38. Pd for putting Chapel in Mourning for William 4th [*d.* June 20,
   1837] 0 6 0

I quote further from Wickham's "Some Notes on Billinge":—

"The singers deserve a short concluding notice. They are not mentioned before 1774, when they received 4s. 10d., nor after 1833, when they were paid £3 "by order of Mr. Bromilow," the then Incumbent. Between these two dates they are mentioned in most of the accounts. They sat in the "old Gallary," which was repaired and fitted with "a Book frame for singers" in 1784; a "new form" was provided for them in 1788, which cost 3s. 6d. In 1832 their seats were furnished with "Curtains and Rods." Their fortunes ebbed and flowed. Some years they received but a very few shillings. In 1794-5 the whole expense of the choir came to £1, 9s., and in 1798-1800 (two years) to £2, 16s., in addition to which no less than £3, 8s. 6d. was paid "to John Hurst for teaching" them. They were visited several times by "Wigan singers," and once by "Newborough singers" to whom 7s. was paid. The Wigan and Billinge singers together got only 5s. In 1800-1 4s. was spent on "Ale for Singers." They were regularly provided with candles. They had "ruled paper" given them in 1825, and their music was repaired at a cost of 16s. The "green base for the musicians," which cost 7s. in 1828, was probably for bags for the instruments. These first appear upon the scene in 1786, thus: "To Mr. Cowley for Green Baze for Bazoon Bag 2/4, and to Taylor making Do. 4d." Henceforward the charge for "Reeds" was apparently the only instrument till 1804 (December), when there occurs the entry, "a sett of Strings for Base Viol, 4s. 8d." and these are afterwards frequently mentioned. A new bow was purchased for it in 1809. In (October) 1805 we read of "a Hotboy for Edward Moyers £1" This was mended in 1808, and again in the following year. But they did not learn to spell it correctly until 1823, when we read of "2 Hautboys and 1 Bassoon Reeds, and for singers 4s. 10d." In 1812-13, 6s. was paid for violoncello strings, but this may be only our old friend the "Base Viol," or, to put it the other way, he may have been only a violoncello, and not a double base. Not before 1826 do we meet with the violin, and again only in 1828, in which year we get the only mention of the flute, thus—"By Jas. Cowland repairing G Flute & Hoop 3s. 4d." "Base Viol" strings and reeds were purchased in 1833, and then the orchestra seems to have come to an end, after doing duty for nearly fifty years. At any rate we find no further mention of either singers or instruments till 1844, when £1, 15s. was paid for tuning "the Organ," and £1 for blowing it. Two years later Charles Williams received £10, one and a quarter years salary for playing it."

And so with these simple, honest documents we see unfolded the story of Billinge Church and its people. It is an incomplete story, as for many centuries records were not kept in the manner they are to-day, and sometimes they were not kept at all, mislaid, burnt or lost forever. But we can derive great pleasures from studying these dutiful entries, for they supply the flesh and blood and tissue to the bare bones of our tale. We see the old Billinge names crop up time and time again – the John Taylors, Betty Cadmons, John Rigbys, James Andertons, Peter Yates, Richard Marsdens, Meyrick Bankes, John Hursts, Edward Moyers, James Cowlands, Charles Williams and the Cowleys. Nearly all these names are still in evidence in Billinge today. The people bearing them can note with pride the honest toil and labour of their ancestors who fetched the wine from Wigan, fixed the Step Stone (requiring great strength), cleared away the rubbish after the flagging was done, cleaned the snow from the Chapel walks, climbed the ladders to the top of the chapel, whitewashed and plastered it, replaced blown-out windows, carted the baskets of coals, propped up the galleries, fixed up the pulpit, adorned the chapel on the 29th of May, sang in the galleries and rang the bell on sundry occasions. Often they were paid their "lowance" in ale, as was the custom, and the three adjoining Inns on Church Brow would no doubt supply refreshment to those of the congregation who had travelled from afar and tend to their horses during and after the service.

For a long time now an important part of the village life has revolved around the solid, original, dignified edifice of Billinge Church. It is a fitting monument to the solid, original, obstinate, humorous folk who built it.

* * * * * * * *

There is an interesting footnote to our story. The 1718 chapel was built by an unknown architect, to whom Billinge owes a great debt of gratitude. As this chapter was being written, Rev. D. W. Harris, the present incumbent, mentioned to me that the Church of St. Alkmund in Whitchurch, Shropshire, bears striking architectural similarities to Billinge Chapel. The old Whitchurch church fell down in 1711, was rebuilt in 1712 and consecrated in 1713. One of the donors present at the consecration was the Rector of Wigan, the Rev. Finch. It is just possible that Finch liked what he saw at the St. Alkmund dedication and asked his colleagues for the name of the architect. If he did not do so at the time, he may have contacted them a year or two afterwards. The re-building of Billinge Chapel was begun in 1717. It is also worth noting that the powerful Bridgeman family, patrons of Wigan Parish Church, hailed originally from Shropshire and that Wigan belonged to the diocese of Chester, only 18 miles from Whitchurch. The Church of St. Modwen, Burton-on-Trent (built 1719-26) is a replica of St. Alkmund's and obviously by the same architect.

Investigation revealed that St. Alkmund's was built by William Smith and St. Modwen's by Francis Smith. These men were father and son but were not, strictly speaking, architects. They were a firm of masons or builders specializing in church construction and they produced work of an exceptionally high quality, as anyone who has seen the churches at Whitchurch and Burton may readily ascertain. It would seem just possible therefore that the reason for our not knowing the name of the architect of Billinge Church may be that no architect, in the strictest sense of the word, ever existed.

CHAPTER SEVENTEEN

1893

By 1893, Gentleman Jim's family had grown up. Five of the twelve children had died in their infancy, but the seven who survived were strong and active. The three boys — Jem, Hugh and Sam — were all bachelors and living at home. The four girls had got married — Mary Ann (Moll) to Teddy Bellis, Elizabeth (Tet) to Seth Martlew, Caroline to Jack Lowe and Wilhelmina to Jem Birchall. Moll already had three children, Tet and Caroline two each and Wilhemina had one son and was expecting her second child. Bellis, Martlew and Lowe had all come to live down Long Fold, so that only Wilhelmina lived in another part of the village.

Jim and Susannah were satisfied with their children. Moll, Tet, Wilhelmina and Jem had the physical characteristics of the Andertons — dark eyes, ruddy hue, curly hair, big bones and strong, energetic bodies. Hugh, Sam and Caroline were typical Parrs — spare in build, fair or ginger-haired with blue, sunken eyes and smooth, delicate skin. Of the girls, Moll, the eldest, was most like her mother. More than any of the others she was defiant in times of trouble, facing up to the many problems that life was to bring her with the same bravery that Susannah had shown. Required to help with the younger children from an early age and sent out to work before she was ten, Moll had never been to school at all. She learned to read at Sunday School in later years, but went through life without being able to write, though she could sign her own name. Of all the seven children she was the quickest-witted, the fastest reckoner and the most decisive. She read a lot and spoke with conviction, but her inability to write was always a source of frustration. The second sister, Tet, who could neither read nor write, could not have cared less about either. A born worker, she was out in the fields from the age of nine and could not have been dragged to school by wild horses. Such was her resistance to any discipline other than hard physical labour that after a time she was allowed to go her own way without advice or interference from others. Tet developed into a stubborn, hard woman who ignored the subtler sides of life. For all this she was capable and intelligent enough not to cross swords too often enough with Moll, who had all her toughness and twice her brains. Caroline, the third sister, was a sweet and calm girl, who followed in her mother's footsteps in going out to help the sick and needy. She was eventually to become the mother of twelve and face considerable hardship and hard work in bringing up her family. Wilhelmina, the youngest girl, was good-looking and fresh with dark curls and gleaming white teeth. She and her brother Jem had wonderful singing voices and they were very close.

Jem, the oldest son, was a bit of a rake. He was big and strong and an excellent worker in the mine, where all the sons were employed. Big Jem spent all his money on beer and went around with women in his spare time. He was a hearty man with a fine sense of humour, kindly nature and hearty appetites. He represented a problem for his father, who was somewhat of a puritan. Jem was the only one of the children who could not be enticed into chapel, for even Tet toed the line there. Gentleman Jim had a long line of preachers talk to Big Jem in order to make very clear for him the dangers of his ungodliness. It was already almost unthinkable for a Parr not to go to church, but to get locked up in St. Helens on Saturday nights for brawling in pubs was considerably worse. Once, when he was returning from St. Helens in a drunken stupor at five in the morning, Big Jem walked straight into Carr Mill Dam and went down twice before being fished out by Bob Barry, a policeman, who took him to hospital on his bicycle. The combined efforts of his father, preachers and constabulary did nothing to change Big Jem's way of life, apart from wringing out of him the odd concession of an appearance in Chapel at Sermons and christenings. He remained a bachelor until he was in his early forties, then married a Billinge girl and had six children. Each child he forced into chapel from the day they could walk till the day they got married. He never stopped drinking.

The second son, Hugh, was everybody's favourite. In most large families there seems to be one child fortunate enough to inherit the good sides of both parents. Though it is no more than a felicitous accident of genetics, it appears as if both father and mother have rivalled each other in conferring both mental and physical gifts upon this chosen offspring and he will inevitably carry the family torch for the following generation. Hugh was such a child. At twenty, he was his father's spiritual heir. God-fearing and upright in all his actions, he was a moral and mental yardstick for brothers, sisters and cousins alike. Thirsty for knowledge, he had been an outstanding scholar and educated himself more than adequately by avid reading at home. In his late teens he was an understanding and perspicacious Sunday School teacher; by the time he had passed twenty he was an inspiring preacher with a fiery style in the pulpit, jabbing forefinger, flashing eyes and courageous voice. Physically, he was extremely attractive. Of less than medium height and small-boned, he had a narrow-waisted, balanced figure which hinted at feline strength in the shoulders, wrists and fingers. The light brown hair was curly and roguish, his eyes piercingly blue under bushy, bristling eyebrows. He had a straight, delicately chiselled nose and a good, dimpled chin. The skin was smooth and translucent, yet with humorous wrinkles at the corner of his eyes and mouth. He smiled easily, sometimes cynically, laughed always with fierce enjoyment. He had his mother's kind heart and loving nature, but also her hot temper if he thought someone had been wronged. He had all his father's righteousness, but was not so much of a Puritan and was not averse to using bad language when he considered someone deserved it. He was sought after by women and dressed always in the height of the fashion of that time. He knew it was no sin to be gay. He could be stubborn but was never hard, and finally was always flexible. When you met him you were impressed by the quickness of his movements, but most of all by the penetration of his blue eyes.

Sam, the youngest son, was all Parr and no Anderton. Similar in appearance to Hugh, he was less intellectual and had not the same drive. A quiet, reserved man, he was entirely without malice and was content to shun the limelight.

*   *   *   *   *   *   *   *

1893 was a time of calamity for the local miners and their families. Disputes between the mine-owners and workers had come to head and the Great Coal Strike was to last many months. Gentleman Jim, his three sons and his four sons-in-law were all out of work. In Billinge the effects of the '93rd strike were widespread, as most of the men and many of the women were connected with the pits. Farm labourers continued to earn their ten shillings a week and those who worked at the Pilkington Glass Works in St. Helens had their livelihood assured, but most of the village went hungry. The six shops between Church Brow and the Bottom End gave people food on credit, though in limited amounts and according to the factor which today would be known as credit rating. To supplement these meagre rations, pea-soup was given out once a day at noon at the Council Offices. After a fortnight of pea-soup the whole village was sick of it.

Down Long Fold the Parrs tightened their belts and sat out the strike. They had no difficulty getting food as their credit was good, but they were wary about using it up as nobody knew how long the strike would last. They settled down to a diet of bread and margarine, potatoes, turnips and tea porridge — traditional Lancashire fare when times were hard.

Up the hill near Church Brow the other Parr — Wilhelmina — was expecting her second child. A sturdy, good-looking girl of nineteen, she was making the best of an indifferent marriage. Jim Birchall drank and gambled and some weeks blew all his wage on the horses before pay-day. During the strike there was no wage at all and Wilhelmina went perpetually hungry. To make matters worse, she could not stand the sight of pea-soup, which she never touched. When the hunger was too bad, she went down Long Field and ate at Moll's.

In December she had the child, a daughter in good health. For a week she fed the child and then was striken by a circulatory defect. She lay a few days unconscious until Susannah came to fetch her and the child with a horse and cab and take them down Long Fold. There she lingered for three weeks alternating between consciousness and oblivion while her parents and brothers and sisters watched her die. Big Jem, whose favourite she was, took it harder than any of them. In her lucid moments she begged him to take care of the infant Wilhelmina. In the years that followed, when he came home drunk at two or three in the morning, Jem would creep into the little girl's bedroom, kneel by the bed and his rough fingers would feel and stroke the tiny arm under the pyjama sleeve and he would say time and time again "Oo asked mit tek care o' thee, an I 'ave done, 'aven't I?" He never did, of course, but the sentiment was there.

Wilhelmina was the sixth child that Jim and Susannah had buried; the rest outlived them by forty years. The baby girl was never returned to the father and was brought up down Long Fold. She was known as Minnie Parr.

Susannah

CHAPTER EIGHTEEN

Long Fold

In 1899 Minnie Parr was a little girl of six. She had not yet started school and she spent most of her time down Long Fold, which to her was the most beautiful part of Billinge, the centre of the world. As you neared the bottom of the main street, a pleasant lane branched off to the left and descended, twisting and turning for half a mile past Greenfields Orphanage and the Sandwash to dip sharply into a small wooded valley which had fourteen cottages. The road was narrow and facing the cottages was a magnificent line of trees — oak, ash, chestnut and the odd beech. A brook babbled behind them and there were only green fields beyond. Smoke always curled from the chimneys of the houses, behind which the gardens sloped up towards London fields. All around was undulating farmland. There was no traffic as we know it — only the occasional horse and cart, wagon or cab. The small front gardens had flowers of many colours. The front doors were brightly painted. The cottages, garden walls and road were all of the same green-grey stone.

Minnie lived with Jim and Susannah and her Uncle Jem, Uncle Hugh and Uncle Sam. Her Aunt Moll, Aunt Tet and Aunt Caroline lived nearby. She was a frail, quick, active child and her earliest recollections were of fetching bread and meat from the village shops and going to all the farms around for milk and buttermilk for Susannah. Long Fold was nearly a mile from most of the shops and the road was wild, bleak and cold in winter. In the days before gas and electricity there were no street lamps and after leaving Main Street there was only blackness and tall trees rustling in the wind. Minnie and her contemporaries were not afraid of the dark lanes, for they knew no other kind. They liked the dark. In the cottages they used paraffin lamps and Minnie would fetch paraffin once or twice a week.

During the course of her errands, Minnie gradually acquired a knowledge of Billinge geography. On her way to the farms she would tramp through Mulks Wood and Hollin Hey Wood, she visited other places called the Rant, Dungeon Fields, Dam Slacks, Brown Heath, Cockle Pit, Marlpit, Startem, Traddle Holes, Poverty Land, Laffuck, Marsh Ground, Turpin Fields, Cockshut, Round Meadow and Top Two Gates. The people in her little world had names reminiscent of the 1860s, though not the same ones. She knew Dancing Jack and Bacco Dick, Owd Pipe and Owd Matches, Neddy Red, Ducky, Thunger, Sall Tazzle, Jogger and Owd Linnet. There was Betty Yallow, Owd Bill Pisser, Barm Johnny, Owd Bottle, Tippet, Red Jem, Togger, Nanny Goat Whiskers, Cock' the Thumb, Hucko, the Slaps, the Cockies and Dolly Blue. She had heard of others such as Dodger, Owd Kelt, the Bumpers, Owd Bill Barebones, and Owd Jack Crow. If you went through Mulks Wood at dusk you had to maintain a good pace and keep looking back over your shoulder or you might be caught by the witch who lived in the shadows there. She was called Owd Nellie Moggie.

Little Minnie knew everybody down Long Fold, as well as every nook and cranny of the fourteen cottages, gardens, yards and middens. She was familiar with each big stone in the wall running along the lane and every tall tree was an old friend. In the early morning, Gentleman Jim and her three uncles would leave for the pit and Susannah and the aunts would start their washing, scrubbing and daily chores. Minnie would be outside before nine, poking her little nose into Aunt Moll's, fetching and carrying between the houses and playing with her cousins of her own age such as Jem Bellis, Jim Martlew and Ben and Tom Lowe. Those were the years of cold, frosty winters, hot, sunny summers and crisp, crackly autumns of brown, red and gold. In spring the air in

A Long Fold group about 1901

Billinge, and especially amidst the natural greenery of Long Fold, was all
dewdrops and dandelions. It was a healthy open air life and the lack of transport
made the Long Fold children wiry, fleet of foot and possessing great stamina.
The food from the ovens was good and the Parr women jealously guarded old-
fashioned English recipes handed down through several generations. Long
Fold was a closed shop, and they judged the rest of the world according to their
own tenets.

Minnie had heard how thousands of people had tramped up and down Long
Fold on the way to Carr Mill Dam to witness the exploits of Our Nell's Jack and
his unlucky opponents. Now and then she would see his nimble figure striding
along Main Street. He had a smile and a nod for everyone and a far away look in
his eyes as though he was thinking about the next big frost. Nowadays only the
occasional stranger passed through Long Fold. There were the regular
tradesmen such as Thompson the butcher, who visited on Tuesdays, Fridays
and Saturdays with his pony and trap. Then there was the Cockle Man, with his
cockles and mussels from Southport, the paraffin man with his paraffin and
firelighters, the rubbing stone man with his chalk, rubbing stones and donkey
stones. On Friday nights came the greengrocer and the newspaper man with the
"Wigan Observer", the "Liverpool Echo" and the "Liverpool Weekly Post".
These men were glad to visit the tight little community for not only did they
have consistent trade, but they were invariably treated to mugs of scalding tea,
slices of egg and marmalade pie and the unspoilt wit and banter of their
anachronistic customers. They were given nicknames and jovially acquiesced to
their use while they were in Billinge, but they were careful to keep them secret
in the other towns and villages on their rounds.

The appearance in Long Fold of any person other than these weekly
suppliers was certain to attract great attention among the inhabitants. If he was
coming down the hill from Billinge, it was likely that his reputation would have
preceded him. If, however, he was coming up the hill from Chadwick Green, he
had probably been on foot through the woods, would not have been scouted by
other Billingers and might have emerged from big cities such as St. Helens,
Southport or Liverpool. You never knew what you were getting from that
quarter. Tramps with long, shaggy beards used to knock on the Parrs' door (for
Susannah had a reputation as a giver) and beg for money, clothes or a hot meal.
Minnie had seen a lot of these men and they no longer frightened her, however
unkempt and wild-eyed an exterior they presented. One day she was alone in
the house, for Susannah had gone to visit a sick person in Rainford, when she
heard a knock on the door. She opened it to one of the tramps, who asked for a
loaf of bread. While she was fetching it from the buttery he came through the
parlour and pulled out a sharp knife. She ran round the back of the big rocking-
chair and stood there transfixed with horror. Fortunately the tramp had left the
front door open behind him and Thompson the butcher chose just that moment

to arrive with the weekly joint. Taking in the situation in a glance, Thompson drew his bloody butcher's knife, let out a blood-curdling yell and charged the vagrant from behind. The latter dropped his knife and ran for his life through the back, up the scented garden, leapt onto the roof of the hen-shed and clambered over the wall into the safety of the cornfield behind.

Another afternoon Minnie was sitting on the old stone wall under the beech tree when a negro came panting up the hill and stopped near her to mop his brow with a large red handkerchief. She ran into the house and fetched Uncle Hugh and Jem and soon more than a dozen people surrounded the newcomer, for a coloured man was a rare sight indeed at that time. When he had recovered his breath, he raised his face to heaven and sang in a powerful baritone:

> "*O Lord send the power just now!*
> *O Lord send the power just now!*
> *O Lord send the power just now!*
> *And baptize everyone!*"

The Billingers applauded him warmly and soon he was leading choruses for all of them, with Hugh Parr conducting vigorously. The tempo quickened, the volume of their voices increased. Everyone began to appear at the doors when suddenly the negro dropped in a dead faint in the middle of the fifth chorus and Hugh carried him into the house where he was revived with brandy and hot tea.

Hunters would occasionally ride through Long Fold, for the woods and undulating fields made good fox-hunting country. Lord Gerard had a fine estate at Ashton Cross and some beautiful horses which he put at the disposal of his guests. One of them was a magnificent white mare, which Minnie remembered quite well. One Saturday afternoon she had been sitting on Susannah's knee learning a new song:

> "*Ride a cock-horse to Banbury Cross*
> *To see a fine lady ride a white horse*
> *Rings on her fingers and bells on her toes*
> *She shall have music wherever she goes.*"

As they were singing this together they heard the beat of horses' hooves outside the window. Running to the door, Minnie opened it in time to see a beautiful auburn-haired woman attired in elegant riding tweeds gallop down the lane on a fine white mare. It made quite an impression on her and thereafter the song always had added meaning. The Billingers used to make gentle fun of the riders on occasion. One of the women living down Long Fold, Blather Hilda, was the mother of a bastard son called Wallop. Not even the Billingers had been able to guess who the father was. On days when Lord Gerard's guests were coming riding down the hill, Blather Hilda would run into the road and scrutinize the huntsmen. When her eye let on a particularly handsome one she would run and grab the bridle of his horse and extend, a fat accusing forefinger. "That's him!" she would shout to the watching villagers, "That's Wallop's father!" The fine gentleman in question would find himself the object of scrutiny not only of the Long Folders, who pretended to jeer, but of some of his own fellow huntsmen. After all, one never knew.

Blather Hilda, who was only half right in the head, used to believe it herself at times and often had to be restrained by her sisters. Minnie found it all a bit puzzling at first.

Long Fold 1907

Main Street

CHAPTER NINETEEN

Father Powell

One of the best known characters in Old Billinge, the Rev. Austin Powell, was not born in the village, but became Pastor of Birchley in 1872 and stayed there nearly thirty-eight years until his death in 1910. His importance as a Billinge figure lies not only in the fact that he was for so long the pillar of the Catholic community, shaping the lives of all those connected with St. Mary's and Birchley Schools, but also in the way he provided a living link between the village at the time of his ministry and the ancient traditions of Billinge stretching back to the 16th and 17th centuries. He was fully aware of his historical role as the latest in an unbroken line of priests serving at Birchley since Roger Anderton's ordination in 1645. The significance of the pre-Civil War Birchley operation, the centuries of struggle to follow, the crises during his own ministry, all gave him a tremendous feeling for the continuity of history

Rev. Austin Powell.

and great affection for the old Hall, the rugged village and its sturdy people. There is little doubt that Austin Powell considered himself to be the Right Man in the Right Place at the Right Time.

It would have been hard to find a better-educated or more erudite leader. Born in 1842 near Liverpool, he was sent to St. Edward's College, Everton at the age of ten, where he studied for six years. There followed a 3-year course at St. Cuthbert's College, Ushaw, after which he went to the English College at Rome, where Roger Anderton had studied more than two hundred years earlier. He pursued philosophical and theological studies for a further six years under the learned Jesuit theologians Ballerini and Franzelin. There were 30 other English students in the College and he himself was delighted with his sojourn in Rome. His own description of the city not only shows his enthusiasm for life, but also the richness of his vocabulary and imagination:

"Is there a man with the least spark of sensibility — be he Christian or Pagan — who would not like it? Obliterate Rome from the pages of history, and what would the annals of the world amount to? How like Rome? — with its hoary memories of king and consul, emperor and pope — with its ruins rich with the fable, the romance, the tragedy, the comedy, the passions, the vicissitudes of 26 centuries — with its priceless art treasures on canvas or in marble — with its three hundred churches, each more noble than the other, culminating in St. Peter's — with its palaces, gardens, villas, fountains? I think it must have been Rome that inspired in me my love of antiques."

In the year 1866 he was ordained priest by Cardinal Patrizzi and ordered to the Pro-Cathedral, Copperas Hill, in Liverpool. He remained there for two years, then spent three years at Newhouse before taking over Birchley a few months after his 30th birthday. He was already a man of the world. Apart from the experience gained from his travels, learning and profession, he came from a well-to-do family and quickly showed his abilities as a businessman. He had already bought a plot of land at Catforth and erected schools costing £800. He had a hand in the building of the Sacred Heart Church in St. Helens and one year after his settlement in Birchley he made an investment of £2,000 in a plot of land at Rainford (and this in competiton with the local bigwigs at an auction) which, on account of coal mines beneath it, realised a profit sufficient for the erection of a presbytery. He financed further purchases of land at West Leigh and Plank Lane, where more churches were built. By 1889, when our three St. Helens newspapermen arrived on their fact-finding mission concerning the impending sale of Birchley Estate, Father Powell was too old a hand in such manners not to know how to manoeuvre the Catholic community out of the crisis.

He told the journalists that when Lord Gerard's agent had informed him that a bid of £10,000 had been made for Birchley Hall and Estate on condition that the schools were moved elsewhere, he had been greatly perturbed. Not only would it be difficult and inconvenient to relocate the schools, but there were the sacred associations of the Hall itself. He lost no time in writing to his Bishop, suggesting that he should purchase Birchley, but, as a second string to his bow, he approached John Middlehurst, a local Catholic, with the proposal that he (Powell) and Middlehurst buy the estate together at once. Middlehurst was immediately willing to buy the greater portion — the 172 acres surrounding the Hall — and Father Powell arranged to take over the land — 25 acres — continuous to the presbytery. Without further ado they submitted a joint bid of £9,400 (Middlehurst's share was £9,000) to Lord Gerard. Austin Powell declared that this was a much better bid than the one of £10,000 made by the mysterious Protestant. On being asked how this could be, he pointed out that it would cost £2,000 to remove the schools — as the new building would have to be put up before the old one came down — and Lord Gerard would therefore get only £8,000 clear from the first offer.

Father Powell was pleased to inform the representatives of the "St. Helens Lantern" that his offer had been accepted and that the Catholic association with the Hall, Chapel and Presbytery would now be able to run on unhindered. He pointed out, of course, that the Chapel was now purely of sentimental value to the Church, since the construction of St. Mary's in 1828 had provided them with a proper place for their services. In connection with one of the newspapermen's querying the initial cost of building St. Mary's, Father Powell had another interesting tale to tell. It appeared that Sir William Gerard, who had died in 1826, gave £8,000 to be apportioned between Ashton and Birchley — £2,000 to go to each for a church and presbytery, and another £2,000 to each as an endowment. The trustees, who were *laymen*, started on the Ashton church first and when it was finished they found it had somehow absorbed £7,000 out of the £8,000, so Birchley had to be satisfied with about £1,000. The Rev. John Penswick — the priest then in charge — managed to scrape together another £400; therefore £1,400 had been the original cost of the church.

"So, practically, Ashton owes Birchley £3,000?" asked one of the journalists.

"Yes," laughed Father Powell, "that's how the matter stands, but when, if ever, restitution will be made is a different thing altogether."

It seems that Austin Powell frequently made a good impression on newspapermen. This was already apparent in 1872 — the year he came to Billinge — when he was interviewed by "Atticus" of the "Preston Chronicle":

"Mr. Powell is medium in build, light in complexion, with a calm, cool, irenic temperament; he takes things easily with equilibrium, has a well-trained mind, which can discourse of any ordinary subject, in religion or literature; is gentlemany and scholarly, and yet free from hauteur and pedantry; has an ancient head on young shoulders; has seen so much, and knows the ways of the world well; can preach a sound and sensible sermon, and can hit off the defects of sinners to a nicety; has in him a quiet, keenly-edged wit and a genial, deeply set vein of humour; once tamed an eagle, and can bring all the sparrows to his doorstep by a good whistle; is generous in disposition, and devoid of everything in the shape of narrow-mindedness; discharges his priestly functions quietly and comfortably, and avoids all meddling, earwigging, and corner cupboard hunting — tricks which some spiritual advisers are very proficient in."

With all these qualities, he was able to handle the Billingers (and not many outsiders could manage that). There are many Billingers still alive who remember him very well. He could be as tough and as eccentric as they were and he quickly gained the respect not only of his flock, but of the Protestants as well. They all knew the story of his catching this young eagle in the Apennines and keeping it as a pet until it was big enough to tear him to pieces: then he had it stuffed and put on a shelf. He loved to take children for a ride in horse and trap, but he would thrash them soundly with his knobstick if he came across them playing truant during his walks through the fields. The villagers knew him as a farmer (he farmed Poverty Land), a mineowner, and a hunter (he rode with Lord Gerard). He was defiant in defence of his faith, but he was the firm friend of Canon Howard St. George and Gentleman James Parr. He loved to appear eccentric or theatrical, leading the Catholic processions on horseback, keeping 4 donkeys and 4 black horses on his land, making bower-like structures outside Birchley school to be used as outdoor classrooms in summer, throwing out quotations from English and Latin poetry and reeling off jokes and amusing anecdotes when he was in the mood.

One good Catholic family at the Rant kept a ferocious dog which bit him every time he went to visit them. It is said that on these occasions he would lose his usual composure and, as he vainly swished at the beast with his knobstick, shouted at his hosts "When are you going to have this Protestant dog of yours done away with?"

As there was no Methodist school in Billinge, Jim and Susannah Parr sent all their children to study at nearby Birchley. Sam Parr, the youngest, was a regular truant and, more often than not, Father Powell would find him among the bushes in Marsh Ground and thrash him with the knobstick. Sam would run tearfully home and hide behind Susannah's pantry door, while the good priest followed on at a leisurely pace up Long Fold and into the Parr living-room. Susannah was often in two minds as to whether she ought to scold the autocratic chaplain or whimpering Sam, for she, too, had a will of iron. Father Powell, without saying a word to her, would go round the living-room and systematically straighten all the pictures. After two or three minutes, when he was satisfied that all was symmetrical, he would say: "Well, how's that, Susannah?"

And Sam would sneak out into the back garden, Austin Powell would take off his hat and coat and Susannah would get out her fine barge teapot.

CHAPTER TWENTY

Ducky

"Jem, I've 'ad me diarrhoea again."
"Well, why dostn't take summat for it, Ducky?"
"What con tha suggest, Jem?"
"Tha boils a pint a wayter till it's down to a quart . . . "
"Down to a quart."
'Then tha rolls it into little pills and tha takes one just after tha goes to sleep and another just afoor tha wakes up."
"Dost think it'll work, Jem?"
'Never fails."

* * * * * * * *

Ducky wore the shiniest shoes in Long Fold. He used to come out at the top of the steps leading up to his front door and spread out his paraphernalia. Huge tin of blacking, two brushes for taking the old polish off, two more for putting the new on and a black rag, a grey rag and a brown rag for boning them up. It used to take him half an hour for one pair and forty-five minutes if he had an audience.

He favoured dark suits with big red carnations in his lapel or even dahlias at week-ends. His shirts had high, starched collars and his ties were gay, but not so gay as his socks. The fashion in Billinge at the turn of the century was long woollen socks with brightly-coloured flowers on them. They were called "clocks". Ducky's clocks were the fastest in the village. A bright green handkerchief always dangled from his breast pocket. He often wore a soft hat. His head, too, was a little soft.

Big Jem made fun of Ducky, Hugh Parr by contrast protected him at all times. Ducky admired Hugh intensely and tried to model himself after him. Let Hugh come out with a blue-striped shirt and the next day Ducky would be in St. Helens looking for one. He copied his suits, hats, ties, collars and cuff-links. If Hugh had started wearing spats to his pyjamas Ducky would have done the same.

The problem of Ducky's simple mentality was compounded by the fact that he was also an exhibitionist. He was never happy unless he was in the public eye and he was convinced that people looked up to him and held him in high esteem. He threw himself into the thick of things, best suit, carnation and all. For instance, there was his obsession with bands. He had never had music lessons but he considered himself to be, like Hugh Parr, a born musician. Nobody would ever let him touch an instrument, but he used to follow brass bands wherever they went. Moss Bank Band was very popular at the time and Ducky walked after them for miles. He was in his element on Field Days and in church processions and he became as much a part of the show as the band itself. He carried a large tin can and went round collecting money for the band. People would give willingly, just in order to exchange cracks with him and pull his leg. He had the simpleton's crafty nature in such matters and those who had mocked him too much were soon approached again with the rattling tin:

"Let's be 'aving your donation to Moss Bank Brass Band!"
"We bloodywell paid thee once, Ducky."
"Well, you con bloodywell pay twice, cawn't yo?"

One year he collected so much money for the band that they made the grave mistake of asking him what they could do to repay him. He said he would be happy if they would let him beat the big drum on their next outing. They were reluctant to agree, but he was not the one to let pass this golden opportunity of showing to everyone what latent musical talents he possessed. The next time the band's services were required, the promise was kept and Ducky was strapped to the big drum at the rear of the band. He had to take out his dahlia, which he passed to Hugh Parr. All Long Fold had come along to see the performance, but it did not last long. Ducky beat in both sides of the drum in the first hundred yards and they had to send back to Moss Bank for another one. He went back to his tin can work the same day. Hugh Parr always said it was a good thing that Ducky had had his chance to get rid of some of his frustrations in this manner. Better an old drum than somebody's head.

*   *   *   *   *   *   *   *

Ducky never had a steady job. He had a lot of unsteady ones. He would be taken on for a few weeks at the pit at certain times when the amount of work available exceeded the supply of labour. It was always a relief to get the sack at the end of a mining episode, for Ducky had no love for coal dust which got under his nails and in his clothes. He preferred odd, seasonal jobs on the farms and occasionally would go as far as St. Helens for a stint at Pilkingtons' Glass Works. When he was hired anywhere, he used to talk enthusiastically about his job and you would wonder how the establishment he had worked for had ever succeeded in getting set up without his assistance, or indeed if it would stay in business if anything ever happened to him. In a while, however, he would invariably get the sack and revert to being self-employed, that is to say, his grandmother would find him something to do.

Ducky's grandmother, Dolly Blue, was not without initiative. The family was poor but somewhere between her middle and old age she had saved up enough money to invest in a horse and cart, with which she went into business. The horse, Owd Dick, was no longer young and the cart had seen better days, but the nature of Dolly's business was such that neither nag nor vehicle carried too great a strain. She would buy vegetables from the farmers and drive round the streets of Billinge selling them door to door at a small profit. Over the years a great variety of objects and articles were hawked around in the old cart, but Dolly's number one line was unquestionably Swaggering Dick. This was not the name of the horse, for Owd Dick's swaggering and prancing days were over, but the term used to describe the style of home-made treacle toffee which was Dolly's speciality.

To make Swaggering Dick, Dolly would heave a great iron cooking pot onto the crow and fill it full of sugar, water, treacle and a gelatinous substance of her own finding. She would boil and stir until it was a thick, light-brown mucilage. After letting this cool and congeal somewhat, she would carve out a great lump of the still glutinous dough and impale it on a big hook fixed on the ceiling. Hanging there, the lump would be allowed to solidify a little more and then Dolly would stand on a chair and begin pulling it down in strips, about one inch wide. The strips would reach to the floor and Ducky, her assistant, would cut it off in sticks about six inches long and put them on the window ledges where they eventually ossified. Swaggering Dick was sweet and brittle and sold well. It ruined teeth of course and there was a lot of toothache in the village. There were no dentists in Billinge. Some people went to St. Helens with their toothache and the St. Helens' dentists pulled their teeth out.

Ducky, who in his early days had been fed a piece of Swaggering Dick every time he opened his mouth, still had a few teeth, but they were light brown like the toffee. He liked to work for his grandmother, for among all his employers she understood him best and made allowances for the way in which he expressed himself.

"Vegetables! Vegetables! I have a cart full of fresh vegetables! Come out and buy what you want. I have potatoes, I have carrots, I have cabbage, I have turmits, I have onions. Take that back! Take that back! I have no turmits! I've left them at home on the dresser!"

"Now Ducky, I want you to go out and sell these cabbages."

"Yes, Grandmother."

"Now we paid twopence for them. You sell them at fourpence."

"Fourpence?"

"That's right."

"Oh, no."

"No, what?"

"I can't do that."

"Can't do what.?"
"Grandmother, tuppence we bought 'em, and tuppence I'm goin to sell
'em!"

And yet those who ribbed him too much would occasionally be bested by the
simpleton repartee. Like when he was going round selling milk:
"Ducky, there's wayter in this milk!"
"Tha what, Jack?"
"Wayter int milk, I said."
"Wayter, Jack?"
"Wayter."
"Int milk, Jack?"
"Ay, in tha milk."
"But Jack, it's not my milk. It's t'cow's milk.
"Aw reet cow's milk. There's wayter int cow's milk!"
"Only what t'cow drunk, Jack."

                    *   *   *   *   *   *   *   *

Ducky fancied his chances with the women. Whenever his grandmother
bought him a new suit he would dress up to the nines and swagger down to the
Parr cottage to show himself off. Gentleman Jim, Big Jem and Sam had not
much time for him, but Susannah and little Minnie were always friendly
enough and Hugh Parr would feel the material between his thumb and first
finger and thump Ducky on the back and tell him he was a gay old dog. Hugh
used to go out on Wednesdays and Saturdays with his friend Tom Halsall and
whenever Ducky had new duds to be christened they would take him with them
one Saturday to Liverpool or Southport and they would go to shows and talk to
girls and Ducky would strut around like one of Joe Middlehurst's peacocks.
    Young ladies who were attracted to Hugh and Tom Halsall would go out of
their way to be friendly to Ducky in an attempt to further their relation with the
others. Ducky always took it for granted that he was the one they were
interested in and he had several romances with these girls, all at different stages
of advancement and all in his eager, struggling mind. It can truly be said of
Ducky that he was never interested in a plain or homely woman; he fancied and
pursued none but the most beautiful. There are many men who fall in and out of
love with monotonous regularity. With Ducky it was not quite the same. He fell
in love afresh every month but, unlike other people, he never fell out of love
again. Consequently the number of ladies for whom he entertained an affection
increased as time went by and if his advances had been returned in any great
measure, it is questionable if he would have been able to stay the pace very long.
Fortunately, however, he seldom made any real progress in his *affaires*, for he

was not exactly the prize which many of these beautiful girls were seeking. Ducky would also fall in love with girls whom he had only seen from a distance, and who had never seen him. Such was the case with leading actresses and chorus girls at Liverpool Hippodrome whom Ducky had espied from the depths of the audience. When the question arose as to how he should contact one of these young ladies and inform her of his feeling for her, it was typical of Ducky that he scorned the idea of waiting at the stage door or trying to attract her with wave or gesture from his seat. His feelings were so fine that there was only one proper way in which he could communicate them to his lady love — by love letter. There was, however, a problem: he could neither read nor write.

He soon hit upon the idea of asking Hugh Parr to do the writing for him. Hugh agreed to help him and Ducky would sit under the huge chestnut tree and stare wildly up into the foliage while he dictated bold, rambling assurances of devotion to his latest Dulcinea. Hugh made a pretty good job of the letters. He had a steady, elegant hand and by the time he had joined up all the non sequiturs, smoothed out the grammar and eliminated various dialect words, the final message would be one of sincerity and appeal, calculated to move any but the coldest of hearts. Indeed, Ducky soon began to get replies and it was not long before half a dozen actresses and chorus girls showed keen interest in his life and fortunes. Like the gentleman he was, Ducky wrote back to all of them, which is to say Hugh was kept pretty busy and soon regretted that he had agreed to act as an invisible go-between.

At Ducky's request, some of the young ladies sent photographs of themselves, often in daring outfits and occasionally in what people of the day would have considered provocative poses. Hugh picked out the two best-looking girls and suggested to Ducky that they confine their correspondence to them alone. Actresses and chorus girls, though undoubtedly busy in the evenings, seemed to have little to do during the daylight hours but recline on couches and answer Ducky's letters. But Ducky would not abandon any of them. How could he just break it off like that? What about the poor girl's feelings? Hugh, being tender-hearted himself, was dragged along in this manner and spent his Saturday afternoons scribbling away under the chestnut tree. His handwriting degenerated considerably and he spent less time than before hunting the right phrase, but the first impression won the day. They kept on writing back.

Happily for Hugh, respite was at hand. Two or three of the young ladies were anxious to have Ducky's picture for themselves and Ducky, after some hesitation, went to Westfield Street in St. Helens and let the photographers do him up proper with a grey flannel suit, starched shirt and striped tie, straw hat and swagger cane. They made him pose with his right hand on the back of a velvet couch and told him to smirk at the camera. He ordered ten postcard sizes in brown and white and sent off three to the ladies who had asked for them in stiff yellow envelopes upon which Hugh wrote in black bold letters "Caution, do not bend!" They never heard from any of these three girls again. Even Ducky was not too thick-skinned to see the connection. When the best-looking actress of them all, Charlotte Tremayne, next asked him for a photograph he was understandably cautious. He temporized and beat around the bush for half a dozen letters. Finally Charlotte got suspicious and insisted that he send his picture the very next time. Ducky studied his photo from Westfield Street for the best part of a week, polished and repolished his shoes and forgot to feed Owd Dick for so many days that he could barely pull an empty cart. At the end of the week Ducky had arrived at a decision. He dictated his long, rambling message to Hugh and they addressed the envelope to the actress. Ducky took it home, put in a photograph and walked up to Chapel Brow to post the letter. When he reached the pillar box he looked up and down Main Street to make sure nobody was watching him, then quickly posted the envelope and went back whistling to Long Fold. On Monday morning Miss Tremayne received the envelope and slit it open with her pearl-handled paper knife. Before reading the letter she studied the picture, with which she was well pleased. It was one of Hugh Parr.

*   *   *   *   *   *   *   *

The months that followed were trying ones for Ducky. The very next letter he received from Miss Tremayne contained an invitation to meet her, in Liverpool, as soon as he could arrange it. Ducky was incredulous, elated and panic-stricken in quick succession. He replied that for the next few weeks he would be unable to travel to Liverpool since the pressure of his activities in a current mine inspection necessitated his uninterrupted presence in Billinge. He turned desperately to Hugh for advice. If he went along for the date she would see that he and the man in the picture were not the same. He could simply not go, which would eventually lead to the correspondence being broken off. Alternatively, Hugh could go to meet her, pretending he was Ducky. They weighed up all the possibilities. Hugh was quite willing to be a stand-in, but Ducky got a bit niggly about it. The pleasure he himself would derive from such an encounter would be altogether too vicarious. Neither was he too keen on just letting the correspondence peter out. In Ducky's universe the world ended not with a whimper but with a bang. He begged Hugh to let him go. Yet the thought of facing Miss Tremyne filled him with terror.

Hugh decided that if Ducky really wanted to proceed, then there was only one thing they could do: they had to make Ducky look like the picture. This was not easy. Hugh was rather fair, blue-eyed and handsome. Ducky was swarthy and approaching ugly. The picture had been brown and white, which helped with the problem of colouring. Hugh, however, sported a moustache and had very curly hair. Ducky was clean-shaven and had hair like black straw. Hugh reckoned that six weeks were needed to grow a moustache like his own, so they wrote to Miss Tremayne and fixed up a meeting on an appropriate date. Hugh then drew two thin blue lines on Ducky's upper lip, denoting the boundaries of a toothbrush moustache and Ducky spent a finicky half hour in front of his grandmother's mirror every morning feeling the stubble with the back of his thumb and trimming it according to Hugh's instructions. Ducky was subjected to not a little ridicule by the Long Folders while these proceedings were taking place, but not much more so than would have been the case with any unfortunate young fellow who tried to grow a moustache for the first time. Only Hugh and little Minnie were in on the secret. Every night when Hugh came home from work, Ducky would rush down the lane and have the day's growth inspected. In fact it came along fine, except that it was much blacker and more noticeable than the one in the picture.

Trying to make Ducky's hair look curly was a considerably more difficult task. First they tried curlers and hair-pins, but although these were to some extent successful Ducky had to stop experimenting with them as all Long Fold was giving him a dog's life. Then they found that if they washed Ducky's hair in salt and water and let his coiffure dry without rinsing, it turned out so stiff that they could press it into waves, and little valleys and hillocks, so that it looked quite curly. But they had to abandon this method as the dried salt began to fall onto Ducky's collar and jacket, and looked like dandruff, and as the salt fell some of the locks were freed, and swung out laterally like stiff little spears or hung down between his eyes.

Finally they were able to achieve a reasonable effect by washing his hair and drying it fast with a towel, then, without using a brush or comb, rumpling it backwards with the fingers and letting it lie loosely in calculated disorder. A touch of pomade held it fast at the sides and Hugh reckoned that if the weather was calm it would carry the day. He lent Ducky the striped shirt and silver-headed knobstick that appeared in the picture and the young cavalier swaggered up and down in front of Dolly Blue's mirror, imitating Hugh Parr's grin and making his moustache twitch from side to side.

"Dost think I'm ready, Hugh?"

"Thar us ready us tha'll ever be, Duck."

On the day of the appointment, Ducky borrowed three pounds from his grandmother and caught the eleven o' clock train from St. Helens to Liverpool. He was wearing his best dark grey suit and Hugh's striped shirt, the collar of which was too tight for him and made him choke if he turned his head too quickly. His large, oval cuff-links were of shining brass with embossed chrysanthemums. In his waistcoat pocket he sported a huge pocket watch secured by a thick brass chain. In St. Helens he had bought a bouquet of orange lilies and a big tin of chocolates with a blue-and-white two-tone picture of Lily

Langtry on the lid. It was a beautiful July Sunday afternnon when he arrived at Lime Street Station.

We shall never know all the details of Ducky's tryst with Charlotte Tremayne. It appears that he met her in front of St. George's Hall and that he recognized her before she recognized him. It was fairly windy, as is often the case in that part of Liverpool and Ducky quickly doffed his straw hat to show her that his hair was curly and quickly put it on again before it was reduced to disarray by the elements. She accepted his presents gracefully and they walked down to the docks and looked at the water for a while. They had a snack in one of the small cafes near the Royal Liver Building and after that they took a ferry to New Brighton. There used to be a tower there in those days and they ascended it to see the view. Later they visited some shrimp stalls and after that graduated to oysters. Towards the end of the day Ducky won a coconut, which he gave to Miss Tremayne. He caught the ten o'clock train out of Lime Street and walked home from St. Helens.

It is to Ducky's credit that he seems to have passed for the man in the picture. Of course the "romance" ended there and then, for Charlotte Tremayne had no shortage of far more attractive suitors, but it is to the actress's credit that she signalled the end of the affair with tact and gentleness of touch. She wrote two or three more letters in a more jovial vein than before, as if the whole thing had just been a bit of a joke, but also as if she and Ducky shared some giggly secret to which others were not privy. Ducky was flattered by her elbow-digging intimacy and Hugh wrote giggly letters back and soon the whole thing petered out in the best of spirits. Ducky dropped his correspondence with far-off actresses and left serious philandering in the big cities to Hugh and Tom Halsall. But at Rainford and Crank and Garswood and Moss Bank when they took him with them on Saturday nights, Ducky was still a hell of a man for the wenches . . . . .

CHAPTER TWENTY ONE

A New Century

As the 19th century drew to close in Billinge, little Minnie Parr started school. Since birth she had been raised by her grandparents, whom she called "Father" and "Mother" and her constant exposure to older people, including her three bachelor uncles who were unused to the ways of children, had made her old-fashioned, serious and watchful. She had absorbed the village scene with a receptivity that few children could match.

The first funeral she could remember was that of Ellen Parr, who died when she was four. For decades Gentleman Jim had presented such a patriarchal figure that it was almost a surprise to learn that his mother was still living quietly in one of the smaller cottages, watching her large brood multiply, marry, live, suffer and die. The news of old Hugh Parr's death down the pit had been broken to her suddenly, without warning, and the brutal shock had caused her head to recoil and then twitch slightly from side to side. Though she was able to work hard and raise her family in the manner we have seen, the twitch continued and did not stop till the day she died, at the age of 82.

Minnie had seen Ellen laid out for three days in bed before being put in her coffin on the day of the funeral. Everything was white – white sheets and pillow cases, one on each side of the face to stop the head rolling, white needlework nightgown and even long white stockings, which Billingers always kept in the bottom drawer to bury people in. It had been an eerie sight and Minnie never liked white afterwards. In later life she always used coloured sheets on beds and even coloured pillow-cases.

Billinge wives dreaded the sound of a spring cart in the middle of the night, for it meant that a collier had been killed on the night shift and was being brought home. For funerals, however, the coffin was always carried on bearers' shoulders up to Billinge Parish Church at the top of Main Street. For Higher End people it was not so bad. For the Lower End it was quite a task. For Long Folders it was decidedly arduous. Catholics carried their dead downhill, since Birchley Chapel was at the bottom end of the village.

After Ellen's funeral there were many others, and Minnie got quite used to them. Suicide was another phenomenon with which she became familar, since it was not uncommon in Billinge at the time. When a Billinger contracted an uncurable disease, such as cancer, he would rarely wait for it to claim him. Poverty and depression also drove Billingers to suicide and it was accepted as part of Billinge life without much fuss or undue ceremony. The villagers' independent nature as well as their preoccupation with the supernatural made it

146

easier for Billingers to understand suicides. Minnie knew there were three main channels of approach. You could hang yourself with a clothes-line; you could drown yourself; you could go and jump down the pit shaft. Long Folders had tried all three methods and found them all effective. Harry Earholes had hanged himself from a hook in the ceiling and Tet had cut him down, tongue hanging out of a black, contorted face. They had barely buried him when Bowls jumped down the pit shaft at Brown Heath Pit, landing on top of the cage, which nearly saved him, but not quite. For those bent on drowning there was a fair choice – Marlpit, Cocklepit, Fratsam's Meadow Pit and Carr Mill Dam. Fratsam's was the nearest, Marlpit the cleanest and Cocklepit the deepest and the loneliest. The Dam was a bit cold at most times of the year.

When anyone disappeared in Billinge, two routine checks would be made. First, the above-mentioned waters would be dragged; secondly the mines would be searched. The bodies were usually recovered quickly, except in the case of Carr Mill Dam, on account of its size. When old Cunliffe vanished, however, the usual investigations failed to produce any evidence of his remains. There was general consternation in the village. Cunliffe had been an agreeable old man in his late sixties, who had retired a few years earlier and was in the habit of taking long walks through the neighbouring fields. On the morning of his disappearence he had taken his pipe and tobacco as usual and left his wife at the garden gate, saying he would be back for lunch. When he did not come back

Boys' School, 1896

that evening, his wife informed the neighbours and later the police. His body was never found and after several weeks the search had to abandoned. It was out of the question that he had left his family, for he was a happy and settled homebird. His wife also discounted the possibility of suicide: he was not the type, they were not unduly poor, he had a weak heart but hardly ever suffered pain. Billinge mulled it over for a while and various theories were advanced. Finally, everybody agreed with Cunliffe's wife: he was no suicide and he had certainly not left her – not intentionally, that is. Wherever he had gone and whatever had happened to him, Cunliffe had disappeared in good standing.

Twenty years passed and the good man's fate remained one of the unsolved mysteries of the village. Minnie had heard it discussed for as long as she could remember, for it was part of Billinge lore. Old Mrs. Cunliffe was now over eighty, still going around swearing that her husband would never have drowned himself. Then one day, as two young boys searched for birds' nests, they found him, sitting there, propped up under a hedge. Two decades had gone by and the old man's body had decomposed, but the bones and clothes were there, deep in the hedge, along with the familar pipe and tobacco pouch. Billingers often went for long walks on their own and when there was a shower they would crawl under a hedge and shelter there until the rain ceased. Cunliffe had crawled further into the hedge than was usual and, as he had smoked his last pipe, his heart had given a little flutter and he had gone....

The old lady died happy.

                *   *   *   *   *   *   *   *

In the evenings Gentleman Jim liked to assemble his old cronies in the Parr cottage and they would sit and tell tales into the late hours, for in those days conversation was prime entertainment. As old people are not so strict about bundling young children off to bed, Minnie would sit like a little wooden hullet in the buttery corner and drink in the stories recounted by the old men. After a while they completely forgot about her and sometimes Big Jem would find her fast asleep in the corner rocking-chair when he came home at two in the morning. Some of Gentleman Jim's pals had been as far afield as London, on excursions to exhibitions and things like that. Billingers inevitably made fun of city-goers and one of the story-tellers related how he had been with half a dozen Billingers who had taunted a London painter painting a sign on a wall near King's Cross Railway Station. They had criticised the sloppy manner in which he was going about his work and had called him a few appropriate names, when the workman had suddenly whipped out a huge pistol and fired three shots at their feet. The villagers had taken to their heels and run to the nearest pub for ale. They had learnt that in a big city they could be faced with a situation with which they could not cope, for there were no pistols in Billinge.

But when it came to drama, there was no shortage of that in the tales of the village itself. Minnie heard of the young orphan girl Ada, who had been adopted by a family at the Rant when she was fourteen. Two years later she was an attractive young girl, sought after by half the lads in Billinge. One day she complained of pains in her lower abdomen and it was rumoured that she was pregnant, for she was plump and well-rounded. The family threw her on the street in disgrace and she had wandered up and down the village a whole day, collapsing on somebody's doorstep as darkness approached. She was taken in, but died in agony a few hours later. Nobody knew about appendicitis in those days. It only became a fashionable ailment after King Edward had had it.

Another Billinger had five sons, four of them fine strapping young lads, but the fifth under-sized, pale and weakly. He never had much time for the youngest son and went about the village saying that the last-born was not really his son and that his wife had obviously found time to dally with someone else. His wife put up with this kind of talk for several years, but finally lost patience with him and told him the truth. He was right: there had been two fathers involved. But the last son WAS his; the other four had been by another sire.

They told about the Hoonan brothers, the elder of whom was quiet and hard-working, the younger ambitious, restless and impulsive. The younger one went abroad, vowing he would return with a fortune and a beautiful wife. The elder stayed at home, worked the farm and supported his aging parents. He led a dull, unexciting life for several years, but had the good luck to meet a red-haired beauty on a trip to Fleetwood. The girl fell in love with his village bluntness and they were married. For two or three years they lived contentedly on the farm, until one day the younger brother returned, penniless and still a bachelor. For a month he ate good meals and then eloped with the red-head. They were never seen again.

By listening to the old men's tales, Minnie received an out-of-school education which was to prove of great value to her. She quickly learned that good and evil existed side by side, that the world was an unjust place where things often went long unrighted and that deception, thievery, lust, jealousy and cowardice were ingredients of everyday life. Once you accept this state of affairs as normal, then disappointments and irritations in life affect you less than if you assume that the world is a well-ordered place where things sometimes go wrong. It certainly helped to make things easier for you down Long Fold. In one of the cottages there lived a man called Red Jem. He was so bad-tempered that he used to scowl perpetually at everybody – including his own family. Minnie used to play with his sons, who quickly inherited their father's ill humour. She delighted in observing their bad temper at close quarters, for they were only five or six years of age and she found it comic. They would go out in the fields and steal a couple of turnips which they would bring back to Long Fold and kick viciously up and down the lane. This would sometimes go on for

hours, without much being said. Now and again one of the brothers would lean over towards Minnie with a savage gleam in his eyes and whisper:
"Min, I wish they could bloody well feel!"

*   *   *   *   *   *   *   *

Minnie started school when she was six and went on and off until she was nine. Susannah's health was beginning to fail and with four men in the house she needed help with the cooking and housework. It was common for children to stay away from school for long periods and the truant inspectors often had the utmost difficulty in achieving any results. Ducky, when younger, had been a notorious truant, for Dolly Blue frequently required his services for taking care of Old Dick.

"Dolly, our inspectors say that Ducky has not been to school for six weeks."
"Oh yes 'e 'as! I sent him every day last week."
"That's not what we have in this report."
"Every fleckin' day I sent 'im."
"Now Dolly, we have to believe our officers."
"Then you'll believe a lot of goddam liars!"

Billinge School is a low stone building right on Main Street, a little more than half way up the hill. It was divided into Infants', Boys' and Girls' Schools. The Headmistress of the Girls' School was a Mrs. Cocker. The most popular

Billinge infants, 1899

teacher was a young woman named Janie Makin, who taught in the school for over forty years and became Headmistress in due course. Minnie sat between two girls who became her lifelong friends – Mary Aggie and Polly Hill. Polly was the daughter of Our Nell's Jack. They were a sharp-eyed trio and were always top of the class. They all wore their hair long, often in plaits down to their waists and used to chew home-made treacle toffee in unison whenever the teachers relaxed their vigilance. They studied Geography and History, Sums and Composition, Sewing and Music. The members of the staff were not particularly strict apart from Mrs. Cocker, who tried hard to be a martinet. She was a Scotswoman with certain determined ideas about the education of young English girls. One of her tenets was that they should be taught as many Scots songs as possible along with a liberal share of Scots poetry. For all her determination, she was quite unable to make any inroads upon the village dialect, but she insisted upon the little girls pronouncing all the words in the poems and songs in the approved Scottish manner. Young people have a great gift for imitation and just as modern Continental singers succeed in intoning English songs with a foolproof American accent so these little Billingers in 1900, while in their normal speech completely immersed in the archaic, aggressive local dialect, burst forth at a moment's notice with "Ye Banks and Braes" or "Auld Lang Syne" with an authentic Scots burr.

Billingers have the blood of many Northern peoples in their veins and they react more kindly to Scots, Irish or Scandinavian influences than they do to the influx of ideas from any southern or Continental origin. For a while this infusion of Scots culture was an interesting and welcome innovation and Minnie was asked to recite "Lochinvar" up and down Long Fold until everybody in the fourteen cottages knew the first half by heart. The little boys, however, had an English Headmaster and they were learning all the old, traditional English songs, so that when Minnie had finished "Lochinvar" her cousin Tom Lowe would follow with a manly rendering of "Hearts of Oak" and generally steal the thunder, in spite of the awesome length of the poem.

Finally Hugh Parr sent a note up to Mrs. Cocker saying that since Billinge was in England and, as long as he had anything to do with it, would remain there, it would be better if a few old English ballads were brought into the syllabus and that the little girls should be told about Shakespeare, who was nearly as good as Sir Walter Scott. Then the girls would be able in later life to discuss literature and music with their husbands, who, most probably, would hail from no further afield than Crank or Moss Bank.

*   *   *   *   *   *   *   *

When Minnie was nine years old Susannah fell ill with her heart and was unable to take care of the family. Minnie had to leave school and see to the cooking, shopping and housework. Susannah had been a healthy, vigorous woman, but she had given birth to twelve children and the hard years of toil in the Sandwash had taken their toll. For three years, as her heart grew progressively weaker, her grand-daughter shouldered the burden. The four men still worked at the pit. While Gentleman Jim's job as a checkweighman kept him on the top, the three sons worked down below and they came home with black faces and black clothes. The daily wash alone was a tremendous task, and the house-cleaning was rendered more laborious on account of the coal dust which found its way into every nook and cranny. The men came home looking like negro minstrels and would bathe in huge dolly tubs, outside in the garden in summer but in the house in the colder seasons, spilling the black water over the flagstones. They used strong, yellow soap and dried themselves on "rough towels" made of yellow sacking material. Minnie always had the water heating up on the hob in large copper kettles or often in large earthenware vessels which were called pan mugs. She washed clothes and sheets in the same dolly tubs after rinsing them out. She became adept at using a rubbing board and learnt the clothes-line routine which in those days was complicated. First she put the clothes out on the line in the garden to dry. After that they were brought in and put on the indoor clothes-line in a certain order. There were special places on the line for sheets, towels, mens' shirts and woollens as well as starched or finer materials. They were left up in some cases for a week or more to ensure that they were properly aired. She had to know when each item had to be put up and when it was permissible to take it down again. Occasionally some clothes would be rotated to make sure they had their fair share of heat. They had some steamy evenings.

Susannah died at the age of 65 in 1906 a few days after Minnie's thirteenth birthday.

*   *   *   *   *   *   *   *

Sam Parr married shortly before his mother's death and Big Jem wed a few months afterwards. This left only Gentleman Jim and Hugh to be taken care of and the School Board Inspector, armed with new legislation, had Minnie sent back to school. She was warmly greeted by Mary Aggie and Polly Hill who had been studying without respite and whom she had hardly seen for three years. Education was compulsory until the age of fourteen, and Minnie completed the two remaining years without incident or further truancy.

On her fifteenth birthday she left school for good and resumed her work at home where she saw to the needs of her grand-father and Uncle Hugh and occasionally worked in the fields when the farmers needed extra hands. By now she was an experienced housekeeper and visiting preachers would marvel at the spread on the table at Sunday tea-time: cold cuts of sirloin, home-picked cucumbers and beetroot, lettuce and tomato salad, apple pie, custard pie, rhubarb pie, jelly, blancmange and home-stewed fruit, even home-made wine. Other specialities were hot potatoes with butter on, coconut or egg and marmalade pie and a flat currant cake called divilsnose, which was a Billinge favourite. The preachers would look round and ask where the woman of the house was and would refuse to believe that the young girl ran the house and did the cooking all by herself.

In the evenings Minnie went to the Council Offices and took courses in Sewing, Cookery and First Aid. Her burden was now somewhat lighter, for Hugh had become pit manager and there were no more black clothes to wash. Gentleman Jim's health remained good, but he was a tired man, and he retired just after his seventieth birthday. Hugh finally took the plunge and married a local girl and his father entered his last, long summer of 1911 when the sun shone brilliantly from late April right through to October. The flowers and green leaves were the most beautiful that Billinge had ever seen and the old man spent most of his time sitting out at the front gate or under the trees. He was not ill, but he was dying, worn-out by the mining toil of his youth. His old cronies came to visit him, and they talked of the mines and the farming, of politics and the results of the Boer War, of places and people they had known.

He died in September, at noon on a beautiful, sunlit Saturday a few hours before the birth of Hugh Parr's first son, who was named Jim. All Billinge lined Main Street on the day of his funeral and in the crowd were many preachers from far and near.

*   *   *   *   *   *   *   *

Hugh, at the age of 36, had been the last of the sons to get married, and the death of Gentleman Jim left Minnie alone in the house. At seventeen she was a cheerful, willing, intent girl, quick with her hands and her head, endowed with a particular wiriness which belied the first impression of frailty. She remained in the house for three weeks while the furniture was divided and the home broken up. It was decided that Mary Ann and her family would move into the Parr cottage, for not only was she the eldest child but the house she was living in was unsuitable for her needs. As two of Mary Ann's children were girls, Minnie moved in with Tet, who had four boys.

The coming generation of Parrs was already quite impressive. Mary Ann had four children: Ruth, Maria, Jem and Ned Bellis. Big Jem had seven: David Piers, Hugh James, Jonathan, Joe, Susannah, Thomas and Nancy Parr. Tet had four boys: Bill, Jem, Seth and Chris Martlew. Caroline had the biggest family – 12 children like her father, ten of them boys. Her children were Ben,

Tom, Jem, Harold, Bill, Jack, Susie Helen, Hugh, Lizzie and Lloyd Lowe. Peter and Joseph Edwin died in their infancy. Hugh was to have four children: Jim, Jack, Beulah and Jessie Parr. Sam had three: James, May and Margaret Parr. Wilhelmina had Jim and Minnie.

This Parr army occupied most of Long Fold and parts of the Bottom End of Billinge from the last years of the Victorian era right through to the Second World War. They were proud, clannish, quarrelsome, God-fearing, impulsive, superstitious, tenacious and very English. They thought the English were the best people in the world, at least the northern English were – especially those to the west of the Pennines in Lancashire. And none more so than the ones living round Wigan and St. Helens, in fact the only man who had the edge on a Wiganer was a Billinger, perhaps not one from the Top End, mind you, but a little lower down Main Street, at the Bottom End and turn left . . . . down to Long Fold, among the proper, old-fashioned, healthy, gradely folk.

Billinge at Work

It was always difficult to make a living in Billinge and it remained so until organized transport enabled people to go to work elsewhere. In the 11th and 12th centuries, much of the land was probably still heavily wooded. As late as the 16th century large tracts of Lancashire consisted of moorland, marsh waste and rough ground. Marling – the process of fertilizing the land with marl found under the soil – produced regular corn crops and enabled farmers to graze their cattle in Billinge, but the hilly nature of the terrain meant that farming was never easy and the Billinge farm workers were miserably paid for centuries, often taking part of their wages in turnips, milk and other farm produce. In spite of these unfavourable conditions, farming has a one thousand-year-old tradition in Billinge, as for many hundreds of years there were no alternative occupations open to the inhabitants.

When jobs first became available in industry – coal mining and nail-making were introduced in Billinge in the 16th century – they proved to be no bed of roses, either. The first local deed in which coal rights were reserved dates from 1350 and about that time coal was being mined in the north of Wigan. Winstanley saw its first coal-mining in the early 16th century and the rich "cannel coal" made the area the leading mining district in Lancashire in the 17th century.

Nail-making was widespread in the district in the 16th and 17th centuries and became a feature of Billinge life at that time. It was a craft requiring little skill and colonies of workers made nails in the cellars or in low sheds attached to their homes. They were supplied by the master-nailers with rod-iron, which they would collect in bundles of 60 lbs each, being debited with the value at the time of collection. This they took home and worked in their own smithies, often located in the cellars on account of the awful noise involved. It was hard on their neighbours. When they had converted the rod-iron into nails, they would take these back to the nail-masters and be paid so much per thousand. The cost of the waste would be borne by the nailers. The work was hard, the profit marginal: consequently nailers were wont to cheat in order to make a better living. Sometimes they would exchange their good iron for bad, and keep the difference. It was not unknown for them to make off with iron and fail to give an account of it. On other occasions they would go ahead and make the nails, then sell them direct to carpenters and ironmongers on their own account. If any unfortunate nail-master happened to overpay them through miscalculation, they kept the information to themselves. Let him underpay them, or criticize

Wm. Melling.
Grindstone. Quarries
Billinge. Nr. Wigan.
Lancs.

their morals and they were quite capable of stoning him. In many other respects, too, they were difficult men to get on with. Sometimes they would not work for a day or two, then they would set to and work day and night until the people living in the neighbouring houses could stand it no longer. When they were not working they were usually drunken and spent their time cock-fighting, bear-baiting and making disturbances. Most of them could neither read nor write and signed the receipts for the iron with a cross. As many of the children were put to work in the smithies at eight or nine years of age, they too became illiterate. We have some evidence that Billinge nail-makers were as dissolute as their Wigan counterparts, who were reported to be pretty bad, and if they were half as cunning as the Billinge poachers, then they were surely quite a bunch. The trade became over-exploited in the early eighteenth century and a long period of degradation for the village nailer set in as the industry became hopelessly over-competitive. John Rigby was well-known as a Billinge nailmaker around 1777, but the trade seems to have been dying out in the village by 1825.

Another cottage industry was hand loom weaving. Hugh Parr, in his "Short History of Billinge" (1953) tells us that his great-grandfather used to carry Billinge-woven cloth on his back as far as Wigan and Prescot, receiving a mere pittance for his labour. This would be about 1805. Quarrying, too, was becoming more important and men were being paid a shilling a day in 1825 to get the stone to the surface ground. (Some of the older Billinge buildings had, of course, been constructed of Billinge stone well before this time, e.g. Malt Kiln House, 1674, the Church, 1718, the Old House at Home, 1740, Eagle and Child, 1745). At least one Billinge legend originated from the quarrying work: George Smith, a young quarry labourer, decided to have a nap on the hill on a hot day in 1720. As he slept he was bitten by an adder, of all things, and continued his snooze in a coffin-shaped tombstone in Billinge Churchyard. The grave is situated right next to the church, which would be only two years old at the time of his demise, and also contains the remains of his wife, Kitty. The tombstone bears a crest depicting a death's head and a pair of bats' wings encircled by a snake, tail-in-mouth. It is unlikely there was much loafing around in the quarry for a few months after George's funeral.

Coal mining became increasingly important to Billingers during the 19th century. The 1786 map shows no coal mines actually located within Billinge itself, though Betty Hodson, the celebrated "Lancashire Collier Girl", achieved her fame less than a decade later in Up Holland (three miles away) and her benefactor and employer, William Bankes, was of the same Bankes family which for so long has been a pillar of Billinge St. Aidan's. In 1795 Betty was reported to have gone down the pit at the age of nine, alongside her father and younger brother of seven, working as a drawer until her father was killed by a falling stone. The mother went out of her mind with grief and was thrown, with her younger children, on the parish. Betty continued to work down the mine and, through her ability to work a double shift, managed to support the family, though it meant she often had to stay fifteen or sixteen hours underground. Her mother and brothers died, anyway, but the tenacious and comely Betty, herself on the verge of collapse, was rescued by the kind-hearted Bankes, who took her on as a cook and left her £50 in his will.

By 1845 the industry had livened up in Billinge itself and statistics show that in that year Sammy Stock employed 87 men and women, 46 adolescents and 37 children down Blackleyhurst. By 1851 Shaley Brow Colliery had 14 men producing 36 tons a day, Ash Grove Pit 6 men producing 21 tons a day and Billinge Colliery 100 men producing 200 tons. Billinge, like most of the Wigan area, was afflicted with the scars of opencast mining and coal cropped out on the surface in many a back garden. Today the mines are worked out, but the scars remain and the pits of the Victorian era played an important part in the development of the village. The 1801 census had shown a population of 1,141 people (an increase of only 33 families since 1717). It indicated that 146 people were employed in agriculture and 477 in handicrafts, trades and manufactures. The 19th century saw a rapid swing to industry, the population began to jump and in 1861 there were 3,066 inhabitants in the village. (In 1961 there was a total population of 6,945, including 3 tramps).

Five of the Lowe brothers – all miners

By the time James and Susannah were bringing up their large family, Billinge was very much a mining community. Employment down the mine of women and children under 10 was forbidden by Act of Parliament in 1842, but this was not strictly enforced and Jake Lancaster, as we have seen, went down at the tender age of nine in 1870. The women of Billinge became pit-lassies, sorting out the lumps of coal on pit-brow, acquiring black faces and bleeding fingers and learning a vocabulary that Gentleman Jim did not altogether approve of. Underground and on the surface, mining was a hard and dangerous job. In the year Jake Lancaster was put on the face, 155 miners had been killed throughout the country, but the previous year before there had been 586 deaths and the year before that 345. In 1879, out of 327 strikes in the country, 67 of them were staged by miners. Conditions improved in the eighties and nineties, but accidents were still rife in the Wigan area, as elsewhere. The degrading nature of the work led to miners becoming coarse and depraved, so much so that John Wesley felt he had to spend a good portion of his time amongst them. The pitmen of the Wigan area were reputed to be among the most backward, foul-mouthed and intemperate of all. What with all this and Billinge's fourteen pubs, Gentleman Jim must have found it hard going at times with the Band of Hope.

One of the few consolations a miner's life had to offer was that his pay packet was thicker than the farm worker's. In 1734 Squire Bankes built three cottages off Carr Mill Road for three of his labourers who had recently married but were too poor to provide houses for their brides. This philanthropic act led to the stone cottages being called "Start Em" – as they had given a good start in married life to the three couples – and they kept the name for over two hundred years, having been demolished only recently. The farm hands, and other Billingers of varying trades, used to supplement their meagre incomes by poaching. In the 17th century, it had been possible to make money legally through catching animals, as Billinge had been infested by foxes and hedgehogs. In 1677 a hedgehog head fetched twopence and a foxhead a shilling. By 1679 the price for a foxhead had gone up to three shillings, which seems to indicate that the foxes were winning. In the nineteenth century, however, the story is not so much of hedgehogs and bounty hunters as of rabbits and poachers. The old files of the "Wigan Observer" and the "St. Helens Newspaper and Advertiser" have several references to Billingers being tried for poaching and indicate little remorse on the part of the defendants. In 1888 one Timothy Shaw (Billinge name: Push) was given the choice of £5 and costs or 2 months' imprisonment. Shaw went to jail, naturally. It was the 58th time he had been "up".

Long Fold had its own poacher in Owd Lint, a practised layabout who poached diligently through the 1890s and kept Long Fold well supplied right up to the First World War. Rabbits tasted good in those days. Lint used to say he was daft, but not daft enough to work. Most Billinge poachers were Ranters, living in the line of stone cottages between the "Labour in Vain" and the "Brown Cow". The Rant kept more ferrets than cats. Minnie would hear the men some nights as they passed through Long Fold on their way to Hollin Hey, laughing and talking quietly, returning even more stealthily at four or five in the morning. One night Owd Lint fell down an open mine shaft in Mulks Wood and that was almost the end of him. They heard his groans the following morning (fortunately Billingers at that time constantly roamed the fields) and he was hauled out more dead than alive with a ruined back and the story that he had just been "going for a stroll". Another night Jake and Tom Lancaster, while still in their drinking days, collided with four poachers in pitch blackness in the middle of Turpin Fields. The poachers, two of them with guns, thought Jake and Tom were gamekeepers, while the brothers, plastered out of their mind after a four-hour session in the "Brown Cow", thought they were being attacked by armed madmen. There ensued a savage set-to with flailing fists, feet and gun-butts, leaving all the men considerably worse for wear before the poachers realised their mistake and made off into the darkness, chased ineffectually by the staggering Tom, now thirsting for their blood. They say that this incident was one of the reasons why Jake gave up drinking and that he and Tom took the same route home at the same hour for weeks afterwards, hoping to meet the poachers again while sober.

A traditional Billinge handicraft for many years was chair-making. Billinge chairs had rush bottoms and were tall and straight-backed, usually with four

slats. They were solid, firm, well-made chairs, not all that comfortable but certainly good for the posture, the back being approximately as high as the occupant's shoulders. One of the best Billinge chairmakers in the 19th century was a man called John Jackson, whose great-grandchildren are still in possession of several of his chairs. Probably the last one he made was for his grandson, Thomas Fairhurst, to whom he gave a rush-bottomed rocking chair about 1870. Jackson normally made his chairs in sets of six and these were selling around 1860 at £2 a set. They were still a bargain at £2 a chair in 1930. After Jackson died, Thomas Fairhurst was in great demand for "re-rushing" his grandfather's chairs as they wore out over the years and from 1890 to 1930 he put new rush seats in many hundreds of them at about one and six a time. As he had a full-time job, Fairhurst rushed chairs only in his spare time and during one period the demand was such that he had almost a hundred of them waiting in his shed on Gorsey Brow. The wood, usually ash, seems to have come from near Blackleyhurst, but the rushes were imported from the continent, probably Germany. Jackson would wash the rushes in the stream flowing past his house and put them in the frames while they were still damp. The chairs themselves he fashioned by hand, drilling the holes for the spindles with an ancient tool called the "old ogre" and "bending" the slats over steam in the smithy.

The smithy itself, situated next to the "Labour in Vain" and run at the beginning of this century by a man called Tom Eaves, was not only a beehive of industrial activity, but also the village Parliament. It turned out everything from horse-shoes to pokers while children and elders would sit around the fireplace or the anvil, trading pieces of gossip, putting Gladstone in his place and discussing such things as pit disasters, funerals, dogs, Colonel Baden-Powell, St. Helens' dentists, the Poor Law, Aspinall's Enamel and Botanic Eye Snuff.

Billinge trades mentioned in the 1825 Directory for Lancashire and the 1861

The "old ogre"

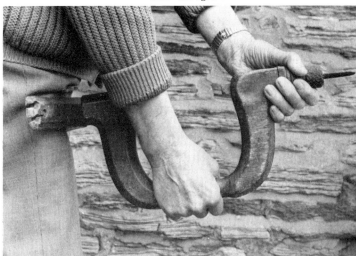

census include the following: wheelwright, joiner, quarry owner, gentleman, publican (many times), tanner, priest, miller, schoolmaster, overseer, yeoman, beer retailer, shopkeeper, farmer, nail master, surgeon, butcher, tailor, clogger, chemist, coachman, shoemaker, storemason, blacksmith, tanner and coal proprietor. By 1900 the great majority of the village population was employed at the pit or at Pilkington's Glass Works in St. Helens. The two men who were perhaps the most indispensable workmen in Billinge seem never to have been mentioned in directories and may have been given a wide berth by census officials, so I will take the liberty of immortalizing them at this point: they were the village's two midden men – John Matches and Owd Jem Muckmon. In the days before flush toilets, somebody had to empty the middens, which contained on one side ashes and cinders and on the other refuse matter discharged from the body after digestion. Every Billinge midden was to be cleaned out once a week, so Jack and Jem worked according to a simple, democratic plan whereby one week Jack would do the ashes and Jem the muck and the following week Jack would do the muck and Jem the ashes. Their equipment consisted of a horse and cart, two shovels and lengths of string to tie round the bottom of their breeches. The job had its unpleasant sides and it was just as well that neither Jack nor Jem was a career man at heart. They were a good pair, for both men were half deaf and consequently shouters. On a normal working day they would shout their way through fifty or sixty middens, so the people of the village usually knew if anything was on their minds. The biggest shouting matches

A Billinge farmer

took place on Monday mornings as they were about to embark upon their weekly round. They would begin with a post mortem of the previous week's work, each man convinced that he had done the muck and the other the ashes. Either it was wishful thinking or they had very poor memories. On one or two occasions they actually came to blows over the issue and the Nuisance Inspector had to be sent for to separate them:

"Ah did t'muck aw last wick, an now 'ee wants me t'do it again while 'ee does t'cinders . . . . "

"Now James . . . . "

"You're listenin' to a bloody liar, it wuz me as did t'muck . . . . "

"Now John . . . . "

"Just let me get at 'im wi' me shovel . . . . "

"Now now James . . . . "

"Ah'll rub his nose int . . . . "

"Now now John . . . . "

And so it went on until Sergeant Mare came down the street and threatened to lock them up for breaking the peace and the Nuisance Inspector appealed to their sense of civic duty. Finally they would settle for half and half that day and start two hours late. By Tuesday afternoon they would have made up the time lost and be right on schedule, to the great relief of those families whose middens were done on Saturday mornings. Apart from when they addressed each other, Jack and Jem were agreeable, good-humoured men who willingly exchanged banter with any Billinger who could shout loud enough. They never let their job get on top of them.

CHAPTER TWENTY-THREE

Billinge at Play

Whatever there may be in the old Garswood joke about the Billingers hurtling out of the Middle Ages at the turn of this century, there seems to be little doubt that from 1900 until the First World War Billinge was a lively centre of entertainment for people from the surrounding villages and townships.

In the days before motorized transport, the lack of a railway meant that access to cities and theatres was a slow and laborious affair, consequently Billingers were used to making their own fun and to entertaining themselves and each other. This they did by their own firesides, in the chapels, in the pubs, at weddings and funerals and, from spring to autumn, in the streets and lanes. They were practised and uninhibited singers, dancers, story-tellers and *farçeurs* who could always be relied upon to put on a performance whether it was to raise a laugh, money for their chapels, or simply a commotion. It is not surprising, therefore, that local impresarios regarded the Billingers as an ideal audience for their shows, for they were guaranteed to flock en masse to such events and inevitably tried to get in on the act, producing a give-and-take ambience which attracted hundreds more onlookers from the less imaginative communities around.

There was a piece of waste land near to the "Druids Arms" at the bottom of Main Street and travelling entertainers usually chose this spot to erect their large tents. Wild Beast Shows were staged every year and Billingers would pay sixpence a time to see lion-tamers crack their whips and pretty girls put their heads into the animals' mouths. Outsiders from Orrell, Pemberton, Downall Green, Bryn, Ashton, Up Holland, Haydock and even Wigan and St. Helens came to see the beasts and the big tent would sometimes be there as long as three weeks at a time. All the cats between the "Brown Cow" and the "Labour in Vain" were nervous wrecks.

The longest run by any show on this piece of ground was one by a certain theatrical company about 1908. The company consisted entirely of "has-beens" – broken-down actors and actresses possessed of talent in their youth, but no longer able, on account of age, ill fortune or bad health, to command parts in theatres with brick walls. They travelled up and down the country in dingy caravans, staging their performances in a big tent similar to that which had housed the wild beasts. They had lost their looks, position and ambitions and had very little money. But they could act. They were made for the Billingers and the Billingers were made for them. The old troupers put on three or four plays a week and the villagers went to see them again and again. The plays were stirring melodramas such as "East Lynn" and "Silver King" – romantic stories of beautiful gipsy girls being taken advantage of by the Lord of the Manor. It was not long before the Billingers knew all the plays by heart and went round the village declaiming their favourite lines ("Cynthia, did I not tell thee not to leave thy tent?") All the money taken at the box office was ploughed back into the Billinge economy, since most of the actors were hooked on gin and whisky and bought all their food in the village stores. After one year there was no sign of their moving and they were still playing to packed tents. During the day they used to walk up and down Main Street and round the fields, practising their parts and chatting with the Billingers. They were fascinated with the Billinge nicknames and many of them learned how to talk just like the locals. They never had enough money to buy new clothes or costumes and when the latter were on the verge of falling to pieces they finally moved on to another part of the country. They would probably have stayed in Billinge forever if the Ranters had not started shouting out their best lines from the back of the tent.

Real gypsies visited Billinge frequently at that time and contributed to the local entertainment by telling fortunes and selling flowers. The superstitious Billingers were easy prey for the fortune tellers and generally bought flowers, as it was well known that if you did not buy any the gypsies would put a curse on you and your house as they left. Villagers tended to be nervous about gypsies and tramps, as in those days many doors in Billinge did not have locks (they were too expensive) and it was not uncommon for such visitors to wander in and help themselves to anything that was going. One night Maria Bellis got up for a glass of water and found a tramp enjoying a pot of tea and scones in the kitchen. Even though such occurrences were frequent, it still remained a custom in Billinge for people to leave their doors wide open, except in cold weather. This was mainly because of their gregarious nature. Two sisters who lived in houses on opposite sides of the street in the Cockshut used to leave their doors open all day so they could see each other. Minnie Parr, who was afraid of tramps, used to leave her door wide open all day as she was more afraid of ghosts from within than of any intruders from without.

After the departure of the theatrical company, the chief attraction on the piece of waste land at the bottom of Main Street was Potts' Auction. Potts was a travelling auctioneer who combined the selling of clocks, pianos, beds, umbrellas, ornaments and many other things with his own variety of show business. That is to say, he employed a regular comic to liven up the audience, had a pretty good line of his own as he peddled off his goods, and held Concert Night every Thursday to give the local talent its chance. He was quick to see the potential of Billinge in this regard and he would leave his tent up six weeks and occasionally months at a time in the village, pulling visitors in from miles around for three or four nights a week.

Jake and Tom Lancaster would occasionally visit the Auction on summer nights and in 1911 Jake actually bought two mug dogs from Potts to grace his sideboard. He was now fifty years of age, the father of five sons, still fit and unscathed after forty-one years down the pit. Tom, who had married a girl from

Joyce Bankes' Wedding

Garswood, had four sons and five daughters and at forty-seven was no less active than his brother. They lived next door to each other and remained inseparable both in and out of the mine. In 1902 Tom had survived a bad roof fall, being pinned under the same rock which had killed his friend John Gorner, but he had recovered completely from a broken shoulder and was still on the face. The two brothers were making good money and forced nearly all their sons into attending grammar school. Tom's boys eventually did well in mining, but Jake kept all his five out of the pit. His fourth son, Dick, had struck up a friendship with Minnie Parr, who was one year his junior. Dick came regularly to Potts' Auctions after that and Minnie used to attend them with her cousin Maria Bellis, although Gentleman Jim disapproved of the whole thing and often threatened to thrash them with his knobstick.

On Auction nights Potts' comic would go on first to soften up the public. The "stage" was not only at the back of the tent, but also ran down the sides and sometimes down the middle too, so that he had an ample access to his audience. His jokes were pure corn, but as Victorians seem to have thrived on this type of humour, he could do little wrong:

> "I would like to take the opportunity this evening of congratulating Moss Bank Brass Band on its fine contribution to British industry . . . . " (What contribution?) Why . . . . look how it has boosted the Cotton Wool Trade . . . . "
> "We all know the worst results of the Boer War . . . . (an accomplice in the audience)
> "Widows – I married one of them . . . . "
> "Tonight we have for you the ideal presents to give to your relations on the occasion of their Golden Wedding Anniversary . . . (???) . . . false teeth, a pair of spectacles, a wig and a pair of crutches . . . . "

The sale would begin by Potts' son Tom giving away two or three dozen articles – pens, pencils, bars of soap – usually to pretty girls whom he fancied, but also to persons who could be expected to buy something later. Then there would be the "mystery" packages wrapped up in brown paper for which people would be asked to pay ten shillings, or a pound. These parcels, on being opened, always proved to be remarkably good value and you could have your money back if you were not satisfied. After that the real auctioning would begin. Mugs, all kinds of ornaments, sheets, drapery and clocks sold best, but Potts sold articles of every description, occasionally to individuals who had no money to pay for them. Billingers in their traditional eagerness to participate, would often bid impulsively for an item to impress their friends, assuming that further bids would ensue and had some shocking surprises when they found that they had been successful in securing the purchase. This type of winning bid occurred one night when Hollow Mon heard Potts knock down a fine upright piano to him for £14. The buyer's family was so poor that it was common knowledge they lived on nothing but stewed fish-heads for months at a time. They told his wife what had happened and the poor woman fainted away in her kitchen, but later threw a screaming fit when they tried to deliver the instrument. Finally Potts consented to put it up for sale again on the following Tuesday.

Concert Night on Thursdays always drew large crowds. Sometimes there would be a Beauty Competition (Maria Bellis won a gold ring) but usually it was singing and entrants had to put down their names one week before in order to participate. Voting was by show of hands and the winner often received a gold watch. It was not unusual for a Billinger to take first prize, since there were many fine voices in the village and the voting could be expected to be sympathetic, but occasionally miners from neighbouring pits would send in a candidate and the whole shift would attend and vote for him and that would be that. As a rule standards were high, for Potts himself was a discerning judge of talent and had a professional piano accompanist to advise him in his selection. It was only natural, however, that the Billingers would take him in in the end and it is unlikely that he ever forgot the performance of Sally Slats, whose candidature had been put forward by a large number of people living at the Rant. The Ranters succeeded not only in persuading Potts that Sally was a wonderful singer, but also in convincing Sally of the same thing. In fact Sally was ugly, looked like a man, had a cracked, tuneless voice and was a halfwit to boot. It had taken the Ranters nearly a month to teach her the words of the song – one which had become popular after the Boer War – and when she finally appeared she was a sensation:

> *"Just break the news to Mother*
> *And tell her how I love her,*
> *And tell her not to wait for me,*
> *For I'm not coming home.*
> *Tell her there is no other*
> *Can take the place of Mother*
> *And tell her not wait for me,*
> *For I'm not coming home."*

As Sally delivered these lines she rocked sideways from one foot to the other, hands clasped rigidly in her lap, squinting at the ceiling in concentration. She sang the verse over and over again, with the Ranters applauding madly and screaming "Encore" until Potts brought the act to a merciful close, leading her offstage by the elbow. He never let himself be duped again in this way.

*   *   *   *   *   *   *   *

Concerts were also held regularly in the chapels. In the days before cinema and television, people looked more to the church for entertainment and if you happened to live with Gentleman Jim chapel-going could be a full-time occupation. There were some weeks when Minnie went every night. Besides three visits on Sundays there was the Women's Class, Christian Endeavour, the Band of Hope, the Men's Class, tea parties, choir practices and other committee meetings on weekdays. The Methodists gave concerts regularly to raise funds. A sit-down tea with ham, tongue and scones cost one shilling, inclusive of entertainment. Somewhat cheaper would be Potato Pie evenings, where the public brought their own pies and ate them during the performance. Most of Caroline's children were musical, especially Tom and Hugh Lowe, and Minnie and Tom would sing rousing duets – "Reuben and Rachel", "Simon the Cellarer" and so on. Tom Lowe specilized in "Hearts of Oak" and Minnie followed this by the tearful recitation "Diamond Wedding" (Min, tha must be improvin', I went cowd dehn me back four times). Minnie decided to be an actress and become famous, but such was the opposition of her grandfather to the plan that she dropped it completely and took a job scrubbing counters and floors at the Top Shop instead.

Weddings were colourful affairs with singing, recitations and good food. When Moll's eldest daughter, Ruth Bellis, got married the guests were treated to jellies and blancmanges, pork and roast beef, ham roasted with onion and sage stuffing, different kinds of pickles, tea, ale and punch served in a new chamber-pot with slices of lemon swimming on top and a broad pink ribbon tied round the handle.

Another interesting custom was to be observed on funeral days when the old woman who laid out the dead person would dress up in a clean, white pinafore, fill a pewter jug with ale, twist lemon peel round the handle of the jug and go round offering drinks to all the neighbours, accompanied by another old woman who would carry a tray of buns.

The first place in Billinge to show pictures was the Conservative Club, which started with stills – many of them upside down – but Hugh Parr had livened up the concert nights in chapel with his Magic Lantern. The locals paid 3d a time to see the same twelve slides – "Anne Laurie", "Bobby Burns" and other similar personages. One of the female subjects, "Highland Mary", was a lady of such breathtaking beauty that the audience frequently objected when Hugh tried to pass on to the next slide and often he would have to leave her on the wall for half an hour before being allowed to proceed. It was not uncommon for the Magic Lantern show to last two or three hours. It was a pleasant way of spending an evening.

* * * * * * * *

A different type of entertainment was to be had in the public houses, which seem never to have been in short supply in Billinge. Not so long ago you could take a walk down Main Street, starting at the "Blacksmith's Arms" just above the Church, and you would pass first the "Horseshoe Inn" then the "Eagle and Child", the "Old House at Home" and the "Stork" on Church Brow, the "Forrester's Arms" and the "Oddfellows" lower down opposite the Methodist Chapel, the "George and Dragon" a little further on, the "Labour in Vain" on the bend, the "Druids' Arms" round the corner and the "Brown Cow" within easy staggering distance of that. The whole walk, outside licensing hours, would take you less than twenty minutes. On top of that there were other pubs on the Cockshut and down Chadwick Green, outdoor licences for those who wished to buy drinks for private consumption, and several other houses which had been pubs in the time of our grandfathers, having either ceded their licences or had them taken away.

In short, a Billinger born anywhere but on the very outskirts of the village in the 1890s had fourteen pubs at his disposal within a mile of his home, which must be something of a record in a community of this size. But why so many pubs? How did they all manage to stay in business at the same time? "Quite simple," the eighty-year-olds will tell you, "Billinge was a drunken place."

I could not accept such a summary description of my own village without pressing for further details, but the evidence of all the old-timers I spoke to seems to support the fact that between 1890 and the First World War Billingers

Shootin' and fishin' men

took their drinking very seriously indeed. Beer was one penny a gill, or one shilling for thirteen gills set out in a row on the counter. Pubs would be packed night after night, log and coal fires would be lit, games and singing would be organized as each hostelry vied with the next for the villagers' custom. Jem Birchall, the publican at the "Labour in Vain" at the bottom of Main Street, had several sons, two of whom, Jack and Wilf Birchall, were top notch singers. Wilf went on to sing opera while Jack, always full of spirits, would start in the pubs at the top of Main Street and work his way down, singing solos in each one until his huge crowd of followers would fill the "Labour in Vain", where he would sing until closing time. The authentic Billinge hero, Our Nell's Jack, then publican at the "Brown Cow", dignified that inn with his presence, while the "Old House at Home" and the "Stork" gained a certain advantage in view of their older construction and historical associations. Most of the pubs would have their "Pastie Nights" about once every three months. Pasties were oblong or triangular, containing pork, onion, salt, pepper and occasionally fat bacon. Eaten hot out of the oven in front of a roaring log fire, they were delicious.

But how could the people of Billinge, known for their poverty, afford all this revelry? "Easy," say the old-timers, "they spent most of their money on drink." And how about food and clothes? "Well, there was a bit of a problem" they reply, "for wages were quite low. Clothes did not matter so much, for many Billingers were used to wearing the same old clothes for years. When it was a question of food and drink, the wages went on drink, which could be bought only for cash, whereas food could be obtained on credit."

"But how did they then pay for their food?"

"They didn't. What money they had left they would take to the shop at the end of the week and for the rest they would run up debts"

"And when did they pay off their debts?"

"Some of them managed to do so when their children started working. Others were content to let their debts run on. Many of them died in debt."

"And what did the shopkeepers think about all this?"

"Well they always managed to collect something, and in this way they never lost their customers."

"Could the shops afford to do this?"

"If Billinge was a drinker's paradise, it was also renowned for good food. The shops never had any difficulty in moving their stock, whether they got paid for it or not. And there was the insurance."

"Insurance?"

"When shopkeepers had elderly customers with huge debts, they would insure them for a hundred pounds or so and collect when they died."

"Were they allowed to do this?"

"As long as they had the signature of one of the customer's children. It was quite a common practice."

The large quantities of drink consumed in the village led to a great number of drunks – a nightly procession up and down Main Street between ten and eleven o'clock. Some of the revellers – such as Big Jem – would arrive home in a more or less jovial mood and after breaking a few ornaments the good-hearted miner would sit in his rocking-chair and sing two or three hours' worth of English ballads till he was sleepy and James, Susannah, Hugh and Minnie were thoroughly woken up. Brown Rabbit used to go straight home to beat his wife until her screams made the neighbours fetch Sergeant Mare. The good sergeant used to take a poker with him inside his tunic as a precaution, for Rabbit objected strongly to police interference. The people living around knew the conversation by heart:

"Rabbit, I hear tha're peylin' thi wife again."

"It's nowt to do wi'thee, Mare, and I can see thi bloody poker."

Another great drinker, a miner called Codger, had an alcoholic wife who did all her drinking at home. Every evening from nine o'clock onwards she would be in a drunken stupor in an armchair by the fire. Periodically, Codger would lose his temper with her, storm out of the house, go and drink fifteen pints in the "George and Dragon", return home and smash up all the furniture. This he did systematically, piece by piece, making a pile of the wreckage in the front garden. For the next three or four weeks he would go round sulking and they would live without furniture until his mood changed. Then he would go to St. Helens and re-furnish the house. He was not a poor man and used to buy pretty good furniture. Three months later he would smash it all up again.

Every time they brought home a new load of furniture, Codger's wife would sober up for a few hours and he would be in a good mood and make love to her. In such circumstances they raised a family of twelve children, and most of them turned out all right. In his middle age, Codger found out that he had cancer and promptly hanged himself by his belt from a hook in the ceiling. He never did things by halves.

*   *   *   *   *   *   *   *

The best preserved part of Billinge to-day is Church Brow, where the four old buildings – the "Stork", the "Old House at Home", the "Eagle and Child" and St. Aidan's itself – form a rough square. This has always been the true centre of the village and it is fitting that the old structures there should have survived intact. In Susannah's day, cock fights took place on the round cobbles in front of the "Eagle and Child" and were left relatively undisturbed by the police until the 1880s. The same space was used for Maypoles and Morris dancing and Moss Bank Band would go through its repertoire there on Bank Holidays. On the same occasions toffee stalls would be erected and Dolly Blue would "perry" her Swaggering Dick and sell scores of bottles of nettle pop. The local shopkeepers would set up stalls and the crowds would mill around all day, many of them popping in and out of the three pubs. In good weather the festivities normally lasted from ten in the morning till midnight.

Both the "Stork" and the "Old House at Home" are coaching inns and mounting stones used to be visible outside both buildings. Now there is only one remaining in front of the "Old House". The "Stork" until a few years ago had mooring rings set in the walls and its cellars were once used as the local jail. Both coaching inns have ghosts – a Cavalier for the "Stork" and a Highwayman for the "Old House". The latter inn is now a private house.

* * * * * * * *

We have seen how Billinge in the late Victorian and Edwardian eras was a hive of social activity throughout the year: in the cold months through its chapels and pubs, in warmer weather with its shows, dancing, processions and picnics (Billinge Hill was a centre of attraction in summer for the whole industrial area around). Two events stood out, however, as the star attractions in the Billinge calendar of festivities. These were the two scoosters held respectively by the Church of England St. Aidan's and Roman Catholic St. Mary's of Birchley. "Scooster" is the local term for walking day, or church procession. The friendly rivalry which always existed between the Protestant

The "Buffs"

and Catholic congregations tended to build up during the winter and spring, culminating in a show of strength on two successive Saturdays in July. They say on the first Friday all the Catholics prayed for rain and on the second Friday all the Protestants prayed for rain, but I am happy to record that most walking days seem to have enjoyed that splendid. old-fashioned summer weather which deserted us in the late 1930s.

The processions themselves were magnificent and attracted large crowds from miles around. St. Aidan's column numbered several hundred walkers, under three or four banners and led by Moss Bank Brass Band and one or two other supporting bands. They paraded in different sections. The Sunday School would lead, followed by the Day School, then the grown-ups and finally the "Buffs" – the Billinge and Winstanley Friendly Society with their splendid blue sashes.

First all these people, dressed mostly in new clothes, would assemble about half past one in London Fields, behind the "Stork Hotel". Just before two, when the ranks had been properly formed, they would proceed to Church Brow, the bands would strike up and the parade would commence. Their route included Longshaw – a Protestant stronghold – and during this part of the walk it was customary for them to halt for the children to have a rest at Longshaw

Catholic Procession, 1906

House. Main Street would be thronged with onlookers from top to bottom. People who had moved out of Billinge years before always came back on that day and the pavements spilled children onto the roadway, waving their flags and clutching streamers and toy windmills. Huge Union Jacks hung out of the windows of the School, the pubs, Police Station, Top Shop, Council Offices and many of the private houses. At four o'clock, when the procession was over, the children and bandmen would take tea in the School and the crowds would disperse to their homes for a bite to eat, before the evening programme got under way on London Fields.

Father Powell and his flock put on an equally splendid display. One of the features of the Catholic procession was a troupe of Morris dancers, eager to perform after their winter training. Other contingents would be the Sunday School, the Men's Society (CYMS), the Women's Confraternity and the fathers and mothers with the little ones.

The column formed at Birchley School, parading along the Rant and up the whole length of Main Street to Church Brow. Father Powell himself led them on horseback, a fine, upright, authoritarian figure on a vigorous chestnut. The Morris Dancers twisted and twirled in the middle of the procession and put on a full show opposite the "Stork" when they reached the top of Main Street. The children would be given soft drinks at one of the pubs and Father Powell would

turn round on his horse and lead them back to Birchley, visiting Greenfield House on the way down. Tea would be in Birchley School and the evening's festivities took place on the field behind St. Mary's.

From four o'clock to six o'clock on both walking days, the out-of-towners would be taken home by Billinge families and fed on meat pies, roast pork, home-grown tomatoes and custard pie. Those who no longer lived in the village would be brought up to date on local gossip over the last twelve months. At a quarter to six, ties were straightened, bows and brooches adjusted, bonnets fixed and those who had bowlers gave them a final brush before they all hastened over to the playing fields for the fun and games. It was a great occasion for the children, because the evening's programme consisted mainly of Races organized for them. The grown-ups would thread their way in and out of the toffee stalls, purchasing odds and ends, shouting encouragement to their infant runners and all the while eyeing each other in their Sunday best. If it was a memorable day for the young ones, it could be no less exciting for their elders, since Scooster Day was known for its romances and if you were unmarried and anywhere between sixteen and forty you went round those toffee stalls with your eyes peeled.

At nine o'clock the children would have had enough, or their parents would have, and one by one the families would gather their brood and slowly make their way home in the evening sunlight. By this time it was customary for the unmarried hopefuls to have conveniently paired off and they, too, would slip away in the fading light, but not yet bound for home. Billinge was blessed with many quiet fields, lonely lanes, sturdy elms and beeches, sheltering hedgerows and scenic walks. The slopes of Billinge Hill itself were covered with an abundance of bramble, gorse and long grass and the whole area was a lover's paradise. Amorous couples and sweethearts melted away in the dusk, arm in arm, fingers intertwined, heading for Billinge Hill and Shaley Brow, the welcoming darkness of Hollin Hey and Mulks Wood and the seductive seclusion of Turpin Fields. And behind them, at a discreet distance, now crawling in the grass, now bobbing their cloth caps above the hedgerows, followed the dedicated bands of Billinge grasshoppers. Scoosters were big days for everybody.

CHAPTER TWENTY FOUR

The Great War

Sarajevo is a bleak, sombre city in March, surrounded on all sides by high, snow-covered mountains and swept by gusty, icy winds which send the Slavs scurrying along the narrow streets and into the dimly-lit bars where they drink thick, sweet, black Turkish coffee.

The river cuts through the centre of the town and I walked along its left bank watching the gusts flatten the ripples on the steel-grey surface. I quickened my pace on account of the penetrating cold, passed two or three indifferent bridges and stopped at an older, hump-backed one further along. It was grey like everything around it, a narrow, quaint, cobbled bridge near the Old Town. It is now called the Princip Bridge and I stood for a few minutes on the spot where it had happened. Almost 60 years had passed, some of the surroundings had changed, but the smell of the old buildings and the solid feel of the bridge under my feet gave me some of the atmosphere in which a 19-year-old Slav, Gavrilo Princip, had assassinated Archduke Franz Ferdinand of Austria at this place in the summer of 1914.

It was too cold to stay there long and I wandered to the left and on into the Old Town where I bargained with Bosnian merchants and eventually bought a Sarajevo pistol — an old, functioning model complete with long barrel, thumb-cocked hammer and elegant, polished handle with elaborate ornamentation of inlaid gold — hardly like the one with which Gavrilo had done the job, but from Sarajevo nevertheless and bought only a hundred yards from the spot where the whole bit of bother started. The pistol now hangs over the fireplace in the Old House at Home opposite Billinge Church.

*   *   *   *   *   *   *

"I bet th'owd Kaiser's sorry he started it, aren't tha, Hugh?"
"Aye, well...."
"Why, they're 'listing i'thousands, it'll only be a matter of a few months."
"Well, I daresay ..."
"I'll go tomorrow if they'll let me. I could do with a month's holiday out o't pit."
"Aye, well pitmen...."
"Grandson o'Queen Victoria, and all. Attacking owd England."
"Well, it started...."
"Come on, Hugh, thee tell us how it started."

A South Lancs. soldier

"Well, first this Slav shot the Austrian Archduke."

"I should think he did too, after what they'd bin doin'to'em. What did t'Germans do then, Hugh?"

"Well Austria blamed Serbia, you see."

"Aye."

"So then Austria declared war on Serbia."

"And th'Austrians are t'same as Germans, aren't they, Hugh?"

"Well, no, you see, first Russia mobilized to protect Serbia."

"But they're on our side, aren't they?"

"That's right. But Austria and Germany are allies, so Germany came to Austria's aid by threatening to march against Russia."

"Aye."

"But Russia and France are allies, so this was the same as threatening France."

"Aye."

"But in order to get at France, Germany would have to invade Belgium."

"They would."

"And England and France said they would fight if Germany went into Belgium."

"And they went in, didn't they, Hugh?"

"Aye, well first they shot this French sentry...."

* * * * * * * *

On the morning of August 4th, 1914, Billinge basked in beautiful Bank Holiday sunshine. As the massive right wing of the German army shouldered into Belgium, Minnie Parr was off early with her friend Olive Williams on a trip to Parkgate to visit Olive's grandparents. Mary Ann went to Llandudno for the day. Minnie heard that England and Germany were at war as they crossed over on the boat to Birkenhead, just about the same time Jake Lancaster and his brother Tom were told they could not buy a return ticket to N.Wales from Garswood station, as the journey back could not be guaranteed.

When Minnie came back on the Monday, the train was packed with regular soldiers and bands were playing at all the stations. Everybody was delighted at the general excitement. Those who remembered the Boer War rather liked the idea of another one. A war fought between gentlemen whose cavalry charges and other adventurous pursuits had been thrillingly recorded by young Winston Churchill. Had not Mafeking been relieved and the war brought to a victorious end? Lord Derby put up a platform with a band on it in front of the "Labour in Vain" and volunteers flocked to sign up, receive one day's pay and one day's rations, and await the call to arms. The recruiters were choosy at first, for they thought, like the French and the Germans, that the war would be a quick, neat affair, disputed by infantry in scarlet trousers and officers in white gloves. Billinge pitmen, anxious for a chance of a couple of months holiday from the mine, with nice uniforms, free food and travel abroad, did not quite fit the picture. Pitmen were declared exempt, railwaymen were held back for a year and the allied armies stopped the Germans on the banks of the Marne, only 30 miles away from Paris. New weapons were being introduced by both sides. The French had a fast-firing cannon which was said to have killed thousands of Germans standing up, as they could not fall for the corpses of their comrades. The British cavalry charged into German machine-gun fire and were mown down by an enemy they could not even see. The French, who decided the best way to deal with machine guns was to send infantry running at them with sabres and bayonets, had to change tactics after they started losing 15,000 men a day and the war soon settled down to an unromantic image of four million men facing each other over two lines of barbed wire stretching from Switzerland to the Channel.

In Billinge, after a while, it became more difficult to get volunteers to rush onto the platform, and when Bill Martlew dragged back his cousin Jem Lowe one night, the sergeant-major went purple in the face and said he would have Bill locked up. They took Jem later, but they were never able to make him wear his cap straight, and he came out undefeated in 1919. As the stalemate continued, the French begged the British to mount a gigantic attack on the Somme in 1916, and the British eventually obliged. At 7.30 a.m. on July 1st, 100,000 men went over the top and charged across no man's land. By nightfall 60,000 were dead, wounded or captured, and by November the casualty figures for both sides had reached 1.2 million — the greatest for any battle ever fought anywhere.

Down Long Fold all the young men, except those down the pit, had gone. Minnie and Maria would get letters from them, jaunty at first, then sadness-tinged and less convincing in their quips, finally full of desperation, longing and heartbreak. For many of them there was to be no return. Telegrams arrived daily during the Battle of the Somme and all over Billinge families mourned. Long Fold, with its fourteen cottages, had four boys killed — Ned Bellis, Harry Lomax, John Shuttleworth and Billy Lowe.

Ned Bellis, Mary Ann's youngest child and second son, was his mother's favourite. From the outbreak of hostilities he had been anxious to volunteer, but his family and friends managed to dissuade him until he was 18. Less than a year later he was sent to France. He was a good soldier and popular with officers and men. He was made a Lewis gunner for the Battle of the Somme in July. He and his team were blown to pieces by a German shell on August 2nd. Minnie dreamt that he was killed on the night before his death. Mary Ann never laughed again. She was one of the first mothers to go over to France in 1919 and visit her son's grave.

Ned's catastrophic death, so cruel and unjust in its suddenness in the flower of his youth, resulted in a remarkable thing happening to several of those who had been close to him. He had been a vibrant personality, for many people the best lad in Billinge, and suddenly all this richness and promise had been cut off at 19. In any community this news would have been unbelievably bad; in Long Fold where the bonds of kinship were so immensely strong, it was simply too bad to be fully assimilated. Consequently, Ned Bellis was not allowed to die. The saying about one's not dying if one lives in the hearts of loved ones left behind can never have been better illustrated. For fifty years Ned has been taken all over and around Billinge, its Chapel and fields and farms and lanes, in the thoughts and words of his contemporaries. His mother and sisters, Jem Bellis his brother, Minnie Parr his cousin, Hugh Parr his uncle and most of the Long Folders would talk about him like they had just seen him go down the lane. It was our Ned this and our Ned that and his picture smiled at you as they talked. I was born 15 years after he died, but I have grown up in his company and my life would have been less rich if I had not known him. I have often seen the merriment in his deep brown eyes and I hope that some of it has been reflected in my own. His energy and youthful zest, his north country bluntness and simple ways, his kindness and *camaraderie* are part of my own heritage. His sturdy blacksmith's frame, though still, has always been there for any of us to lean on, his level gaze has never wavered. I have been influenced by his sunny temper and winning ways. I have heard the deep baritone of his voice and have shared, with his family, his innate sense of fun. By knowing him in this way I have had some insight into the secret of his universal popularity.

Of course part of Ned's importance for me and for some of my own cousins is that he symbolizes the young British soldier who gave his life unselfishly. We had a little wooden cross with a poppy in the centre and every year, on November 11th, we would attach it to Ned's picture and say a few words. What happened was that Mary Ann and Minnie and the others, by clinging fiercely to his memory, had made him live twice. His impact, through their intermediary, was so powerful that his influence on people turned out to be no less than that of other men who survived, indeed it was possibly equal to what it would have been had he come back from the war. What power can ever tarnish his image?

When I was twenty I went to France and visited Ned's grave on the Somme, as Mary Ann had done in 1919. The beautiful cemetery is completely isolated, surrounded by rolling countryside — it was a peaceful summer day of sunlight and greenery. As I spent the afternoon there, alone by the grave, I found I had never got on so well with anybody in all my life. There we were, two Billingers of the same age, both away from home, both knowing the same quaint people, the old grey cottages, the rugged hill, the jokes and stories, the fields and ponds. We talked the same dialect.

Of course his mother and Maria had told him a lot thirty years before, but I had to bring him up to date on Jem Bellis and his sister Ruth, as well as Minnie and Uncle Hugh. He was much as I expected — unassuming, humble and uncomplaining. It wasn't so bad out there: quiet, nice scenery, good weather in summer. He missed everybody, naturally, and wanted to know every detail I could recall, but he was tranquil and smiling, at least while I was there. I could feel how glad he was to see me; he had not seen a Billinger for thirty years. It was our first meeting and in a way I felt shy. In the end I felt he liked me and it was hard for me to leave. I know he wanted to come with me and I pedalled off furiously without looking back.

If I had turned my head he would have dropped his gun and run after me.

＊   ＊   ＊   ＊   ＊   ＊   ＊   ＊

The 2nd South Lancs were spread out in a long, thin line along the left bank of the river in the April sunshine. They had ten men on the bridge and another dozen or so pushed out on the right bank, lying flat on their stomachs in the long grass about twenty-five yards apart. It was 1918 and the Germans had been advancing steadily since March, The South Lancs had been retreating, sometimes marching twenty miles a day with a heavy pack and five minutes rest every hour.

Dick Lancaster, the last soldier on the flung-out right flank, today was thinking of his heavy pack with something approaching fondness. The day before he had received a parcel from the railway at Wigan containing 50 packets of cigarettes. Even after sharing them with his friends he had twenty-odd

In France

packets left and he inhaled contentedly, blowing the smoke through his nose and watching it seep, mist-like, through the blades of grass a few inches in front of his face. This was one of the better days, out of the trenches in the sunlight, with a well-stocked pack and no orders to march with it. After 4 years he was sick of the war, but like a lot of others he had reached the conclusion that it would never end. The German advance had made the prospects of victory more remote than ever, yet a British defeat was to him also quite unthinkable. He knew about the Thirty Years War and the Hundred Years War and he supposed he was involved in something similar. A lot of the men were so sick of it that they wanted to be killed or wounded or at least taken prisoner and he suspected that there were a lot of self-inflicted wounds about. Though without any hopes of release, he had not yet reached any of these stages of desperation. Assuming the war would go on, he had adapted to it as a way of life and got through it one day at a time. On most days there was enough to eat and, being lean, he found that the marching gave him no trouble. He disliked the shells and the barbed wire and the lice and the drills and the officers, but he did not hate the enemy particularly and reckoned that old Jake at home had it just as bad squirming and hacking his way along the coal face.

He raised his head six inches and peered over to the left. He could just make out the next man in the line, Tranter from Runcorn, who was nearly thirty yards away. Tranter had been waiting for three months now for the chance to give himself up. Dick could not see the next man on account of the length of the grass, which gave good cover but limited one's own visibility. He lifted his head another six inches and scanned the fields to his right, wondering where the Germans were. All he could see or hear were two skylarks. He thought of scrambling over and having five minutes with Tranter, then changed his mind and lit another cigarette. He might as well enjoy the chance to rest. Sometimes when they took you out of the line for a week's "rest" they drilled you so hard that you were glad to get back to the trenches and the cockroaches. He cast his thoughts back to his training: four weeks in Crosby and then fourteen weeks in Barrow, rifle practice, bayonets, parades. Now his brother Tom had been rushed through the whole thing in seven days. God, he hoped Tom would be able to take care of himself in France.

Dick stubbed his cigarette and lifted his head again. The field to the right was full of German soldiers. They were scampering forwards in their hundreds, stopping to crouch every twenty yards or so, and even as he watched he saw a group of them set up a machine gun and train it on the bridge. They still had not seen him, so he began to wriggle through the grass towards Tranter, rifle in one hand, dragging his pack behind him in the other. As he began to move he heard a dry crackling sound and he saw that the bridge ahead of him — his escape route over the river — was going up in flames. By the time he reached Tranter both knew what had happened: there had been orders to retreat and they had not been passed down the flank. The scouts on the bridge had seen the Germans coming and, thinking all their men were back on the other side, had set fire to the bridge. Poor Tranter had not even seen the Germans and almost fainted when Dick told him their bank was crawling with them. "That settles it; I'm giving meself up".

Dick knew his man and did not bother to argue. The bridge had not yet collapsed and he thought he had a good chance of running over it. The problem was reaching it. He had two hundred yards to go in full view of the Germans and there was not time to wriggle the whole distance. He gave Tranter a quick pat on the back, got to his feet and ran the first fifteen yards. When the machine gun opened up on him he threw himself flat and waited. He thought of how all the tall soldiers usually got shot in the head and of the time when there was a gap in the trench and seven men got shot in the leg. He decided to leave his precious pack behind and did another twenty-five yards before the scream of bullets forced him to drop flat on his face once more.

He thought of the officer from Bryn who had given him a tin of bully beef and got shot an hour later and of Ned Bellis meeting Tippy who had been rejected by the army nine times before they took him and Ned shaved the poor lad in Arras the day before they were both blown to pieces. He ran another twenty yards marvelling at how so many bullets could miss him and hit the sweet grass again and remembered when he had gone out with another man and a corporal on his first night patrol. Go out and scout the German trenches the officer had said and the corporal had taken them off into the darkness, over the wire and twenty yards on in the blackness and the corporal had stopped and tugged at their sleeves and said now you lie quiet here you buggers till I tell you to move, and after an hour they had crawled back and the corporal had said everything was quiet sir.

The Germans were waiting for him to get up again and as soon as he began to run bullets whistled close to his head and ripped into the turf near his flying feet. He felt hotter than he had ever been in his life, increasing his speed up the incline, feeling the searing heat of the flames in his face, crashing down once more to deprive the willing gunners of their target. The 8th South Lancs had been wiped out and they had transferred him to the 2nd. They said the 3rd was a "feeding" battalion filling up those that got wiped out. When there was a full battalion there were sixteen men to one loaf, but after a skirmish there had sometimes been nearly a loaf each.

He did another ten yards and this time hit the earth, as the long grass had run out on the approach up to the bridge. The firing slackened as he lay flat and he wondered if Tranter had managed to give himself up without getting shot. He had seen Ghurkas come back from night patrols with Germans' ears on strings and had heard Germans did some funny things to prisoners, but he felt that in many ways they were quite like the English. They had a tenor called Paul who used to sing to the South Lancs when the trenches were only a hundred yards apart and when Paul got shot the British missed him as much as the Germans did. Personally Dick could not stand their black bread, but the Germans certainly cleaned out Jim Martlew's home-made jam one night and Jim saw them neither come nor go. He calculated he could make one more break, throw himself down ten yards short of the bridge, and then get his breath for the run through the flames. The whole structure was now crackling merrily as he zig-zagged up the ramp, now a clearer target against the slope. He still was not hit and dropped for his last wait, only a few feet from the gathering inferno. He could see a coloured poster on a wall in Wigan somewhere, showing a broken old man in a chair with his wife at his side and an officer, stiff at attention, addressing them both. The caption was "The Tale of a Glorious End". He thought of the night he and Clark had buried Eccles — his right arm had been stuck out stiff at right angles and they had to break it to be able to stuff him into the narrow grave in the moonlight. Jem Cotton had lost one of his mates from his side on a dark night, his pockets stuffed with Mills bombs and never so much as a whisper.

He ran over the bridge with his rifle clutched firmly in his right hand. He tried to run straight through the smoke so that he would not go over the side into the river. He could not swim and preferred roasting to drowning. First the flames seared his hand and then the side of his face, but there was nothing to do but go straight on. He ran faster and faster, gasping and coughing, and suddenly he was out of it, uniform just singeing, his body drenched in sweat, his heart pounding in his ears. Khaki-clad figures ran up to him, beating at his tunic, grabbing at his arm. "Why didn't you throw your ammunition belts away before coming through those flames?" shouted a sergeant. Dick looked down at himself, bristling with hot cartridges. An orderly ran up and examined his burns: "Jump into the lorry, you need treatment."

Dick climbed in among the others. It was a strange feeling, going to get a wound treated after three years' fighting, but he had not asked for it. Somebody offered him a cigarette and, as he smoked it quietly, he thought of Garswood and Billinge and Wigan and Bolton and of his last leave and his next parcel.

*   *   *   *   *   *   *

Min said to Dick, "They'll never take thee in'th'army. Look at thi black big toe."

In November the Belgian sentry ran over to him:

"La guerre finie"

"Let's hope it bloody well is."

CHAPTER TWENTY-FIVE

The Top Shop

Halfway up the Main Street of Billinge, exactly opposite the Methodist Chapel, stood a big, stone building which used to be the village general store. The official name of it was the Blackleyhurst Co-operative Society, probably named after Blackleyhurst Hall since it appears that Sammy Stock was one of the founders. It has been set up by a handful of Billinge men when Jim Parr was young and at the time of the Great War was owned by a hundred customers, more by some than by others. The minimum share was for one pound and the dividend was paid every three months, usually at a rate of about two shillings in the pound. The name of the store was too long for any Billinger to attempt on a daily basis, so it was always called the Top Shop.

After the beginning of the War in 1914 a position became vacant at the shop for a girl to scrub counters and floors one day a week for a wage of two shillings. Minnie Parr applied for the job as she thought there would be a future in it, and as nobody else applied she was appointed. Her scrubbing was so efficient that after one month they took her on three days a week and raised her wage to 8 shillings. Between scrubbing she served customers and spent most of the day running up and down the steep, open wooden stairs fetching hams, bacon, corn, bran and pigmeal, which were never kept below. Minnie was the fourth and most junior employee under Liz Giddy the manageress, Alice Haselden and Hetty Rigby. The hours were from 8 in the morning till 11 at night, as they closed after the last customer had been served. The last client was usually an old Irishwoman in a cottage on Gorsey Brow who used to snooze in her armchair in front of the fire and they would have to go and wake her up and take her back to the shop to get the order, so they could close up and go home. The old woman used to doze on the bench in the shop while they were wrapping up the food. Mrs. Brimelow, another customer, often fell asleep in the shop during the day while you were talking to her.

After 6 months, Hetty Rigby left and Minnie graduated to full-time employment and one pound a week. It was ding-dong all week long, for the shop sold most of the everyday necessities and many of the people nearby would drop in four or five times a day, ordering this and that sporadically, trading news and gossip, fetching their tales of woe, begging credit, eyeing the travellers and escaping for a few precious minutes from the drudgery of their grates and flagstones and cooking meals.

The shop would buy three or four pigs a week from the local farmers and cut these up to sell pork, bacon and ham. The bacon and ham was cured and put in the cellar. Friday night was Pig Night, when all the customers used to assemble to witness the distribution of the different cuts of pork. For years there had been constant quarrels and arguments over who got what and finally the management decided to divide the pieces according to a Pig Lottery, and even then there was bother. All the cuts of pork were displayed on a big wooden trestle in full view of the contestants. Those present were counted and the same number of pieces of paper were put into a hat. Everyone dipped and drew a number which indicated the order of choice. Number One had first pick, and so forth. The one who had first choice usually paraded up and down in front of the goodies for a full minute or two, aggravating the humour of those low down in the picking order. If you were in the middle or high forties you knew you were getting ribs or neck and if you came too late to draw out of the hat you wound up with the trotters and pig's tail. The Irish used to make an excellent stew out of pig's tail. The shop kept the head and boiled it to sell, while the liver and lights went into the savoury ducks and the blood was used for black puddings. Billinge has always made the most of its pigs.

The Top Shop sold sugar, rice and flour, kept in two-hundredweight sacks upstairs. Downstairs there were potatoes, peas, most other vegetables, coffee, tea, bread, sausages, eggs, pies, savoury ducks, black puddings, big barrels of treacle and syrup, curtains, towels, stockings, crockery and fancy mugs, aprons, chair-covers, rubbing stones, the softer donkey stones, chalk for doing the

The Top Shop

borders, yellow scouring soap for scrubbing the table tops, blue mottled soap for washing clothes, soda for boiling, whitewash for walls (later green, red and yellow "colouring"became more fashionable). The great hams were hung from the hooks at the top of the stairs and paraffin was kept in big tanks. The paraffin man came once a week on Thursdays. By Wednesday most of the Billingers were running out of paraffin for their lamps and they would drop in on Wednesdays and Thursdays to leave their bottles in a long line round the skirting boards, where they would often get knocked over by rats playing skittles with them during the night.

Billinge was infested with rats at the time and Sergeant Mare one morning saw a whole army of them marching up Main Street, otherwise deserted, at half past six. Seeing that they were"moving house", he prudently stepped aside to let them pass and then followed them up the street to watch them wheel right and all disappear down a grid just a few yards behind the shop. For a long time afterwards they played havoc with the stores, as they could gain access through the wooden floors almost at will. Minnie often used to run across them in the morning when she opened the shop and saw how they carried eggs and tomatoes down through the holes. She took on cats which were frightened to death (for the rats were huge and well-fed) and another called Timmy which did little but eat the cheese in the rat-traps, but finally along came a little black and white cat called Rudolph, an undersized specimen if there ever was one, and the situation changed radically in a few days. Cats are much quicker than rats, which meant that while these vicious rodents could not catch fleeing Timmy, neither could they escape from advancing Rudolph. Rudolph not only pounced on rats, but ate them up on the spot, and the word soon got around. He liked heads, but used to leave tails, which Minnie found on the shop floor in the morning. For a month or so he got through two or three a night, now and again leaving a body upstairs when he had tummyache. He peered down the holes in the floor during the day and hid among the sacks of food upstairs at night. Then one memorable night he caught five and that settled the issue. At dawn, with Rudolph safely locked inside the shop, the huge rat horde came up through the grid and marched purposefully down Main Street to wherever they had come from. Neither the Top Shop nor the unfortunate Rudolph ever saw them again.

The War dragged on, Alice and Liz Giddy got married and Minnie became manageress at 30 shillings a week. Sugar was rationed at half a pound a head, butter at a quarter pound. Bacon was scarce and the shop started getting torpedoed bacon, which arrived covered in thick green slime. They spent hours scrubbing and scouring it with boiling water. The colour was never right, but people would eat it in the end . There were more objections to the wild boars' heads with their big ears and teeth. They used to chop it up as well as they could but customers used to bring the pieces back if they found teeth in them. Jam started to taste funny and folk swore it was made of turnips, but the most scandalous and oft-repeated rumour was that the corned beef was made of dead soldiers. It was sold in big seven-pound tins and one afternoon Sall Tazzle streaked into the store in a frenzy, waving a calico bag which she held under Minnie's nose, and then threw down on the counter. It was a soldier's cutlery bag, which she had just pulled out of the corned beef for Tuesday dinner. Minnie said it must have been a joke on the part of some workers in the canning factory, but she was eyed suspiciously by the village women for the rest of that week.

In fact, some of the regulars were quite a handful at the best of times. Often short of cash, under pressure from hungry, bad-tempered husbands coming back from the pit, they would fly into the shop in a panic, wildly scrutinizing the shelves, rummaging in their purses and grabbing anything that took their fancy.

"Ee, Christ, they're comin wom an ah've nowt ont table. Min, han yo any bloody chops?"

Women would send up their envoys four or five times a day to report on the state of the ham.

"Hag thee up tot Top Shop an see if th'am's it middle."

"Hey, Min, how's th'am?"

"It's not so good to-day" or

"Oh, it's sittin up and pickin' a bit."

One fat woman from the Rant throughout the whole of her married life used to make all her meals sitting at a table next to the fire. There was an oven in the grate and she used to have all her children and relations fetch everything to her where she sat — potatoes, flour, water, milk, meat, pepper, salt and so on. Her family would go all the way up Main Street to the Top Shop to buy what was needed. She traded there for years and Min never even saw her. The table had a long woollen stocking round each leg — a common sight in Billinge at the time. They said that it protected them from wear. Well-off families used new stockings; poorer people had to use darned ones.

People brought their problems as well as their orders:

"Min, Min, I've lost me false teeth — I've looked everywheer and cawn't find 'em. Dost think I've swallowed 'em?

"Polly, if tha'd swallowed 'em tha wouldn't be standing here, go an look under t'sofy."

"Min, somebody's shit in our front garden again. What shall I do?"

"Sergeant Mare says keep it for now, an if nobody claims it i'three days it's yores."

The good sergeant, too, occasionally had his problems:

"Min, somebody stole sixteen o' Joe Middlehurst's lambs int middle ot neet — hast any idea who it could be?"

"I've no idea, Sergeant."

For the next two weeks there were three families in the Cockshut who bought

no meat at all. When Mare dropped in again he said:
"Ave they towd they who did them lambs, Min?"
"No, Sergeant Mare."
"Aye, but ah bet it shows on thi bloody books."

*   *   *   *   *   *   *   *

People came in the shop and sang out their orders not in English, or
Lancashire dialect, but in the strange code which old-fashioned Billingers used,
which was not slang or jargon, but more like a type of argot — completely
incomprehensible even to folk from the next village. A typical order sounded
something like this:
"Ah'll take a bottle o'sausage alicker, half a pound o'round rings, a jar o'
pussarves, two bovanas, a pound o' wide wash, some pay-cock blue, a bottle o'
Harry Paddy, a pound o' stutters and a gill o' stinkers."
Most of the women concerned would not have been able to call these things
by their proper names, any more than they could have called each other by their
proper names. They lived in a world of their own with the "Labour in Vain"
and Birchley to the south and the "Stork" and "Eagle and Child" to the north.
People who lived beyond these boundaries were regarded as foreigners,
including the travellers who brought their soap and fancy mugs.
In Billinge at the turn of the century, as in Japan during the isolationist
Tokugawa period, "foreigners" were ridiculed at the slightest excuse, and even
people from nearby Garswood and Downall Green had to have all their wits
about them whenever they visited the village. Hugh Parr and Min and a few
others, more outward-looking with their trade contacts and keen on travelling
further afield themselves, were much more lenient and even friendly to
strangers, but could not always protect them from the inhabitants. Travelling
salesmen were often easy meat. Now, in all the time that Min had been in the
Top Shop she had found that she could sell virtually anything these men
brought her, except one particular product. A few years earlier, they had
bought in a fairly large consignment of a new ointment called "Mustavit",
which sold in threepenny tins and was supposed to cure rheumatism and,
actually, anything else which might ail you. The ointment was hot to the skin
when it was applied and the first Billinger who bought a tin condemned it
outright as a quack remedy. Nobody bought any after that. As the years passed,
the ill-fated tins went higher and higher on the shelves and lower and lower in
price. Finally they ended at a halfpenny a tin, still unsold, on the top shelf under
two inches of dust. There they remained until one day the quaintest travelling
salesman ever seen in Billinge came prancing down Main Street with his
suitcase. He was a midget of a man, wearing a black bowler hat, black suit, white
shirt, red waistcoat, blue tie and spats. His suit was so much too big for him that
he had to roll up both the sleeves of his coat and his trouser legs. His bowler hat

came down over both ears. He bobbed up and down as he walked and by the time he had covered the distance from the Church to the Top Shop he had a Pied Piper following of a dozen layabouts, all of whom stuck their heads round the door to see what he was selling. There were several customers in at the time and the man plonked his suitcase on the counter with an air of confidence and told Min and the rest of audience that he had brought a sensational new product which was going to revolutionize the life of the village. He went on about this for some time and indeed it began to sound as if people's lives really were going to be brightened up considerably by this new invention, for he had a persuasive way of putting things, in spite of his high-pitched whine of a voice and his habit of saying "sh" instead of "s". In fact he kept them all on tenterhooks for five minutes or so, and some of them began to wonder how they had managed to live to the age they had without the help of this thing that he had in his suitcase. It seemed incredible that you could get something as beneficial as this for as little as sixpence a tin, so that when he finally clicked back the fastens of his case and unveiled his marvellous product ("Mustavit") he was greeted with ten seconds of unbelieving silence before the whole assembly burst into an uncontrollable fit of laughter, jeers and taunts. Suffice to say that he was subjected to every imaginable verbal indignity and fled back up Main Street as fast as his short legs would carry him, pursued by such comments as: "Yesh, and it'sh good for making you shit, too!"

In the midst of their poverty, the Billingers usually managed to pay their bills in the end and Min knew how long she could wait for the money and whom she should give credit to. The only thing they would not pay for was their drapery. You do not eat drapery and so, while the food was paid for regularly, drapery remained for ever in the "receivables" account. Min finally got sick of this, so she asked one of the travellers to introduce "Coupon Tea". This was normal tea but you paid threepence extra for the coupon attached and when you had so many coupons you paid for your drapery with them. The scheme did not work very well until the traveller hit upon the idea of charging the threepence extra for a *special* tea (in reality the same as they had been buying for the last twenty years). He had printed on the packets "This tea is specially manufactured to suit the water of this district". From then on, that was how the people of Billinge paid for their drapery.

*   *   *   *   *   *   *

During the 1926 Strike, Min had some difficult decisions to make. Some of her customers were able to carry on paying their bills, but it was only a small minority. Most of them did not know what a bank account was and for years they had simply been paying for their food out of the wage that their husbands brought home at the end of the week. Neither did they have any stocks of food, since there were no refrigerators (only cold "slabs") and in any case they were eating food as a rule within hours of its leaving the shop. After the first week of the strike, practically all of them were flat broke and many had families of seven or eight to feed. They were quite bewildered in the situation and asked Min what they should do.

Min knew that the only thing was to extend credit immediately, for these people made up ninety per cent of her regular customers. Not only did they have to eat, but they would remember every move she made. She convinced the Committee that she had to have a free hand and after that the customers simply signed for what they took. Nobody expected the strike to last for twenty-odd weeks. It was beautiful weather and there was hardly any rain for 6 months. The strikers hung around, went for walks, talked, argued, hoped — and waited. In the Skitters, Dick Lancaster and his friends sailed matchsticks downstream at tuppence a race and a lot of the men got brown all over for the first time in their lives.

The Top Shop's bank balance sank lower and lower and finally went into the red. Min then took out all the shares and used them up for more food. Finally she asked Higgson and Ormrods and Collins (the suppliers) for credit, and they, like Min some months earlier, had no alternative but to comply. She promised she would never marry or leave her job until every penny had been paid off and every share restored, although the rumours were out that the shares had been disposed of, and the shareholders (some of them with one pound in) bobbed in daily to ask how their investment stood. She fended them off with white lies and pointed out that the building itself as well as the stocks (including "Mustavit") all belonged to them.

That way they all got through the Strike without mishap and, in fact, they paid the Shop back every penny. In the months that followed, entire families' wages went straight to Min and everything but absolute living necessities was cut out until the debts had been repaid. With all the shares in the safe, a new shop floor, new lamps, a thousand pounds in the bank and a roaring business once more in being, Min eventually left and got married.

Within three months of her departure, half the custom was gone and the Top Shop continued to decline through the thirties and the Second World War until it collapsed completely and the hulk of the building was sold to someone in another trade. With broken windows and boarded-up doors, it presented a sad sight to those who had known it in its hey-day.

One thing is for sure — if the rats ever come back, Rudolph's ghost will haunt them.

CHAPTER TWENTY SIX

Hugh Parr and the Methodists

Hugh Parr was born on the 1st March, 1873, the seventh of James and Susannah Parr's twelve children. He quickly became the favourite of both parents, on account of his good looks, intelligence and zest for life. He was, in return, devoted to both his father and his mother, declaring he would never marry while Susannah was alive and consequently remained the most eligible bachelor in Billinge till he was 36.

A contemporary of Winston Churchill (whom he admired greatly), Hugh resembled his famous compatriot in the way he brimmed over with life force and tried his hand at virtually anything. Leaving school at the age of twelve, he began as a stable boy at Greenfield House. At fourteen, he took it into his head to emigrate to America and spent several days trying to get a boat at Liverpool docks before his parents located him and hauled him back to Billinge. He decided to educate himself further and for the next fifteen years rarely went to bed before three, taking one exam after another and reading anything he could get his hands on. He became a miner, an insurance man, a pit manager, a coal merchant, a Mine Inspector, a co-op manager, a shopowner and eventually a farmer (he bought Slack Farm). That was just to make a living; on top of this he was Sunday School Superintendent, Church Trustee, organist, choirmaster, local preacher (50 years), J.P., official of the Red Cross Society, the National Savings Movement, the Workers' Education Association and Billinge District Council. In his later years he became Chairman of the Council and his writings on various subjects earned him the reputation of being the Village Poet. In April, 1953, just after he had turned 80, he took his pen and wrote "A Short History of Billinge", which is the most complete description of the village that has come to my notice.

Hugh showed his sense of humour already as a boy. One day he was given a raspberry jam sandwich at Greenfield House and found three wasps fighting for their life in the jam as he was about to eat it. He took the sandwich back to the kitchen saying, "This 'ere wasp butty, I don't think you warmed it up enough – three o'mine are beginning to pull round." So they took out some very old cheese to make him another sandwich. When he had caught a whiff of the cheese, he said, "You needn't have fetched that cheese from t'larder. If I'd have whistled for it, it would have come runnin' and jumped ont table. Leave it another two days, an I'll have to fetch me gun and shoot it for you."

When he preached, his eyes laughed at you. In a way he was a bit of a hot

Billinge Methodist Chapel

gospeller, though less so than his father, for he had much more time for human weakness. He would tell the congregation what they had probably done wrong that week, and he was probably right. After Hugh had discussed your various foibles, you did not feel so bad about them. There was nothing you could tell Hugh about drinking or gambling or deceit or vanity, for when a man has been brought up in Long Fold he is likely to be an expert on all of them. Hugh, furthermore, was one of those psychic Billingers who only had to take a good look at you to know where you had been last night. He never drank or gambled, but you felt that if he had done, he would have enjoyed it. Following the straight and narrow path himself, he had boundless compassion for those who fell by the wayside and at times seemed quite fond of good, solid sinners. You felt that when Hugh Parr went to Heaven (and there was not much doubt about that) the first thing he would take up with St. Peter would be the question of a few extra places for wayward Billingers.

Those of us who knew him in his old age remember many things about him: his sprightly figure and proud swagger, twinkling eyes and delicate nose, his hoarse shout and righteous anger, the occasional engaging profanity; but above all, you remember him as the man who loved his village. He was not just a Billinger, he was *the* Billinger, and seems to have been the first Billinger to feel the urgent need to produce a portrait of Billinge and its inhabitants. He had seen Billinge during the seventy most interesting years of its long history and at the age of 80 he felt compelled to put some of it together. He writes in the beginning of his "History":

> "Musing, this April evening in 1953, with the red glow of the setting sun permeating my very soul and body with a warmth and fragrance inexpressible and uncomprehended by anyone but a native of this place .... the fragrance of living ...

Hugh knew what a special place Billinge was and he was determined to tell people:

> "I have often said this is my native place – Billinge – but saying this has never given me the satisfaction I hoped for – I wanted something deeper, higher, nobler. It has not, nor ever can be attained, or my hope realised until I adopt something definite and concrete. Therefore, I intend to put on record not merely what I have said about my native place, Billinge, but rather to reveal what is indelibly engraved on my heart and in so doing, other lives may be enriched and my joy enhanced .... "

His poetic "Short History of Billinge", in his flowing, Victorian style, is available for all to read. His father, Gentleman Jim, had, 60 years earlier been obsessed by the beauty of the village. He had written:

> "On the 25th of May, 1892, when viewing the scenery around my cottage home at Long Fold about eight in the evening, my whole soul and mind were entirely wrapped up in the thought of the goodness and mercies of God. The beautiful green fields, the foliage on the trees, filled me with praise and thanksgiving .... "

Hugh, at the age of 80, was still entranced by the Billinge landscape:

> ".... this village of ours, with its shady, leaf-bedecked lanes and by-roads, fragrant

with the perfume of wild flowers on every copse and in every cranny, carpets of bluebells beautifying the paths we tread, as we drink . . . . refreshing goblets filled with a pure and uncontaminated energising atmosphere . . . . "

Walking down Shaley Brow he writes:

"Look, there lies our Promised Land . . . . reaching to the sea, which can be seen on the one hand and the hills of Wales before us, encompassing a fertile plain to supply the needs of man and beast . . . . "

Like his father, he felt that all this beauty was his birthright:

"You and I may stand on Billinge Hill and view the landscape o'er, seeing with delight the rolling meadows, woodlands, streams, pathways, houses large and small, church and chapel, hearing the song of the birds, and can say: all these belong to me, not because I own them, but because I love them".

While the natural beauty remained, Hugh Parr felt that much of the old Billinge was slipping away. He fought for the retention of the name "London Fields", when streets were being named, he objected to the cutting down of the age-old chestnut trees down Long Fold, he is nostalgic in his writings about the passing of some of the traditional features of the village:

"Alas, the smithy is no more. Gone, the village parliament. Gone, the laughter of children, only the memories of days that were rough and happy remain to sweeten the lives of the old folk, but to the modern generation, just nothing . . . ."

His fears for the youth of the village in the 1950s were well-founded. From being a centre of social activity up to 1914, Billinge had declined to the point where in 1955 (though still possessing 13 pubs) it had become a community of

6,000 people with no cinema, no bank, no public hall, no barber's, no chemist's shop, no park, no railway station, no taxi services, no clothes- or shoe-shops, no cricket or football field, one solitary public convenience and virtually no amenities for recreation or self-betterment.

Things have, of course, changed since then and modern comforts have come in to temper the old, rugged life style. What Hugh wanted most of all was the people of the village to know their past and to keep their character as Billingers. In his own words:

> "Let us then, ye people of Billinge, for the love of the parents who bore us, and the glory of God who created us, ever strive . . . . to maintain, worthily, the heritage we have received, and to pass it on, unscathed, to future generations; as Gradely Folk."

* * * * * * * *

In this century, Hugh was Billinge's leading Methodist, a role inherited on his father's death in 1911 and for which he was well suited.

We have seen that Billinge, though predominantly Anglican, never fully abandoned the Roman Catholic faith, and saw the erection of Birchley St. Mary's in 1828. In the early 1840s, the first rumblings of Methodism were heard in St. Helens and a few years later a certain Miss Jackson was sent to extend the campaign to Billinge, where she travelled round in a caravan and organised Camp Meetings. Hers was not the most difficult task, since Billingers would always listen to someone who had something new to say and the independent nature of some of those who heard her speak led to the formation of a small congregation, who rented two stone cottages to hold their services. These became known as "The Cottage Rooms" and stood in close proximity to the site of the present Chapel. One of the most ardent believers in the new faith was Joseph Anderton, Susannah's grandfather.

To begin with, preachers from St. Helens (where the St. Helens Society was designated a "Branch on Trial") came on foot to deliver their sermons, and it is said that some of them failed to arrive for their appointments and were ticked off soundly by the angry pioneers who had missed their week-end entertainment. They were mainly coal miners and nail makers and by 1864 they had grown sufficiently in number to ask the landlord to build an extra room for a Sunday School. In 1866, however, money was raised for the purchase of a piece of land on Main Street, upon which a permanent place of worship could be erected. The cost of the land was £32.0s.0d. and the deed for the land was signed by all the original trustees – Edward Webster, Henry Burrows, John Holland, James Shaw, John Harrison, William Knowles, Thomas Heaton, William Fishwick and John Bradburn. Webster was sent to St. Helens to discuss the matter of a new chapel at Billinge and a mortgage was negotiated to enable them to complete the present chapel at the end of 1868 at a total cost of £326. 0s. 0d.

Hugh Parr

Members of the Society contributed £1 each towards the building of the chapel (almost as much as a week's wage) and each man laboured in its construction. The stone was local (from the Delf at Crank) – a quarry owned by a Yorkshire business man known as "Yorkshire Charley".

The chapel is a small, rectangular construction, austere and unadorned, but set high above the road and not lacking in simple dignity. Lighting was supplied by oil lamps suspended from the ceiling and also smaller swivel oil lamps attached to the pulpit. Heating depended on a 4ft 6ins. stove which stood on a round iron plate at the right hand side of the chapel. The pews standing nearest to it had their paint scorched off at intervals and it is said that little boys sitting close to the stove in winter used to drowse off in the heat and were only prevented from falling on it by watchful mothers in the pews behind. Gentleman James Parr became the first Sunday School Superintendent after the chapel was built and his second daughter, Tet, was the first girl to be baptised there in 1869, sharing the honour with Levi Heaton, the first boy. (It was not until 1948 that the first couple were married in the church – Mr. and Mrs. W. Roby, (the bride being Gentleman Jim's great-grand-daughter.) The descendants of the Parr family formed the bulk of the congregation (his daughter Caroline, who married Jack Lowe, had twelve children, most of whom became pillars of Methodism) but the chapel was supported by different branches of many of the old Billinge families, among them the Mathers, Heatons, Cadmans, Wildes, Grimshaws, Winstanleys, Andertons, Martlews, Bellises, Cunliffes, Bradburns and Cartwrights.

The first Harvest Festival Service was a great success and such were the quantities of fruit and flowers stacked around the newly-decorated chapel, that fears arose about their premature removal before the service on the Sunday. Thomas Heaton, one of the original trustees, hit upon the idea of nailing up the back door, as well as locking it, to make things even more difficult for would-be intruders. This was done with great ceremony by the member in charge of driving in six-inch nails and they all trooped righteously homewards, leaving the front door wide open all night. God watched over the fruit anyway.

Edward Webster, the first organist, was another trustee who did not trust absolutely everybody. It is said that he used to stuff his harmonium with newspapers before leaving it unattended. He did not like anyone else playing it.

In 1914 the Platt family came from Cheshire to work the Arley Mine Coal Seams in Billinge. They were strong Methodists and Mrs. Platt formed a Women's Meeting, which thrived for many years. Her daughter Peggy founded the Women's Guild in 1945. A Church Hall was erected in 1959 on a piece of land purchased at the bottom of Main Street, almost on the spot where the "Labour in Vain" had housed its happy gatherings for many a decade.

Not long after his father's death, Hugh Parr became Sunday School Superintendent and began his long rule as torch bearer for Billinge Methodism.

He had learnt a lot in his youth from the frequent encounters he and his father had had with other religious leaders such as Dean Powell, Canon St. George and Canon Miller – all men of great character and considerable intellect. Hugh revelled in the flexibility which the Methodist form of service allows. In the pulpit he could dress as he pleased, say what he liked and vary the length of his talk at will. The warm intimacy of the smaller chapels and the proximity of the congregation suited his rhetorical, humorous, almost roguish style. His arguments were classical and there was always poetry in what he said, but it was poetry close to the earth, or emanating from it, and the pitmen in the congregation always knew what he meant, and remembered his words.

It was only natural that as a local preacher, he should be a favourite in the chapels for miles around. One of the places he liked to preach at best was the Methodist Chapel in Downall Green, where the front three pews on both sides were solid with miners, among them Jem Eaves, the son of Tom Eaves the Billinge blacksmith, Jem Nicholson, John Wildman, the formidable Lancaster brothers, John Houghton, Tom Hampson, Tommy Woods, James Gorner, Jimmy Fazackerley, David and Tom Grimshaw and many others who worked in the pits of Billinge, Winstanley and Ashton. These impressive rows of face-workers, regular as clockwork every Sunday night, presented a fine challenge to a visiting preacher, and Hugh Parr felt that at Downall Green he really had something to get his teeth into. Jake Lancaster, in the meantime, had graduated to Sunday School teacher himself and Hugh knew that to make any impression at all on Jake and his colleagues you had to give all you had got. It appeared that Jake had his own inimitable style of teaching youngsters in Sunday School and Hugh Parr always maintained that he told the story of David and Goliath in a manner the boys never forgot. It was supposed to go something like this:

"To-day I'm tellin' you about a giant called Goliath and a little lad called David."

"Go on, tell us, Mr. Lancaster."

"Israelites were feighting t'Philistines and they stood on top o' two hills facin' each other. Now, the idea wuz, instead of everybody feightin', they would pick out one mon apiece and these two 'ud have combat. And whoever won – his army would triumph and spoil the others' tents."

"Go on."

"Now, t' Philistines, they had a huge champion named Goliath, a giant wi' a face as could stand cloggin', an he would do their feightin' for 'em."

"How big was he?"

"Six cubits and a span."

"How big is that?"

"He was twice as big as I am."

"Gosh."

"So he comes with all his armour an helmet o' brass an coat o' mail, an he wuz frickenin' fert see, I can tell you. An he sez, I defy the armies of Israel this day; give me a man, that we may fight together."

"And what happened?"

"Nobody moved. They were frickent deeath on him."

"What happened next?"

"Well, there was this shepherd lad David, mindin' his father's sheep. His three brothers were in th'army on top of th'hill, and his fayther sends him wi'some jackbit for his brothers."

"What was it?"

"Bread and cheese. They needed somethin' when they'd had an eyeful of Goliath. Anyroad, David comes wi'this meight, and they're all in a bad mood, an tell him off a bit, an try fert send him wom again, seein' as he's only a little lad. But he has plenty of pluck, see, an when he hears about Goliath, he goes to Saul an sez as he'll take him on, just like that."

"Gosh."

"Well, Saul laughs, an his brothers laugh, an old Goliath nearly guffaws hissel sick, but David goes down to the brook and takes a staff to show 'em he means business and goes and draws near the Philistine."

"Go on."

"Well Goliath sez, well, little lad, am I a dog that thou comest to me with staves? An he gives David a black look, reckonin' he'll turn tail an go back to his sheep, but David stares him in the eye and cusses him good and proper, just to get him to come a bit nearer."

"An what happened?"

"Well, t'giant has had enough o'this, an he pulls himself up to his full six cubits and drew nigh."

"An then?"

"Well, David puts one o'these smooth stones in his sling an he whirls it round and round, and round and round, just like this, round and round and round and round, and you could fair hear this sling hummin' and hummin' and then, aw at once . . . . whish . . . . he lets it go and slang it . . . . an . . . . *busho* . . . . it hits Goliath smack in the middle of his forehead, an sinks in, two or three inches."

"Two or three inches?"

"That's right."

"Whew . . . . did it hurt?

"Did what hurt?"

"The stone sinking in, did it hurt 'im?"

"Hurt 'im? Hurt 'im? It fleckin' well kilt 'im!"

Hugh loved to tell this story as an example of Jake's dry, Lancashire humour, for he greatly admired this blunt, independent miner and his simple, courteous

brother. Jake and Tom, who remembered Hugh's promise as a youngster and
the eloquence and verve of his father, were delighted to have him planned at
Downall Green once or twice a year and there would be few empty seats when
Hugh climbed up to the pulpit. There would be the two dozen miners, best
suits on and in stiff white collars, their arms folded across their chests and sitting
bolt upright like so many pit props. If they were enthusiastic about the choice of
speaker, they did not show it. Immobile and attentive, their eyes remained
rivited on those of the preacher for the whole of the service; not once would they
betray what was going on in their minds. It was an unnerving experience for
many a visiting minister, used perhaps to adjusting his message according to the
feedback he was getting from his congregation. With Hugh it was different, for
he knew the psychology of these men. He adapted simile and metaphor to their
taste, took his parable from the mine or the mill, shared secrets with them,
showed them the masculinity of his humour, re-phrased the text and its
messages in words they enjoyed, laughed over their sins like the whole thing was
just a mental aberration, for men the stuff they were made of all had their tickets
booked on the Hugh Parr char-à-banc to Heaven, which in any case differed
little from Billinge or the Miners' Home in Blackpool.

Halfway through his sermon, they would begin to melt. Tom Lancaster
would be the first to show his appreciation, nodding morosely every time Hugh
made a point of some significance. Jimmy Fazackerley would smile and chuckle
in approval and one by one the pitmen would discard their impassivity, flashing
Hugh the odd grin, relaxing imperceptibly in their pews and occasionally
unfolding their arms and putting their hands on their knees. The Grimshaw
brothers would be among the last to bend, often only during the summing up.
The only man who remained completely inscrutable throughout the whole
performance was Jake Lancaster. It was one of Hugh Parr's secret ambitions to
extract a smile out of Jake in church. He had once thrown the book at them for
an hour and a half – a sermon Wesley himself would have been proud of – and
Jake had sat through the whole thing like a stone statue. Hugh swore that he
could go into the pulpit and preach standing on his head and Jake would not bat
an eyelid.

*   *   *   *   *   *   *

Hugh never did manage to get him to show any outward sign of approbation,
but achieved his ambition in a roundabout kind of way one Sunday night in
1935. As the Billinger mopped away the perspiration from his forehead in the
vestry after a no-holds-barred service, Tommy Woods popped his head round
the door and whispered he had seen Jake put half a crown in the collection.

Four Billinge women

Jem Bellis

CHAPTER TWENTY-SEVEN

Jem Bellis

And so time moved on. Jake and Tom and Hugh became old men and their children grew up and had children. Jake's eldest son, Bob, inherited the eloquence of his grandfather, went into politics and became the Mayor of Wigan. Taciturn, humorous Dick Lancaster, the fourth of the five sons and the one who most resembled Jake in character, married Minnie Parr, his childhood sweetheart.

Tom, getting weaker in his old age, retired after 60 years down the mine. Jake, still on the coal face and as strong as a horse at 74, completed 65 years in the pit, before suddenly quitting at the end of a morning shift.

The thirties came to a close and the war years and those that followed were ones of transition for Billinge and its inhabitants. The village grew rapidly, old stone cottages were pulled down, red brick houses were put up in their place. Nail-making and chair-making had gone forever and, as the coal seams in Billinge, Ashton and the Wigan area were worked out, the Billinge miner, too, disappeared. The Bankes family still occupy Winstanley Hall and the Mather family continue their long tradition as physicians of Billinge, but the Lowes, Heatons, Birchalls, Andertons and other old Billinge families are now greatly outnumbered by those who have moved in from elsewhere. I hope these few chapters will help our new Billingers to know their village and its past a little better and serve to enrich in some way their own experience here.

In 1968 St. Aidan's celebrated its two hundred and fiftieth anniversary and the same year marked the centenary of Billinge Methodist Chapel. About that time Jem Bellis was one of the few surviving great story-tellers of Billinge and I would like to end my account of the old Billingers by writing a few words about this man, who perhaps typified the people of the village more than any other.

* * * * * * * *

Mary Ann Parr, the eldest child of Gentleman Jim and Susannah, married an unassuming collier from St. Helens named Teddy Bellis and their four children were brought up in Long Fold. Ruth was the first, then Maria, Jem and Ned. Ruth was quiet like her father, as was Jem in his youth, while Ned bubbled over with life and Maria was the family beauty. When Ned fell in the Great War, Mary Ann died inside, too. She never laughed again and spent most of the day standing at the garden gate looking towards France. She had been a fighter by nature, a fierce and possessive mother, the toughest of all the Parrs along with Tet, but she lived her last fifteen years in a personal twilight.

Maria and her mother were inseparable. The younger daughter had much of Ned's liveliness, she could sing and mimic, and had beautiful regular features and rich, auburn hair. In her mid-twenties she had rheumatic fever, which left her with a weakened heart, a condition shared by her mother. At the end of 1930 both Maria and Mary Ann were taken ill and confined to bed. They lay in the two upstairs rooms at 37 Carr Mill Road for six months, each one on her deathbed. Mary Ann, at 68 years of age, felt old and weak and knew she was dying. Maria, on the other hand, was in full flesh at 42 and had every intention to live.

As their hearts grew weaker, they were unable to leave their beds and for the last six weeks they never saw each other, but shouted back and forth from where they lay. They had never been apart for over forty years and each one was terrified that the other would leave her alone. Every hour one called to ask how the other felt and Mary Ann kept on living to spare her daughter the shock of her death. Poor Jem, Ruth and Teddy were besides themselves in grief as the last cries became more pathetic:

"Don't leave me, Maria."

"Don't leave me alone, mother."

They both died on the same day but the end was merciful, for neither knew that the other had gone. Maria went unconcious on the Wednesday and Mary Ann died on Sunday at noon, to be followed by Maria at midnight. They were both buried on the following Wednesday.

*   *   *   *   *   *   *   *

The family had seen its share of tragedy and Teddy, Ruth and Jem all lived to be old. When Ned and Maria had been alive, Jem had seemed shy and retiring by comparison, but when he eventually took over as head of the family something quite remarkable happened. Year by year his character developed and he seemed to incorporate all the qualities which his dead mother, brother and sister had possessed, as if he had to do the living for all of them. He showed Mary Ann's fierce temper and her quick tongue, Maria's generosity and powers of mimicry, Ned's good humour and sense of fun. As Jem grew older, the twinkle in his eye grew merrier and he developed a style of oratory and story-telling which made him the centre of any gathering he went to. He had only to poke his bald head round a door, wag a reproving finger at someone, look fearfully over his shoulder, tuck his chin in and glare at somebody and everyone present would hold his breath to hear what he had to say. He was an old Billinger through and through, with all the beliefs, prejudices, legends, wit and superstitions that went with it. He knew more jokes, tales, puzzles and conundrums than any man I have ever met and he never told me the same one twice. He had a manner of telling tales all of his own and a strange way of stringing together non-sequiturs so that they made sense – if you were a Billinger, that is. It is impossible to give an accurate discription of the effect he would have on a listener, since so much depended on his sense of timing and timbre of voice, but the following examples of his dialogue may convey some idea of the enjoyment I gained during hundreds of hours of conversation with him: (dialect diluted)

"Jem, what was Billinge like in the old days?"

He would frown at you hard for several moments without replying, as if he were wondering which newspaper you were from. Then he would go over to a chair, point to its seat with his right forefinger, arm extended:

"Why....sit thee dehn here while ah tell thee."

You would think he was going to tell you the way you wanted to hear it, but he would jump straight into the driver's seat with the non-sequiturs:

"What, wi'me soon turnin' eighty and booath me dowters down wi' flu and our Rachel sayin' as I'm hard t'live with, tha wants t'know abeht th'owd Billingers, dosto?"

"Well, I...."

"There was Barm Johnny, he wore t'same nasty cap for fifteen year and Sergeant Mare towd him it 'ud make a bloody good stew and Dancin' Jack, he used to go round all the pubs and do his clog dance for free booze."

"You mean he...."

"And t'same mon used to keep pigeons for racin' and there was a sparrow come every day for three months and sat on top of his pigeon coop – it wuz allus t'same sparrow – so finally Jack went off to St. Helens to buy it a cage, an when he come back wit cage t'sparrow had gone."

"Incredible."

"An they say as Dick Turpin's mare Bess is buried in Hamilton's Wood, thanose."

"It is?"

"They're cawd Turpin Fields, aren't they? And what about Belter?"

"Belter?"

"Belter an his horse."

"What happened?"

"He had an owd horse cawd Bill, as used pull his spring cart back from Wiggin. And it wuz gettin' a bit long int tooth, and one neet he arrives wòm jiggert and says to th' owd woman: "By Christ, yon Bill wouldn't pull t'cart up Winstanley brow – ah've had to push it up meself". "You should have thrown him down t'mineshaft" says th'owd woman. "I bloodywell have done." says Belter."

"He...."

"An then there was Owd Post Jack an his horse, in them days all t'mail in Billinge wuz delivered wi'a pony and cart, thanose. An at Christmas and whenever it wuz a special occasion Jack would have a drink at every house and after t'first hour he'd be pollatic drunk in the back of the cart, but t'pony knew t'road anyway and used t'follow route and folk would get their letters out and t'beast would take him wom afterwards when t'cart wuz empty."

"It...."

"An what other place but Billinge would have a pub called t' "Labour in Vain" wi'a sign hanging outside showing a white woman trying to scrub a black lad white in his bath, and Dolly Blue sayin' as 'oo had a bladder in her stones and Harry Danny standing in the middle of the lane lookin' up at the sky for hours and when they asked him what he was looking at, he said "I'm lookin' at nothing."

He would go to the mantelpiece, take a packet of "Park Drive" out from behind the clock and offer you one, like it was nothing unusual.

"I keep telling 'em, it's aw reet bein' eighty, but it's mighty hard work gettin' theer. Now we have Dr. Jim's son Charles to bring us round if out ails us and I could do with some of that dandelion brew wine like all th'owd Billingers used to make, and rhubarb wine, and beetroot, and blackberry, and potato, too, and that we made out of petals – White Rose Wine – that was it!"

"What do you think of the Billinge nicknames, Jem?"

"Why, they're gradely names – there's not a village in the country can put a name to a mon like Billinge con – look at names like Pipe and Matches, and Main Root and Hairy Man and Red Jem and Nanny Goat Whiskers."

"They're marvellous, but how did he get a name like Main Root?"

"Listen while I tell thee. This mon (ah've forgotten his real name) used fert go round and weed gardens for folk to make a bit o'beer money. Well, one afternoon he doesn't half have a tussle with a badly overgrown garden, but when he comes in for his cup o'tay, he says to the woman as had given him t'job, "You don't have to worry now missus, you'll have no more weeds in that garden, I've pulled up the main root." Dost know what he'd done?"

"No."

"He'd pulled up all their rhubarb."

"You don't say."

"Art good at sums?"

"Yes. I mean, no. Why?"

"What's half of two and two?"

"Two."

"Rung."

"How much is it, then?"

"Three."

"How's that?"

"Half of two is one, so half two and two is one and two, which is three."

"You're dead right."

"What was the biggest island in the world before Australia was discovered?"

"Greenland."

"No."

"New Guinea."

"No."

"Borneo."

"No."

"I give up, what was it?"

"Australia." When he won a conundrum like that, he would give you a tired smile and poke the fire a bit. He could sit closer to a coal fire than any man I knew.

"Tell me some more tales, Jem". I knew he had hundreds.

"There was this owd Billinger – he used to go for walks every mornin' at six o'clock – he wasn't a good sleeper. And this partikler mornin' it was foggy, thick as a bag, an as he wuz walkin' across t'graveyard he fell down a newly-dug grave, and try as he might he couldn't clamber out of it. Well, he reckons t'best thing fert do was sit at one end of the grave and wait for the fog to clear, and when folks started gcttin' up and walkin' round, he'd give 'em a shout and they'd send a rope down for him. Well, theer he wuz sittin' peaceful, when who comes but a stranger and faws dehn t' same grave. Anyroad this stranger doesn't see t' Billinger and he starts trying to clamber out like t'first mon had done. So t' Billinger amuses hissel watching this mon keep slidin' dehn, and when he'd been at it for abeht five minutes, he shouts to him "Ah don't think tha'll manage it." But he did, thanose."

"Fancy, falling down an open grave."

"We had some fogs i'them days. Some folks used t'like 'em an others geet depressed. One of the Ranters wuz comin' back with a hare one foggy mornin' o'er th'Hollin Hey fields, an he sees this woman wi' a black shawl coming along t'waggin road. So he gets behind a bush and keeps out of her road and lets her go past. She wuz off to Fratsam's Pit to drehn hersell – he'd of stopped her if he'd known. It wasn't a month after that as th'Hollow Mon wuz comin'back o'er t'same fields, drunk as a lord after playin' cards till midneet. It wuz a foggy neet and he nearly stumbled into Fratsam's by mistake, so he has a bit o'sense and he lies dehn under t'bushes near t'pond and he decides fert have a snooze theer until t'fog clears. He lies theer half an hour an he hears some ghostly footsteps comin' through t'fog, and knowin' abeht this woman drowning herself a month earlier, he reckons it's her ghost going through all the motions again. So he lies theer under t'bush, too frickent fert move and sure enough t'footsteps comes right up to Fratsam's and....SPLASH....in 'oo goes, just like it was real, and he hears these bubbles comin' up for two or three minutes and then he can't stand any moor on it and he gets up and runs through t'fog and makes his road to Tom Abbott's, but Tom was drunk, so he spends t'neet theer and t'followin' mornin' they go and look at t'ghost's footsteps and they find another mon has drehned hissell i't'Pit."

"So it wasn't a ghost?"

"No, it was a mon fer Garswood."

"Who was Tom Abbott?"

"He wuz t'nicest farmer as ever lived i'Billinge. When he wanted to get drunk, he used to go down to his cellar where he had a barrel of beer and he would just lean against t'barrel and try to finish it off. One neet owd Cockey went and asked him for a rappit as Tom had promised him, so Tom gets up from his barrel and takes his shotgun which he kept behind t'stable door and they booath go out over t'fields, nearly pitch dark, and Tom stands behind a tree wi'his gun ready. And after abeht five minutes, Cockey says, "Tom, there's a rappit o'er theer, dusn't see it?" and Tom says "Aye, but thee wait a minute", and they wait a minute and another rappit comes and stands near t'fust 'un and Tom shoots booath on 'em wi' one shot – and nearly blind drunk at that."

"Did you ever go poaching, Jem?"

"Me, poaching? Wi' a respectable job at Pilkington's Glass Works? No, me lad, no jail for Jemmy. I once asked Lizard what it wuz like bein' i'jail an he said it was like going upstairs and never gerrin' to the top. No, I used to go and shoot me rappits on Uncle Hugh's Slack Field."

"Don't Billinge fields have funny names?"

"The finest in the land. Look at 'em: Milkin Hey, Mad Meadow, Poverty Land, Sour Hey, Middle Cutlet, Coal Pit Hey, Pingot, Ash Tree, Three Nook Croft, Little London, Marl Pit Meadow, Lower Farther Field, Gorsey Croft, Three-hawpenny Croft – what moor could we ask for?"

A neighbour stuck his head round the door and squinted at Jem: "What time is it Mr. Bellis?"

Jem looked up at his old clock: "Ten minutes to four."

"With the clock?"

"No, wi't'fleckin' waw."

The neighbour disappeared and Jem went on as if there had been no interruption:

"I wuz so poor when I was a lad, I used to go to St. Helens and back on foot to fetch yeast for me grandmother from the brewery. She used to give me a penny and I'd go to St. Helens market on the way back feelin' like a millionaire. One day I bought a penny jelly and brought it back to Long Fold and scalded it in a bowl as soon as I landed, for I hadn't had a jelly for months. An all t'other kids heard about it and were hanging round t'door waitin' for it to set, so I grabbed a big spoon and ate it hot, and burnt all the inside of my mouth.

Then Charlie and me went and did some decorating to make a shilling apiece to go to Southport. It was in a house up Cowley's Lone and the fashion at the time was Willow Pattern borders, so I did the painting of the lower part and Charlie stuck the borders on, and when they came round to inspect, they said it looked very good, except it was the first time that they had ever seen men and horses walking upside down under bridges. Well, they paid Charlie anyway, and folks used to come from miles around and go and look at their borders, so it turned out fine in the end."

Jem went for more coal and built up the fire. It was getting dusk outside and, in the darkening room, the old man's red face glowed brightly as the flames took hold of the new coal. He cackled quietly for a while and slipped a "Park Drive" in my direction.

"There was this Billinge woman, she had a husband who was so good, she could trample on him and he never complained. But he wasn't so fond of one of her sisters, who used to visit her from St. Helens. One day, this sister was visiting and the old man was in the back kitchen doing the dishes, and the wife says to her sister "He's such a good husband, I could throw that jug of cold water over him and he wouldn't say a word." So the sister says, "Well, when he comes in, just throw it over him, and we'll see if what you say is true." In a few minutes, when he's finished the dishes, he comes in for a quiet smoke and his wife throws the cold water all over him."

"And what happened?"

"He knocked her to the floor and broke two of her ribs."

He jabbed a stubby forefinger at me, which meant another stream of non-sequiturs was on the way:

"Talk about charcters we had, there was Blue Bottle used go for a swim every neet in Carr Mill from April to September – he said it was good for his circulation – he wuz so frickent o'drehnin' he took a clothes-horse in with him and used to swim up and dehn for half an hour, pushin' it in front of him. And we used to go t'Top Shop i'summer i'hot weather when t'sides o'bacon and t'round hams were turnin' a bit, an our Min used scrape t'maggots out and fill our tins up for bait, an Liza come into t'shop one mornin' and Min seed this great rat sittin' on her foot an shouted "Liza!" an t'rat ran off an Liza sez "What is it, Min?" an Min sez "There was a huge rat on thi foot" an Liza feels her clog an it wuz all warm where t'rat had been sittin', but it was gone and neither she nor any of t'customers had seen it, only Min, an they never found out where it bored, neither, but thanose...."

"What?"

"Liza was dead and buried within a week."

This time he sat quietly, staring into the fire, as if pondering poor Liza and the eerie event which preceded her early death. I studied his face in repose

Jem was approaching eighty and had magnificent wrinkles, especially humorous ones round the eyes. He often said he had no wish to live the first part of his life over again ("We kids down Long Fold were so poor, we used to go to Abbotts' farm and steal the potatoes they had boiled for the pigs – and they were *good.*") but he had enjoyed his middle and old age as few men do. He worked first as a miner, then as a gardener, but as he grew older he got involved in all that went on around him. He would spend hours in discussion with his uncle, the eloquent Hugh Parr, on Sunday nights, and in doing so rounded off his own powers of oratory. Jem would go to all kinds of social gatherings in the evenings and at week-ends – Old Folks' Association, Civil Defence, hot-pots, jumble sales, church socials, concerts, slide-shows – he loved them all. During the formal part of the programme he would sit shyly somewhere near the back, though he would grin or wink at anyone who turned round to have a peep at him. Five minutes after the meeting had been thrown open, you would see him being surrounded by a circle of admirers and from that moment on he would run the show until they locked everybody out. It was only natural that this sort of thing would happen in Billinge, where in his later years he was the Grand Old Man, but I once saw him do the same thing in St. Helens, at a church social we

Old Pingot

visited for the first time, where he organized Obstacle Races all round the schoolroom for so long that half those present missed the last bus home. On his first trip to Butlin's, they took one look at him as he checked in his bags and made him Chairman of the Entertainments Committee. The next day he won the first prize at the Knobbly Knees Competition.

Jem was also mad about sport. He played football till he was 40, supported the Saints at Rugby, played a canny game of snooker, enjoyed darts, organised airgun competitions, was unbeatable at draughts, shot rabbits and hares and fished in all kinds of weather. Apart from puzzles and conundrums, perhaps fishing was his greatest love. He would get up at four or five to catch the misty, clammy dawn over Carr Mill Dam, usually finding his uncle, Big Jem, there before him ("What are they takin', Jem?" – "They're takin' no bloody notice."). They say Big Jem ruined his kidneys with many a long night sitting on the cold banks of Carr Mill. In later years Jem Bellis used to go fishing with Sam Mather – a witty, good-looking miner from the same pit. They used to go to elaborate lengths cooking suet puddings down Long Fold, dyeing them in cochineal and other bright colours to make attractive bait for the fish. Sam was still learning the difficult art and Minnie Bellis, Jem's daughter, recalls how one morning as she took them their sandwiches down to the Dam, she caught them in the act of pulling out the biggest trout that had ever been seen on the end of Jem's line. Jem was staggering up and down the bank, trying to swing it in and Sam was making a frantic attempt to get it into a net on the end of a pole. After Sam had struck the fish two or three times with the net it fell off the hook and returned to its watery habitat, leaving Jem and Sam to curse each other blue. The following Saturday morning the inexpert Sam, angling on his own, caught the same, huge fish and ran a mile and a half back to Long Fold, rod extended, the fish – still on hook and line – tucked under his left arm. On reaching Jem's, he bundled the whole lot through the front door and parlour into the living-room where Jem was breakfasting on bacon and eggs. "It's him!" shrieked Sam.

Jem always said it was the biggest trout ever to come out of the Dam and he and Sam (after eating it) spent years afterwards regretting they had not stuffed it.

*   *   *   *   *   *   *

Now kindly, original Sam Mather had been gone for more than twenty years and my old warrior Jem was one of the last of a dying breed. In his retirement he was always trying something new – Nightwatchman at Billinge Quarry, School Crossing Patrol, Civil Defence – but above all he held his forum in the bungalow on Pingot Road, like Hugh Parr and other old Billingers had done before him in days when radio and moving pictures had not been invented.

I gave him a nudge and he came out of his reverie:
"Where art gooin' next, lad?" he asked me.
"Tokyo."
"What wi'aw them crowded trains and earthquakes?"
"They're not so bad."
"Earth'll swallow thee up one o'these days."
"I'll send you a card, so you'll know if I'm all right."
"I'll write thee a letter" (he always signed himself at the end of his letters:
". . . from False Teeth, Bawd Yed, Hearing Aid, Spectacles Jemmy.")
"Tell me one more story before I go."
He had that cunning look again: "Tha wants another tale?"
"Just one".
"There wuz this Billinge farmer, he'd been married twenty year, one neet he was gooin' wom wi'his wife by horse and cart, an they were attacked by some ruffians, who threw them into the ditch, stole his wallet and her rings and necklace, and drove off with th'horse an cart. Farmer did some cussin' and towd his wife as thieves had made off wi' everythin' they had. "Nay" says his wife, "not everything, I still have my purse." "How dit manage that?" asks t'farmer. "I put it in my mouth", says his wife. "By Christ", says t'farmer, "I wish thi mother had been with us – we might have saved th'horse an cart."

*   *   *   *   *   *   *   *

Reluctantly, I took my leave and he stood at the door as I made my way down Pingot Road. As I turned to go up Main Street, I heard his voice for the last time:
"When tha gets to Tokyo, keep away from them holes!"

Anatomy of a Dialect

Readers who have managed to get so far will have noticed that the people of Billinge speak their own dialect which, until recently, was passed on from generation to generation. In fact, dialogue occurring in previous chapters has been watered down and standardized to a considerable degree, in order to make the speech more comprehensible to the general reading public.

The Billinge dialect is akin to that of Wigan, which was so admirably described by Clifford Webb in a series of articles a few years ago. Like several coalfield dialects, it is not only almost incomprehensible to the southerner when spoken at speed and in its unadulterated form, but it is one for which there so far has been devised no adequate system of phonetic representation. It is true that some pure dialect forms such as **sackless, cornish, jillet** and **prigmeet** give no problem, but we encounter more difficulty with such words as **slerr, pow, tronnin'** and **meyt (meight?)** and find it quite impossible to do full justice in normal print to the local pronunciation of such non-dialectal forms as house, about, want, better, butter, down, butcher and war. We can get so far with **hehse, abeht, dehn** and **werr,** but how can we convey the open Northern "a" in want (like rant or Kant) or the double "lean" on the intervocalic consonants in better, butter and butcher?

Let us, however, put aside phonology for a moment and start to examine the various characteristics and peculiarities of the Billinge dialect. To begin with, we must mention its variety of forms. This is not unexpected on account of the village's central location in the coalfield and in the Lancashire plain. We know that Billinge was an Anglo-Saxon stronghold and both Billinge and nearby Ashton have Saxon names, but nearer still are Celtic Bryn and Pemberton, while Viking Ormskirk and Skelmersdale are only a short horse-ride away and the Danes were at one time not far to the south. All these cultures (and, indeed, the later mining culture) contributed to the dialect of Billinge. **Skrike** (weep or cry) is Scandinavian (cf. mod. Swedish "skreka") but **clem** (starve) is Germanic, **hoo** (she) probably Danish ("hon") and **brat** (apron) certainly Celtic (cf. Old Welsh "brith" = swaddling clothes). **Kench, jackbit** and **rived** show the influence of the mining community.

For many centuries, before mechanical transport, Billinge was a very isolated place. The language of isolated communities usually features archaic forms and, occasionally, locally invented words and expressions. These characteristics are evident in Billinge speech in such examples as the archaisms **fain, harken** and

wench and the invented forms **pindert, bortert** and **Ah'll watch Haddy for thee.**

There is also the phenomenon of semantic change. Small villages often take a normal word in standard speech and use it in their own dialect with another connotation. Billingers use the word **tackle** as an adjective, moreover with two different meanings. **That pie was tackle** means "good and tasty" but **Yo mun watch yon mon, he's tackle** means he is a "rum 'un". Similarly **clod** (of earth) is used as a verb (**to clod** = to throw) and **ill off** in Billinge means "sad" or "regretful".

The self-reliant Billingers have always been doers or men of action. It is not surprising therefore to find that the dialect is extremely rich in verbs. **Hahmin', jaftin', pinkin'** and **slancin'** are particularly local vintage. Also we have noted earlier that Billingers were very keen story-tellers, hence the richness and expressiveness of the home-grown adjectives, e.g. **fawse, tittle, brossen** and **yammerin.**

Before taking a close look at the actual mechanics of Billinge speech it should be pointed out that the dialect is typically Northern and, as such, incorporates the usual features of most Lancashire dialects. This applies particularly to pronunciation and the assimilation of the definite article. It is clear, therefore, that cat, dance and last will have the same vowel sound and the "u" sound will not vary in push button and the butcher cuts. Fall will be **faw,** wall will be **waw,** out and about will be **eht an abeht,** sound and found **sehnd** and **fehnd,** (but less common trout, snout and clout retain a near-standard form), fine and sign will be **fahn** and **sahn** and so on. "The" is assimilated with the following noun or adjective on both sides of the Pennines and in Billinge, predictably, the barn, the oven, on the floor, in the field, in the house, go to the market, with the dog, along the canal, the old man emerge as **t'barn, th'oon, ont flewer, it feelt, inth'hehse, gut market, wit dog, alunk canal** and **thowd mon.**

In addition to these general northernisms, which in the great majority of cases may be taken for granted as existing in Billinge speech, the local dialect has a considerable number of peculiarities which on account of their originality and diversification merit a closer scrutiny. Let us first take a look at the general vocabulary, that is to say, how the Billinger uses nouns, verbs and adjectives on a daily basis, how he selects them and where he got them from. These words seem to fall roughly into three classes: firstly, those close to standard speech; secondly, those which have undergone considerable change; thirdly, pure dialect words with no equivalent or source in standard English.

*   *   *   *   *   *   *   *

In the first category nouns predominate, verbs are few and adjectives almost non-existent. This ratio is an interesting point which we shall discuss in a moment, but first let us see a few examples:

NOUNS: **poss** (purse), **comm** (comb), **chonge** (change), **bally** (belly), **hommer** (hammer), **ankicher** (handkerchief), **bonk** (bank), **lone** (lane), **sofy** (sofa), **sluch** (mud), **steel** (stile), **chimbley** (chimney), **appo** (apple), **yed** (head), **mardi** (softie), **th'oon** (the oven), **een** (eyes) and **pitee** (pit-eye).

ADJECTIVES: **chonched** (changed), **skew wiff** (askew)

VERBS: **lap up** (wrap up), **met** (might), **manish** (manage), **prow eht** (prowling at night), **scrawpin'** (scraping a living), **coddin'** (kidding), **favver** (look like) and **seech** (look for)

OTHER: **favver as if** (seems as if), **'oo can noather poo ner scawd** (she can't make a decision), **afoor** (before), **sin** (since), **sithee** (look now), **thanose** (you know) and **varneer** (almost).

All the above examples are easily traced to standard speech, though occasionally might slip by the southerner when delivered at speed. Why are there so many nouns and so few verbs and adjectives? The most probable explanation is that dialect users take words from standard speech only when they have to. The dialect-rich Billinge story-tellers could afford to spurn adjectives and to some extent verbs from normal usage, as they had hundreds of more expressive ones of their own. A noun, lacking altogether in poetry or expressiveness, would be borrowed more frequently. They are considered "loan-words", however, and are given only a slight, derisive phonetic twist. This style of borrowing is not unfamiliar to the student of linguistics who will have seen how such strange languages as Japanese and Finnish have loan-words from English in great number, but take almost exclusively nouns, seldom verbs and will not touch our adjectives.

In the second category, we have words which derive from standard English, but which have been deformed or moulded sufficiently by time and usage to make them more acceptable or palatable to the local speakers and consequently are more in use:

NOUNS: **cosy** (from causeway = pavement), **meyt** (food), **moggie** (mouse), **storr** (from stir = party or "do"), **hess** (ash), **hess-hole** (ash-hole under a coal fire), **yure** (hair), **wom** (home), **awom** (at home), **breyd** (width of material or grave) **fettler** (rum 'un or devil-may-care individual), **brawth-yed** (fool), **coms** (from combination = knickers).

ADJECTIVES: **pown** (beaten, well-used, beaten up), **gradely** (good, worthy), **wichert** (soaked, from wet-shod), **nowt** (angry) **nangy** (angry).

VERBS: **slerr** (slide), **bargein'** (arguing), **warch** (ache), **sken** (squint), **hacklin'** (equivocate, not say "yes" or "no", possibly comes from "haggle"), **ah'm pikin' off** (I'm going, derives from a miner with pickaxe being called a pikeman).

OTHER: **beht** (without), **owt** (anything), **nowt** (nothing) **tethee agate** (go part of the way with you), **oo's agate agen** (she's on about that again, or on with that again).

If this second category has given more trouble to southern English gentlemen, it is the third which will rout them completely. Here we enter the realms of pure dialect and any connection between the words that follow and word in their own southern speech is entirely accidental:

NOUNS: **chowf** (face, derogatory), **jillet** (loose woman), **pow** (haircut), **brat** (apron), **ginnel** (entrance or alley), **powse** (rubbish), **baggin** (lunch), **rigut** (fold or wrinkle), **jawm** (vertical part of door-frame or fireplace), **cornish** (shelf above mantelpiece for pictures, candlesticks), **scorick** or **skerrick** (bit, scrap), **sheppie** (starling, from sheep's eye), **peggies** (teeth), **poot** (woman, chick), **bo-bos** (sleep), **quarrel** (pane of glass), **jonock** or **janock** (black bread), **nerr** (fool, cf. Swed. narra), **fililoo** (din), **petty** (toilet), **roozer** (troublesome person), **gansey** (pit-vest), (from Guernsey, cf. Jersey?), **butty** (sandwich, but "friend" in South Wales).

ADJECTIVES: **powfagged** (exhausted), **widdert** (wrinkled), **powsy** (lousy), **sauvy** (deceitful), **prigmeet** (just it), **pindert** (brittle, burnt away), **fleed** (chapped), **bortert** (covered by thick layer, e.g. shoes with mud), **fawse** (clever, cunning, crafty), **reemin** (excellent), **fehh** (ugly, from Span. or Portuguese "feo"?), **wick** (lively), **tittle** (it only just fits), **jiggert** (tired out), **wasty** (draughty), **sackless** (fidgety, can't settle), **brossen** or Garswood variant **broasen** (fat and bonny), **tackle** (tasty for food, rum for people).

VERBS: **maitherin'** (bothering, pestering, irritating, going on and on about something), **hahmin'** (answer angrily), **reemin'** (stinking), **yammerin'** (making a din, maitherin'), **pinkin'** (hinting) **fradgin'** (gossiping), **tootin'** (peeping, spying, ferreting), **slancin'** (stealing food), **maulin'** (messing about, sometimes equivalent to Yorkshire "lakin'"), **consterrin'** (arguing), **mankin'** (fooling around), **tronnin'** (doing useful things around the house, e.g. repairs, carpentry), **clem** (starve, from Dutch "klemmen"), **skrike** (weep), **perr** (kick), **peyl, pole, pown** (beat, beat, beaten), **peyl off** (rush off), **scratch** (make or do, used only in top half of village), **rawm** (reach), **thrutch** (push in), **deg** (water plants), **cahr** (sit down on haunches), **perry** (to throw treacle toffee), **jaftin'** (going about having a good time), **mooed eht wi'** (inundated with), **trankle** (touch, interfere with), **mee-maw** (act silly), **kale** (to get in first, to forestall), **snape** (to scold).

OTHER: **a laht** (a few), **no shenanigen** (stop making fun), **'oo** (she), **live i' tally with** (live in sin with), **spon new** (brand new), **divvilsnose** (currant cake), **leet** variants **leef** or **least** (various meanings) e.g. **they're leet be somewheer** (they must be somewhere), **ad us leet go wom** (I'd prefer to go home), **ad us least nor** (I'd rather not).

*   *   *   *   *   *   *   *

In addition to this general vocabulary, much of which clearly derives from Anglo-Saxon, Scandinavian, Celtic and other sources, having been handed down directly and independently of normal Standard English development, Billinge dialect has also picked up the words coined more recently by the mining industry, such as **londin, kench, rived, daytlers, drawers, scuftin, scotch** and **shotties.** Less technical mining words such as **jackbit** (food), **tommy tin** (container for food), and **take thee hooks** (be off with you) remain in the dialect in everyday use. It is also said that **moggie** for "mouse" originated down the pit, although the same word means "cat" in Liverpool. Mining provided an interesting verb-plus-preposition combination in the expression **fawed up,** used to describe the roof of a tunnel which had, in fact, fallen down.

As far as archaisms are concerned, the most important feature in the dialect, as in several parts of northern England, is the retention of the second person singular forms when addressing a child, friend or inferior. Though modern English has dropped "thou", thee" etc, it is of course not the case in other modern European languages, where French, Spanish, Italian and Portuguese *tu*, German and Scandinavian *Du* and *du*, Finnish *sinä* and so on are as widely used as ever. In Billinge the pronouns are **tha** (you), **"thee"** (you, object) **"tha** (your) and **thahn** (yours). The corresponding forms for strangers or superiors are **yoh, yo, yore** and **yose.** In the second person singular the verb, too, takes the archaic form, so we have **tha goes, tha comes, thanose** as well as interrogative combinations such as **dusto?** (do you?), **arto?** (are you) **art gooin'?** (are you going), **ditto?** (did you?), **ast?** (have you?), **assn't towd 'im?** (haven't you told him?) and so on. People in the Wigan area use the second person singular basically in the same way as the French and other Europeans do, with the exception that children never address their parents in the familiar form, though this would be normal in France, Spain, Sweden, Germany, Finland and most European countries.

Other archaisms in everyday use in Billinge are **fain ('oo'd bi proper fain t'sithee), harken** (for listen to), **wench, yon, yonder,** and **ouzel** (for blackbird). **Yon mon** is very often used for "he" or "him", as in the frequently-heard **Harken yon mon** (Just listen to him). By coincidence, this use of **yon mon** as the third person pronoun is very reminiscent of the Japanese word for him, **ano hito** which means, literally, "that man".

Shives and **threap,** the Billinge words for "slices" and "contradict" might also be considered somewhat archaic, although they enjoy currency in other parts of the North. Certainly "threap" (from Anglo-Saxon **threapian** = to rebuke) extends as far as Scotland. **Jangling** is provincial and is the old Billinge word for "chatter" or "gossip". The expression **let on** is colloquial for "divulge" in many parts of the country as well as in Billinge, **(Tha mawn't lerron sowot tha does,)** but has the secondary meaning in the village of "encounter" or "come across" (**Oo lerron 'm dehnt lone**) that is, "she ran into him down the road". Still another situation is inferred in the expression **Owd mon, ooze norrafe lerron wi' yon mon anter?** which a southerner could hardly be expected to known means "I say, she's been frightfully lucky in landing that chap (for marriage), hasn't she?"

*   *   *   *   *   *   *   *

Vocabulary can undergo semantic change in different circumstances. Sometimes the change in meaning of a word occurs simply because of the passage of time. Thus we have seen that the original meaning of the word **threap,** for instance, was "rebuke", whereas to-day it means "contradict" or "argue" in the areas where it has survived. Sometimes a word passes from one language to another and changes its meaning in the process, as in the case of the word "kimono" which means a particular Japanese garment in English, but was the general word for "clothing" in Japanese. In other circumstances a dialect can borrow a word from the standard language and use it in a completely different sense. Billingers have done this to some degree, so that the word **starved** means "freezing cold" in Billinge and not "starving" which has been driven out by the dialect word **clemming. Tha's bin starvin' it lone agen beht lappin' thisell up proper** is not so bad as it sounds. Similarly **clod** means "throw", **rattle** means "spank or give a beating", **flit** means "to move house", not necessarily in a hurry or by moonlight. **Side** is used as a verb – **Let me side them mugs** (Let me clear the table), also for eating prowess – **He can side summat** (He can eat a lot). **Champion** becomes an adjective meaning "first rate" or "excellent" (that tripe's **champion**) and **happen** an adverb (perhaps) as in **'oo'll happen sahn thee on when ooze eyed thee o'er** (perhaps she will approve of you when she has had a good look at you). "**Carry on**" has the general colloquial meaning of having an illicit affair, but in Billinge is also used to signify a scolding or telling off, as in **He's behnt carry on when he eights them brunt chips. Chops,** for some reason, is used to describe the side of the face – **Oo giddim a belt it chops** (she gave him a blow to the face or slapped him), while **ill off** means "sad" or "regretting". When someone does not go to work in Billinge, he **plays him** or he **wags it (they've done sum playin' 'um them lot). Slopstone** means "draining board" or even "sink" and the primary meaning of **closet** is "toilet". **Nasty** is seldom used with the meaning "unpleasant" but refers directly to dirty things **(Ah doest nasty pots i this hehse).** The word "nasty" is in the Concise Oxford Dictionary, but the word **nast** is not. **Nast** – meaning "dirt" or "soil" is in current usage in Billinge and Wigan.

Besides numerous examples of semantic change, the Billinge dialect also displays certain syntactical peculiarities which prove puzzling to the southern listener. Several years ago in London a very nice young lady asked me what I did on Sundays. I replied **"I follow going to church"** – an answer which seemed to confound her, since she asked me what I followed to church or whom I followed to church, and even after I had taken considerable pains to explain to her what this fine expression meant, she appeared far from convinced. Billingers and Wiganers know that **to follow** plus the gerund means to be in the habit of doing something. Similarly a southerner would not realize that the word **called** in the expression **Ooze cawd gooint pictures toneet** means "is supposed to be". If a Billinger tells his host in another town **I'd be liked t'stop here aw neet** he is not saying what he would like to do, but what he would be obliged to do if, for example, they got snowed in.

Other Billinge expressions which defy classification are **Ah'll watch Haddy for thee** (I'll keep an eye on things while you are away) and **owd snuffocker** (a derogatory term describing catarrhal individuals). Both seem to have been invented locally. While the inference in the second one is obvious, it would require an old Billinger to tell you that there had once actually existed a dubious character named Haddy who, in point of fact, took quite a lot of watching. Billinge uses the widespread colloquial expressions **he's no oil in his lamp** and **three sheets in the wind** (nautical) to describe someone eccentric, but prefer their more picturesque **he's not getten aw is cheers awom** (all his chairs at home). Also worthy of notice are the expressions **all of a rook,** meaning "in a mess" (vaguely reminiscent of awry) and **owd mon sorrie** which is virtually untranslatable, being used to attract your listener's attention and possibly to enlist his sympathy. **Boggarts** are ghosts and when a horse bolts, Billingers say **By gum, he's ten boggarts** (ten = taken). **Cahr thee dehn an sit like a little wooden hullet** was old Billinge talk for "Sit down and keep still". The dialect makes the use of general slang superfluous, but two somewhat slangy expressions used in the village are **Put t'wood it th'ole** (Close the door) and **He's not much bottle** (he's not up to much, though he might think he is).

* * * * * * * *

Relative pronouns are quite simple – there are only two – **wot** and **us.** The standard relative pronouns "who", "whom", "whose", "which" and "that" have all been discarded, "who" because it conflicts with the Billinge word for "she" (**oo**), "whose" because of the conflict with **ooze** (she has or she is), "whom" as it was already dying in standard English and "that" and "which" losing the battle to **us** (much more easily pronounced). **Us** is used more with people and **wot** more with things. Consequently:
Mon us cum (The man who came), **Wench us tha seed** (The girl whom you saw), **That's th' hehse wot tha wants** (That is the house that you want), **It's brass wot kehnts** (It is money that counts). **Us** and **wot** are in many cases

interchangeable, just as are "that" and "which" in standard speech, so that **T'waw wot fawed dehn** and **T'waw us fawed dehn** are equally correct (= acceptable). There are, of course, interesting combinations and contractions such as **worrid** and **usood** in sentences like **He towd us abeht t'book worrid read** and **Oo showed us scones usood baked.** The famous northern contraction **wottle** is current in Billinge when the relative pronoun is required in the future tense. No doubt many readers have heard the story where Jack says to Bill **"Heh dost spell 'Wottle'?"** Bill asks him **"Heh dost use it int sentence?"** Replies Jack: **"Han yoh a nahf wottle cut proper?"** Answers Bill: **"Lad, it's not 'wottle' us tha wants, but "uzzle".**

If the dialect has simplified relative pronouns it nevertheless slightly complicates Reported Speech. Normally this is introduced simply by the word "that", as for instance: "I am going" which becomes "I said that I am going". We have already seen how the dialectal **"us"** has displaced "that" in relative clauses. This substitution is carried over with Reported Speech, therefore "She says that she is coming" becomes **Oo sez us ooze comin'.** This would be simple enough, but unfortunately **wot** also seems to want to get into the act, so that we have another variation **Oo sez us worrooze comin'** which has a certain inelegance about it. Other possible combinations are:
Oo sed us worrud bake (She said that she would bake) **He sed us worree knowed nowt abeht it** (He said that he knew nothing about it). Another less

Milkin Hey

than graceful intrusion appears in the Negative of the Imperative in Reported Speech. *In standard English :* Don't eat the food becomes "He told me not to eat the food". *In dialect :* **Doan't eight that meight** becomes **He towd me not fert eight t'meight.**

It is interesting to note that such clumsy features are the exception rather than the rule in dialects, which generally survive because of their ability to express thoughts in a quicker, more supple and frequently more expressive and picturesque way than standard speech.

The use of **fert** leads us to the question of prepositions, since the word is a contraction of "for to". (**Oo axed me fert go** = She asked me (for) to go). Dialects do not normally interfere with prepositions very much since they are vital link words and clarity of meaning is essential. Consequently we find words such as "on", "under", "in", "among," "across" retaining their standard form in most parts of the country. In Billinge "with" drops the "th", but of greater interest is the local word for "without" which is **beht.** Cliff Webb recounts how a stranger went into a shop in the area and asked for a certain item, to be told, **We han noan.** "What do you mean?" he asked. **"It means were beht"** was the reply. In general the preposition "of" is substituted by the preposition "on". So we have:

He took it eht on his pocket (out of his pocket)
Booath on 'um (both of them)
Noan on us (none of us)

The expression **Oo fawd eht wi'er dowter** (She fell out with = quarrelled with her daughter) must also be regarded as unusual, while the word "off" is left out in the expression **they haven't been hitting it,** meaning hitting if off, or agreeing. Another strange local use of prepositions is seen in the expression **he went for a doctor,** meaning he was studying to be a doctor.

*   *   *   *   *   *   *

When learning a foreign language we often find that one of the major difficulties is acquiring mastery over the verbs. They are not so great in number (in fact we achieve reasonable fluency in everyday conversation in French, Spanish or Italian with a command of fewer than 200 common verbs) but they tend to fall into different categories or conjugations, all with their own rules. There are regular verbs, irregular verbs, main verbs, auxiliary verbs, reflexive verbs and defective verbs. It should no longer come as a surprise to the reader to learn that the Billinge dialect enjoys the use of all these phenomena and that the irregularities of the local verbs constitute a formidable hurdle for any stranger wishing to imitate or penetrate local speech habits.

One can observe various characteristics: firstly, the tendency to regularize irregular verbs in standard English:

	Dialect			**Standard**	
Present	*Past*	*Past Participle*	*Present*	*Past*	*Past Participle*
know	**knowed**	**knowed**	know	knew	known
grow	**growed**	**growed**	grow	grew	grown
faw	**fawd**	**fawd**	fall	fell	fallen
see	**seed**	**seed**	see	saw	seen
catch	**catched**	**catched**	catch	caught	caught
howd	**howded**	**howded**	hold	held	held

Less frequently, we see the opposite tendency, i.e. to make a verb irregular which was regular in Standard English:

heave	**hove**	**hoven**	heave	heaved	heaved
dive	**dove**	**dove**	dive	dived	dived
ask	**axed**	**axed**	ask	asked	asked

The most common type of verb used in the dialect is irregular in its parts, but differs from the irregular forms in the Standard version:

give	**gid**	**gen**	give	gave	given
speyk	**spooak**	**spokken**	speak	spoke	spoken
get	**geet**	**getten**	get	got	got
peyl	**pole**	**pown**	beat	beat	beaten
steyl	**stow**	**stown**	steal	stole	stolen
tek	**took**	**ten**	take	took	taken
brun	**brunt**	**brunt**	burn	burnt	burnt
breyk	**broke**	**brokken**	break	broke	broken
hide	**hud**	**hudden**	hide	hid	hidden
eyt	**et**	**etten**	eat	ate	eaten
sez	**said**	**sen**	say	said	said
mon	**et**	**monna**	must	had to	must have
met	**—**	**metta**	might	—	might have
tell	**towd**	**towd**	tell	told	told
clod	**clod**	**clod**	throw	threw	thrown
cum	**cum**	**cum**	come	came	come
sit	**seat**	**sitten**	sit	sat	sat
fit	**fit**	**fit**	fit	fitted	fitted
poo	**pooed**	**poon**	pull	pulled	pulled
fahnd	**fond**	**font**	find	found	found

While some of the above variations look relatively harmless in print they are extremely difficult for the stranger to understand when they are used at speed and particularly in combination with other dialect forms and with each other. These examples illustrate the point:

ast hoven um eht th'oon?	Have you taken them out of the oven?
ooze beht getten beht um	She has probably got rid of them
ah met a clod this powse it flash	It would have been as well if I had thrown this rubbish into the pond.
ah deht ooze font noan	I don't think that she has found any
ast towd um ooze pown it bits?	Have you told them that she has smashed it to pieces?
ooze poon it varneer eht o'shape	She has almost pulled it out of shape
ah metta thowt ad be teed lap up	I might have realised that I would be obliged to wrap myself in warm clothes
astet axe um wot thi pole off fo'	I shall have to ask them what they rushed off for.

Another characteristic of the dialect is the intrusion of a Germanic "n" in the third person plural of the present tense of the verb:

Thi sen its gerrin wuss awt tahm	They say it is getting worse all the time
Thi han nowt	They have nothing
Thi drinken thersel dee-ath	They drink themselves to death
Thi ten wot thi want	They take what they want
Thi gin thi owt tha wants	They give you anything you want
Thi fawn ore thersel t'elp thee	They fall over themselves to help you
Thi sitten aw day fradgin'	They sit all day gossiping

Reflexive verbs are almost non-existent in Standard English (where the sense is conveyed by introducing the pronouns "myself", "oneself" etc.) but, as most of us know to our cost, they are rampant in most European languages. The Billinge dialect not only has reflexive verbs, but invented one of its own. When learning French, we are told that "I wash" is translated not by "*je lave*", but by "*je me lave*". Similarly, Billinge conjugates the verb as follows: ("**wash**" pronounced with "a" as in "cash, rash")

I wash me   **wi wash us**
tha washes thee   **yo wash yo**
ee washes 'im   **thi wash 'um**
oo washes 'er

The Imperative form is: **Go un wash thee**

Other examples of Billinge reflexives are **cahr thi dehn** (sit thee down), and **Hag thee.** The latter means "Hurry up" and may have originated from a word meaning "sweat". By far the most original reflexive verb in the dialect is exemplified in the expression **Ah umbethowt me,** deriving from the verb "to umbethink oneself": (used in the Past only)

Dialect speakers

ah umbethowt me	wi umbethowt us
tha umbethowt thee	yo umbethowt yo
he umbethowt 'im	thi umbethowt um
oo umbethowt 'er	

In fact we occasionally hear this fine verb in the Present, e.g.: **Howd thi din wha ah umbethink me** (Be quite while I try to recollect).

Another interesting and original verb of local invention, though this time not reflexive, is the verb **to oerfawse** (somebody). We have seen how the dialect adjective **fawse** means "crafty, clever or cunning". If you are craftier than someone, or if you outwit them, you **oerfawse** them. (**By the fleckin' heck, yon mon's oerfawsed me agen**).

Dialects tend to play havoc with auxiliary verbs and Billinge is no exception. The following table shows the most usual forms of some of the local auxiliaries:

Dialect		**Standard**	
ah'm	**wur**	I am	we are
thar	**yore**	you are	you are
eeze	**there**	he is	they are
ooze		she is	
amma?	**ar wi?**	am I?	are we?
arto?	**ar yo?**	are you?	are you?
izee?	**ar thi?**	is he?	are they?
izoo?		is she?	
ah wuz	**wi wuz**	I was	we were
tha wuz	**yo wuz**	you were	you were
eewuz	**thi wuz**	he was	they were
oowuz		she was	
ah snot	**wi snot**	I shan't	we shan't
thallnor	**yo'llnor**	you won't	you won't
illnor	**thi'llnor**	he won't	they won't
oollnor		she won't	

ah yav	**wi yan**	I have	we have
tha yas	**yo an**	you have	you have
ee yas	**thi an**	he has	they have
oo as		she has	
av ah?	**an wi (on wi?)**	have I?	have we?
asto? (ast?)	**an yo? (on yo?)**	have you?	have you?
azee?	**an thi? (on thi?)**	has he?	have they?
azoo?		has she?	
avnor	**win-nor**	I haven't	we haven't
thasnor	**yon-nor**	you haven't	you haven't
eeznor	**thin-nor**	he hasn't	they haven't
ooznor		she hasn't	
astet (mahnd)	**wistet**	I shall have to (mind)	we shall have to
thallet	**yoh-let**	you will have to	you will have to
eellet	**thi-let**	he will have to	they will have to
oollet		she will have to	
ah monna (lost it)	**wi monna**	I must have (lost it)	we must have
tha monna	**yo monna**	you must have	you must have
ee monna	**thi monna**	he must have	they must have
oo monna		she must have	
(alternatively):			
av beht (lost it)	**win beht**	I must have (lost it)	we must have
thasbeht	**yun beht**	you must have	you must have
eezbeht	**thin beht**	he must have	they must have
ooze beht		she must have	

The above tables are hardly complete, since there are several other tenses to be represented and a variety of dialectal contractions in the negative and interrogative. The following examples are the most frequent: **wutto?** (would you?), **mawn'ta?** (mustn't I?), **mettoo?** (might she?), **ditto?** or **dit?** (did you?), **arto?** or **art?** (are you?), **wilto?** or **wilt?** (will you?), **dusto?** or **dust?** (do you?), **dersto?** or **derst?** (dare you?), **wusto?** (were you?), **didoo?** (did she?), **asto?** (have you? or do you have to?), **connoo?** (can she?), **cutto?** (could you?), **on-thi-nor?** (haven't they?).

* * * * * * * *

People who are not born into a dialect and who use Standard English as a matter of course may well ask themselves why dialects are necessary or even useful. Queen's English, albeit the Northern version, is taught in the schools of Billinge and Wigan and the local people are no less skilled in grammar, spelling and so on than anyone else. Why, therefore, do they bother to cling to their bilingualism? There are probably three reasons: one traditional, one emotional and one aesthetic.

Firstly, we have mentioned earlier how dialects perpetuate an historical tradition. Why do the people of Barcelona and the surrounding province of Catalonia speak Catalan, when they are all fluent in Spanish – one of the great world languages? It is because they regard Catalan not as a bastard offshoot of Spanish, but as a legitimate daughter of Latin, no less so indeed than Italian, Spanish, Portuguese, Rumanian and French. The dialects of northern England have a continuity of evolution from the sources which made up the speech of the English nation equal to that of any other, and we must remember that Standard English is no more than just another dialect which happened to gain ascendancy towards the end of the 15th century. We might also recall that the great mother tongue Latin itself was at one time a dialect of Latium, a small area south of the Tiber.

Secondly, a dialect is an emotional matter. It is noticeable how a dialect speaker may use only Standard speech in a calm discussion with strangers, but will accentuate his local pronunciation and lose control of grammar as he gets excited, finally lapsing into pure dialect and haywire syntax as he becomes overjoyed or outraged. It is no accident that the emotive content of a large number of Lancashire dialect words is strongly derogatory or disparaging. A dialect reflects the life and mood of the area in which it is spoken. The pits and the mills of Wigan, the isolation, climate, hardship and poverty of Billinge bred a dialect with a ring of despair. The geographically kinder south might leave a man tired at the end of his day's work, but the utter exhaustion of the miner is conveyed in the words **powfagged** and **jiggert,** he returned to a home of **clemmin** and **skrikin** kids, a **maitherin** wife, **yammerin, fradgin, slancin** relations, he would react by **hahmin** and **consterrin** and gave them a **porr,** if need be. Can we part a man from the vehicle of expression of his rage? On the other hand emotion is equally bound up in such terms of endearment as **mi owd fettler** and **owd taw** (marbles) both words unsurpassed for conveying the depth and essential nature of the northerner's affection.

We finally come to the question of the aesthetics or expressiveness of a dialect. When it snows on the Isle of Man we are told that Manxmen say "They are plucking geese in Scotland". This is a wonderful example of the way a local saying can reflect the soul of the people – in this case the poetry and imagery of the Gaels. Harsh conditions, poverty and no doubt the ills of the Industrial Revolution served to eradicate most of the poetry, in any lyrical or epic sense, from the dialects of Billinge and Wigan; but there is another kind of poetry, picturesque (almost picaresque) in the compound, synthetic effect of such words as **jaftin', slancin'** and **maitherin'.** The word **jaftin'** contains four elements. It means someone is going about from place to place; the moving about must be taking place out of doors; there is the social element of other people being involved; and the person jafting must be enjoying himself. Take away any one of these four elements and the word **jaftin'** would not be used. **Slancin'** means "stealing", but the thing being stolen must be edible and the word also conveys a surreptitious action. One also understands that not too much was taken and that the accuser has partly forgiven the slancer. It is becoming clear that in order to explain fully one dialect word, one often has to resort to several sentences in Standard speech. Take for instance the word **maitherin'.** In order to tell a southerner exactly what is happening, one would have to say "a **maitherer** is a person who complains about something, who pesters us with it, who goes on and on about the matter, even though it be of no great importance and even if there is nothing we can do about it; it is a bee in his or her bonnet and the culprit is either moronic, ignorant or simply getting senile. After a while it gets on your nerves".

Powfagged means "exhausted" but in the expression **stop powfaggin' me** we have the extra meaning of being irritated; **sackless** describes an uneasy, restless person, one who through physical or mental discomfort fidgets his way through the day, moves from place to place, never settles. The Lancashire **tron-ner** is a jack-of-all-trades, a man who in his spare time makes himself useful about the house, turning his hand to all things, not necessarily a skilled man, but one who can "fix" anything. How more expressive are dialect words such as **oerfawse, umbethink** and **fililoo** than their Standard counterparts "outwit", "recollect" and "din"! "Rubbish" is a fine word in English, yet does not quite convey the same amount of disgust as the Billinge **powse** (spat out for proper effect). Anyone can tell a child to stop pulling his face, but **Wilt stop poo'in' thi chowf** has something extra. When a Billinger says **chowf** his face actually becomes a **chowf.** Why say just "things" when you can say **tranklements,** "spy" when you can say **toot** or make a cake when you can **scratch** one?

Hag thee, or tha'll loyse thi kale seems to me to be a shade ahead of "Hurry up or you won't be among the first in the queue" while "I'd better be going, it is getting rather cloudy" lacks the punch of **Ah'm pikin' off, it's thickenin' up.** And if Celtic imagery is lacking, the dialect is not without its similes. A Billinger eats till he is **as full as a fitch** and then sits in the corner **like a wooden hullet.** Of course he can be as drunk as a lord and as sober as a judge, just as they can down south, but now and again the northern version creeps in. If our southern cousin ransacked his vocabulary to describe an unlovely woman, he would probably say "she was as ugly as sin". A Billinger would say **Oo wuz as fehh as a dolly-tub.**

REFERENCES

E. Baines. *"History of the County Palatine of Lancaster."* (various vols.)
T. Baines. *"Lancashire and Cheshire, Past and Present."* (various vols.)
J. F. Giblin. *"The History of Birchley Hall and the Mission of St. Mary's Birchley, in Billinge, Lancashire."*
J. J. Bagley. *"History of Lancashire"*, *"Lancashire"*.
P. E. H. Hair. *"The Lancashire Collier Girl, 1975."*
"Transactions of the Historic Society of Lancashire and Cheshire" (various vols.)
J. D. Marshall. *"Lancashire."*
Lt. Col. H. Fishwick. *"A History of Lancashire."*
Austin Powell. *"The Tenth Annual Report of the Birchley School."* 1883.
Austin Powell. Appendix, Birchley Schools. 1890.
Transactions of Lancashire and Cheshire Antiquarian Society. (various vols.)
D. Anderson. *"The Orrell Coalfield, Lancashire 1740-1850."*
W. A. Wickham. *"Some Notes on Billinge."* 1909.
D. W. Harris. *Further Notes on Billinge, 1968.*
J. P. Rylands. *"Lancashire and Cheshire wills and inventories."* 1897.
Final concords of the County of Lancaster.
Sir William Dugdale. *"Visitation of Lancashire."* 1664-5.
"Endowed Charities (County of Lancashire). Parish of Wigan. excluding the County Borough of Wigan." 1899.
F. Gastrell. *"Notitia Cestriensis."* 1850.
D. Sinclair. *"History of Wigan."* 1882.
J. E. Bailey. *"Inventories of goods in the Churches and Chapels of Lancashire in 1552."* (1888).
H. Fishwick. *"Lancashire and Cheshire Church Surveys."* 1879.
Schools Inquiry Commission. North Western Division. 1869.
Joyce Bankes. *"Winstanley Hall."* Historical Notes on the Winstanley Family.
St. Helen's Lantern. No. 43 Vol. II and No. 44 Vol. II.
Hugh Parr. *"A Short History of Billinge."* 1953.
J. Brown. *"Billinge Bazaar, 1834."*
Billinge Methodist Church Centenary Pamphlet. 1968.
Billinge Methodist Church Centenary Tableau (Narrative, Mrs. M. Ward).
Commission for Inquiring into the Employment and Condition of Children in Mines and Manufactories. 1843.
"The Wigan Observer" February 1860. January 1957. et. al.